From Grand To Grove

Entertaining South Bedfordshire

A History of Theatres and Cinemas in Luton,
Dunstable, Leighton Buzzard and Toddington

Eddie Grabham

The Book Castle

To Rosemary, Christopher, Susan and Timothy

First published June 2007
by
The Book Castle
12 Church Street
Dunstable
Bedfordshire LU5 4RU

ISBN 978-1-903747-83-4

Typeset and designed by Caroline and Roger Hillier
The Old Chapel Graphic Design
www.theoldchapelivinghoe.com

Printed in Great Britain by Cromwell Press, Trowbridge, Wiltshire

FOREWORD

By John Buckledee, former editor of The Luton News and The Dunstable Gazette

This is a book of magical memories for those of us who, in the days before TV and DVD, enjoyed a twice-weekly film-fix at the cinema as well as variety shows and plays at the old Alma and Grand theatres in Luton.

Eddie Grabham is the ideal person to tell the story of entertainment in South Beds. He's acted in local rep, helped to manage a theatre, written drama reviews for *The Luton News*, and presented programmes on movies and musicals for BBC Three Counties Radio. He also went to the same school (in Dunstable) as film star Gary Cooper. He and Gary were not there at the same time, of course, but it's a nice reference for a film buff to have on his CV!

Eddie, as I well know from his regular visits to *The Luton News*, is a walking encyclopaedia on movie icons from every era. He can talk, for instance, with equal knowledge about Cameron Diaz or Jeanette Macdonald (no generation gap here!) and is an authority on the buildings in South Beds where their work is best seen. But his book is more than this...it records the pioneering entertainments of travelling showmen, the star-spangled variety bills, the struggles of weekly repertory companies and the visits of such show biz luminaries as Valerie Hobson, Maurice Chevalier, Petula Clark and Lillie Langtry.

Everyone will have different memories triggered by the names of venues featured here. For me (at random) there will always be Billy Cotton's band show at the Alma, Molière's Tartuffe at Dunstable Town Hall, Pride and Prejudice at the Grand, and even Gene Autry films at Kensworth's WI hall.

I queued to see the young Marlon Brando, singing with a snarl in Guys And Dolls at the old Savoy in George Street, Luton. I caught a bus to the old Oriel in Leighton Buzzard to watch the brooding passion of Laurence Olivier in Wuthering Heights. The old Union Cinema in Dunstable, now a nightclub, is the place where, as a schoolboy, I first saw Gary Cooper (that Dunstable schoolboy!) in For Whom The Bell Tolls. The enormous Ritz Cinema in Luton was packed for ticket-only screenings of Gigi. There was Joe E. Brown's immortal closing line ("Nobody's perfect!") in Some Like It Hot at Luton's old Gaumont, where trains on the neighbouring railway line shook the building as they passed. And at the old Odeon in Luton's Bury Park, as the audience sat stunned after the desolating final voyage of Gregory Peck in On The Beach, the manager played a recording of Ravel's Bolero instead of the usual interval music. His inspired choice remains in my mind all these decades later.

Alas, the buildings which provided those enchanted evenings have now vanished or are being used for other things. A warm welcome, then, for Eddie's comprehensive reminder of so many marvellous times, published in the year when Dunstable's new Grove Theatre aims to add a further exciting chapter to what is, clearly, a never-ending story.

ABOUT THE AUTHOR

(CG)

BBC Three Counties broadcaster Eddie Grabham has been involved in the local arts and theatre scene since performing with the Dunstable Grammar School Dramatic Society in the early fifties. After school, he joined the Dunstable Repertory Company and later became involved as both actor and director with the Library Players and Wheatsheaf Players in Luton. He attended an Associate of the Drama Board course to learn more about theatre and, unable to continue his direct involvement with local drama due to his duties as a director of ABC Travel Guides in Dunstable, he turned to reviewing theatrical productions, both amateur and professional, for *The Luton News*. When he finally left ABC Travel Guides after twenty-nine years service, he devoted himself to broadcasting for BBC local radio and various management duties at Luton's St George's Theatre. He also wrote a syndicated video column for a range of newspapers stretching from Whitehaven in the north to Portsmouth in the south. He is a former Chairman and Vice President of Luton Arts Council and is currently a member of the Cinema Theatre Association . As an active member of the P.G Wodehouse Society, he regularly contributes to their journal, *Wooster Sauce*. Born in St. Albans, he has lived and worked for most of his life in Luton and Dunstable and was familiar with many of the theatres and cinemas described in this book.

Contents

INTRODUCTION

Although this book is concerned with the many theatres and cinemas which have existed in Dunstable, Leighton Buzzard, Luton and Toddington, I have also highlighted various buildings which have presented live performances or film shows before any dedicated venues were built. I have shown the various changes which have taken place, noting that cinemas have become bingo halls, night-clubs, ballrooms, churches and, in one case, a synagogue and then an Islamic Centre. In too many cases, they have been demolished. A number of buildings which were not strictly cinemas or theatres, such as the California Ballroom and Cesar's Palace, have been touched upon simply because they largely took the place of variety halls in terms of the acts they presented. However, the detail for these is necessarily brief.

I was tempted to list all the famous stars and personalities who have appeared at the various venues, but such a list would have doubled the size of this volume. They say the devil is in the detail and that has proved true here. The devilish detail with regard to seating and the many changes which have taken place in the various venues would, I feel, have taxed the patience of the reader. Therefore, in the case of both the visiting personalities and the various changes, I have highlighted the most significant, sometimes confining additional information about changes in the buildings to the list of venues in Appendix I.

A Note Regarding Currency

There are a number of occasions where I have given ticket prices in pre-decimal currency which will be familiar to older readers. To offer a conversion to decimal currency on every occasion in the text would be misleading, for continuing inflation means that the true values are not comparable. After the Second World War, five pounds a week would have been a respectable living wage; it would have been even lower before the First World War when a shilling would have been a considerable sum for working people, the main audience for the cinemas.

For reference, 1/- (one shilling) would convert to 5p; 1/6 (one shilling and sixpence) to 7.5p; 6d (six-pence) to 2.5p and 3d (three-pence) to approximately 1.2p. £1.0.0. (one pound) was made up of twenty shillings, while a shilling comprised twelve pence (thus, a pound contained 240 pence). A guinea was £1.1.0 (21 shillings).

A Note About Sources

Wherever possible, I have endeavoured to study primary sources to be found in plans, council minutes and contemporary correspondence lodged in various council premises, museums and the Bedfordshire & Luton Archives & Records Service in Bedford. Gaps exist in these sources, especially in Luton where many were destroyed in the Town Hall fire of 1919. I have therefore also relied upon contemporary reports in *The Dunstable Borough Gazette* (later *The Dunstable Gazette*), *The Leighton Buzzard Observer*, *The Luton Times*, *The Luton Weekly Reporter*, *The Luton News*, *The Tuesday Pictorial*, *The Saturday Telegraph*, *The Luton Leader*, *Herald* and *Post*, *Luton/Dunstable on Sunday* and other relevant journals. I have also considered the excellent articles in *Bedfordshire Magazine* and local histories (see bibliography) whilst attempting to verify the facts given in these wherever possible. Every effort has been made to trace the the ownership and copyright of photographs and these have been noted.

I have also been very gratified by the interest shown by so many people who recall the various buildings; their memories have added much to this history.

I apologise if any inadvertent errors in spellings, omissions or details in the text or ownership of photographs should be found; if the attention of these be brought to the publishers, they will be corrected in any future editions.

Eddie Grabham

ACKNOWLEDGEMENTS

I acknowledge with gratitude and appreciation the help, support and encouragement I have received throughout my researches. It would be impractical to name everybody who has shown an interest, but without all of them, this book would not have seen the light of day. I must nevertheless extend special thanks to the following individuals and organisations.

First, my thanks go to The Book Castle and its staff who have given their support to this venture.

Luton Museums Service allowed me to inspect many relevant items and documents, made more meaningful due to the expertise of the curatorial staff, including Dr Elizabeth Adey, Dr Stephen Bunker, Dr Robin Holgate and Marian Nichols as well as Photographic Officer Chris Grabham, all of whom gave of their time generously and with enthusiasm.

The relevant items held in Dunstable, Leighton Buzzard and Luton libraries were made available and the help of the staffs, especially Mark Stubbs in Luton, proved invaluable. Equally, archivist Nigel Lutt and the staff of Bedfordshire & Luton Archives & Records Service in Bedford, were most helpful in the identification of documents.

Staff in Luton Town Hall planning department, especially Stewart Cuff, were always helpful, while Brian Waller, formerly in Luton Town Hall legal department, also offered important information and support. I am also grateful to Richard Walden, Dunstable's Town Clerk, and his staff for allowing me access to the town's archive. I am also grateful to South Bedfordshire District Council and Clair Thomas for keeping me informed of progress with the new Grove Theatre.

Managers and staff in various relevant locations, even though some of them no longer operate as theatres or cinemas, have been most helpful; in particular, I acknowledge the enthusiastic support of Stuart Antrobus, former manager of Leighton Buzzard Theatre. Members of voluntary bodies such as the Dunstable 'Rep' Theatre Club, Toddington Amateur Dramatic Society, Luton Arts Council, Luton Community Arts Trust and other associated bodies have also offered valuable information.

I am also grateful for the expert assistance given by Clive Polden and the Cinema Theatre Association Archive and to the management team at Luton's Cineworld.

I must also thank Barbara Benson, the late Fred Benson, John Buckledee, former editor of *The Luton News* and *The Dunstable Gazette*, Ken Cooper, Jo Cross, John Dandy, Dr James Dyer, Andrew Grays and members of his staff at the

Hat Factory, Roy Joyner, Tom Lawson, the late John Lunn, Eric G. Meadows, Sid Rutstein and Brian Yates.

Last, but by no means least, I wish to give particular thanks to the editor, Geoff Cox, and the staff of *The Luton News* and *The Dunstable Gazette* and associated publications. David Ainsbury gave special support and help in finding so many of the photographs in this book, often with the collaboration of Chris Grabham at Luton Museums Service which holds a massive collection of Luton News, Dunstable Gazette and other photographs from the past.

Many others, including my long-suffering wife Rosemary, have also given their generous help and I am no less grateful for their support.

Eddie Grabham

CHAPTER ONE

The Beginnings of Theatre in South Bedfordshire

The true history of the theatre in South Bedfordshire started in Dunstable. During the early years of the twelfth-century, a future abbot of St. Albans, Geoffrey de Gorham, directed a play described as "The Martyrdom of St Katherine". Geoffrey de Gorham was from Caen in France and the abbot Richard of St. Albans had called for him to govern the school there. However, during a time when travel was hazardous, Geoffrey arrived late and another master had been appointed to govern the school in his place. As a result, he was sent to teach at "Dunestaple" until he could take over the school he had been promised. It was while he was in the town that the play, which depicted the conversion and martrydom of St. Katherine of Alexandria, was performed. It is recorded that "to add glamour to the play", he borrowed choristers' copes (ceremonial vestments) from the sacristan in St Albans. Sadly, Geoffrey's house caught fire and the copes along with the master's books were all destroyed. He was distraught, but when he eventually became Abbot of St Albans, he arranged for new copes to be made.

No known script for the miracle play, which may have been destroyed in the fire, has survived. Also, opinions vary as to who actually performed the play. It seems most likely that it was performed by the pupils of Geoffrey de Gorham's school, but Dunstable historian Worthington G. Smith has it that it was performed by "Dunstable rustics". Perhaps they were one and the same; in any event, it is probably the earliest account of a play being performed in the vernacular language of twelfth-century England. Indeed, the thirteenth-century monk Matthew Paris claimed that Dunstable was the "cradle of English drama". Thus, Dunstable has an important place, not only in the history of theatre in Bedfordshire, but also in England. It is particularly interesting to note that this play was performed long before Latin ceased to be the language of the Church.

Entertainers at Medieval Fairs

As the medieval fairs came into being, so the entertainers moved in. Luton had been granted its fair at the beginning of the thirteenth-century; the town's market had been established since 1066. The fair was a much grander event than the weekly market. It was held for three days in August to coincide with the festival of the Assumption. Goods from far and wide were sold in the grounds of St. Mary's Church. Beer flowed and entertainers in the form of jugglers added to the sense of occasion. People tended to visit all the fairs in the district; South Bedfordshire had fairs at Dunstable and Leighton where entertainers presumably also accompanied the trading which was the real purpose of the fair. The jugglers in Luton probably provided the first form of secular performance to be enjoyed by the ordinary folk of South Bedfordshire. The age-old technique of attracting people to buy goods through entertainment continues to this day as clowns open super-markets and magicians demonstrate intriguing boxes of tricks to wide-eyed youngsters in the run up to Christmas. The most notable form of selling through entertainment today is, of course, the television commercial.

During the fourteenth and fifteenth centuries, Luton was an agricultural centre. As well as much wealth, there were fine houses which would almost certainly have provided entertainment for themselves and their guests. Travelling performers would entertain the rich and influential, while ordinary folk would have to wait for the annual fair and those jugglers. As the straw-hat trade developed in Luton and Dunstable, so plait markets – and with them, more wealth – came to both towns. Dances were held in the bigger houses and strolling players became regular visitors to Bedfordshire.

Dunstable Drama

Dramatist Elkanah Settle was born in Dunstable in 1648. He was destined to become a restoration dramatist, having written his first play, "Cambyses, King of Persia", in 1671. His plays were mostly tragedies, but it has been claimed that his comedies with music anticipated the musical theatre typified by John Gay. His "Beggars' Opera" was produced in 1728, four years after Settle's death.

Towards the end of the eighteenth-century, travelling players became more commonplace. There were no theatres as such for these rudimentary touring companies, but there were inns and other suitable premises which could be "fitted-up" as theatres. In 1797, a notice announced the performance of 'that most favourite play "The Mountaineers; or, The Maniac of the Cave"'. It was to be performed 'For the benefit of Mr. Sylvester Daggerwood at Theatre, Dunstable

(Licensed by Authority)". It may have been the Town Hall (which was demolished in 1805) or possibly an inn which became "Theatre, Dunstable" on the night of Monday, June 21st.

Advertising for the piece was florid to say the least. The play was a revival – it had not been performed for thirty-nine years. The eighteenth-century copywriter wrote these words to convince Dunstablians that they should part with their cash:

> "Any attempt to be particular in the praise of this Piece would be at once difficult and unnecessary; no Play every (sic) succeeded better, on the Stage, since the memory of man. The fertility of the Author's incomparable genius never appeared to greater advantage; presenting an assemblage of all the beauties of
>
> Desperation, Execration, Detestation, Perturbation, Humiliation & Ostentation".

"By desire of several Persons of Distinction", audiences were promised that Mrs Daggerwood would attempt a recital of "Collins Ode on the Passions", accompanied "on the Bladder and String" by Mr Sylvester Daggerwood. This recitation was to take place between the first and second acts and would be followed by a "Grand, Superb, Splendid and Magnificent Spectacle, called DON JUAN: or The Libertine Destroyed". This piece offered "Mirth and Sorrow, Joy and Horror, With Rage and Despair most pleasingly blended". A variety of scenery was also promised, which included "A Dreary Cave most beautifully decorated with Skulls, Skeletons, Bones and Monuments". Nine years old Master Apollo Daggerwood also got into the act "in the character of a skeleton". This spectacle was also described as a ballet which would conclude with "a pleasing VIEW of the INFERNAL REGIONS", after which there would be a "Farewell Address to the Town of Dunstable, by Mr Sylvester Daggerwood, In the Character of the Devil".

Even then, the entertainment was not over. Mr Daggerwood had engaged:

> "the celebrated Don Trigola Toxicordendria who is just arrived from the Continent, with a most curious Casket of Black Beetles, They consist of Seventeen in number, viz. Fifteen Males and Two Females; and will perform between the Play & Farce".

It was clearly quite an evening. The notice concluded:

"Owing to the extent of the Night's Performance the Doors will be opened at FOUR o'CLOCK, and the Curtain to ascend peremptorily at Five. Those Ladies and Gentlemen already taken Places, are respectively entreated to send their Servants at Half past One. ***Tickets to be had of Mr Sylvester Daggerwood, at the Mouse and Tinder-box, near the Theatre. To prevent confusion the Nobility are entreated to order their Coachmen to set down and take up, with their Horses' Heads towards the Cow and Snuffers. N.B. It will be Moonlight".

Thus were the people of Dunstable entertained at the end of the eighteenth-century!

In his fascinating *Bedfordshire Magazine* article, "Dunstable and the Drama", R.P. Mander draws attention to an announcement for the comedy "John Bull or: An Englishman's Fire Side" to be performed at "The Theatre, Dunstable" on Wednesday, 4th July, 1804. Like "The Mountaineers" a few years earlier, a full evening was offered at whichever venue became "The Theatre" that summer evening so long ago. A playbill held in the British Museum collection outlines the full programme; in addition to the play, there was a comic song and a comic opera. One member of the cast for both the play and the opera was a certain Mr. Carey which, claims Mander, was the name used by the teenage Edmund Kean (born in 1789) whilst working with travelling companies of the period. It is entirely likely, for the illegitimate Kean's mother was actress Ann Carey. Although Kean was a child prodigy who had appeared as a child at Drury Lane, he became a strolling player with various companies before returning to London and wide acclaim for his portrayal of Shylock at Drury Lane in 1814.

Fit-Ups and Conversions

For South Bedfordshire as a whole, the age of the fit-ups and conversions had arrived. Luton historian William Austin refers to Frederick's Travelling Theatre being a regular visitor to the town. In 1827, it was Luton's turn to find advertising bills headed "Theatre, Luton", but on this occasion the building used can be readily identified. Once again, the style was flowery in the extreme:

"To the Nobility, Gentry, Inhabitants, and Visitants of Luton and its vicinity.

MR. BREWER of the Theatres Kentish Town, Barnet, and Hemel Hempstead, respectively announces that he has fitted up as a temporary

Theatre, a building situated on the premises of the RED LION INN, which tho' as an Edifice, it may be found more allied to the ORIGINAL, than the MODERN ones of Dramatic Entertainment; yet, as every attention has been paid to the Comfort and convenience of the AUDIENCE, and every effort will be exerted that limit and talent will allow, to add respectability & effect in the Stage department; he, with the utmost deference solicits that Patronage it will be his study to merit, although he is aware the "tout ensemble" may not be worthy of the Town, whose auspices he covets, yet he assures the Public, that the humbleness of the Edifice holds no alliance with his ambition, in rendering every satisfaction within it. It has been acknowledged by all, that the Drama "holds as't were, the Mirror up to Nature, shews Vice its own Image, and the very age and body of the Time, its form and pressure. And while properly conducted, and for a limited period, it is hoped will meet the approval of the Liberal Mind, and give offence to no one.

On Monday Evening, May 28th, 1827"

Sadly, the title of the play itself has not survived!

Henry Jackman's Touring Company

It was around this time that Henry Jackman's touring company brought plays to towns in Bedfordshire and other counties in the South Midlands. Northampton historian Lou Warwick has recorded the activities of this remarkable company in his book "Theatre Un-Royal". Jackman's daughter Louisa was born in Luton around 1828, so it is not unreasonable to assume that she was born "on the road" as it were and that Jackman and his company performed in the town at that time. Unfortunately, there seem to be no local records to confirm this.

Warwick also refers to a letter Jackman wrote from Leighton Buzzard in 1841. He mentions business being good at Woburn, but could not say the same for Leighton where, he bemoaned, "they think of nothing here but drinking"! The attitude in the town today is entirely different; recent threats to close the Leighton Buzzard Theatre caused an uproar, but that's a tale to be told in a later chapter. It would be interesting to know where the Jackman company performed in Leighton Buzzard. Judging by the date of the letter, it would not have been at the Corn Exchange as this did not open until 1862. When the Corn Exchange was built, it did include a space suitable for the performance of plays and no doubt provided a stage and auditorium for various touring companies which came after

Jackman.

As late as the 1890s, however, Leighton Buzzard continued to enjoy an age-old form of entertainment. In the fourth in his series of fascinating *Bedfordshire Magazine* articles, "The Itinerants", Thomas W. Bagshawe refers to the "merryanders or clowns" at the annual statty fair. The term "merryander" probably derives from "merry andrew", an old term for a clown or buffoon.

Various rules and regulations controlled the performance of plays; touring companies needed a licence to perform, but they didn't always bother. *The Luton Times* reported such indiscretions; for example, they highlighted a play which was performed in the town without a licence in March, 1858.

Left **Author's impression of the Corn Exchange in Leighton Buzzard before the top section was removed. (EG)**

Prince of Wales Mammouth Theatre, Dunstable

In Dunstable during the late 1860s, Mayor Samuel Burgess was one of the distinguished patrons supporting a production of "Macbeth" at the "Prince of Wales' Mammouth Theatre". This so-called theatre was almost certainly a fit-up in the Town Hall or one of Dunstable's many inns. It is particularly interesting to note that Shakespeare's Scottish play was accompanied by a full programme of incidental music, a comic song from the Prince of Wales' proprietor "Brother" E. Wildman (for whose benefit the whole evening was promoted incidentally), a "Characteristic Dance" by Mr. Harry Hamilton and a "Favourite Song" by Miss Nelly Foreman. As if that wasn't enough, it was announced that the evening was "To conclude with the fashionable Farce entitled "Boots at the Saracen's Head"".

Prince of Wales Theatre,

DUNSTABLE.

PROPRIETOR—MR. E. WILDMAN, M.U.I.O.O.F.

A SELECT

FASHIONABLE PERFORMANCE

WILL TAKE PLACE

On WEDNESDAY evening, APRIL 21st, 1869,

Under the Distinguished Patronage of His

WORSHIPFUL THE MAYOR,

SAMUEL BURGES, ESQ.,

THE OFFICERS AND MEMBERS OF THE 4TH BEDS. RIFLE
VOLUNTEER CORPS.

AND THE LOYAL PHILANTHROPIC LODGE OF

ODD FELLOWS.

THE BRASS BAND

Of the above Corps will attend and play several popular Airs.

BEING FOR THE

BENEFIT OF BROTHER WILDMAN,

Who trusts that his humourous efforts to amuse during the season he has
had the honour to appear before the inhabitants of Dunstable have given
satisfaction, and that his friends will rally round him on this the occasion
of his BENEFIT.

" 'Tis not in mortals to *command* success,
But I'll do more, endeavour to *deserve* it."

Admission—Boxes, 1s. 6d.　Pit, 1s.　Gallery, 6d.

Tickets to be had of Mr. MERRIFIELD, Saracen's Head ; and at the
THEATRE.

The Entertainments will commence with Shakespeare's
sublime Tragedy, in 5 Acts, entitled

MACBETH!

KING OF SCOTLAND.

Macbeth	...	...	...	...	Mr. N. HARTLEY
Macduff	...	...	...	Mr. MONTAGUE KEELEY
Hecate	...	...	...	BROTHER WILDMAN
Lady Macbeth	...	...	Mrs. MONTAGUE KEELEY
1st Singing Witch	...	...	...	...	Mrs. SYKES

Comic Song	...	...	BROTHER WILDMAN.
Characteristic Dance	...	Mr. HARRY HAMILTON
A Favourite Song	...	Miss NELLY FOREMAN

To conclude (by desire) with the Fashionable Farce,
entitled

BOOTS AT THE SARACEN'S HEAD.

Boots at the Saracen's Head　..　...　——

Stage Manager—Mr. MONTAGUE KEELEY ;

Leader of the Orchestra—Mr. CHARLES POWELL.

Door open at **7** *; Curtain to rise at a quarter to* 8 *o'clock.*

D. TIBBETT, PRINTER, DUNSTABLE.

The actual venue described here as "Prince of Wales' Theatre, Dunstable" is not known, though the concluding farce, "Boots at the Saracen's Head", may provide a clue. This contemporary document shows the extent of the programme performed on that Wednesday evening in 1869. (LMS)

(Does this give a clue to the inn which hosted the Prince of Wales, I wonder?). The leader of the orchestra was a Mr Charles Powell.

Quite apart from the exceptional value this programme offered, it is instructive to consider why a Shakespearean tragedy should be accompanied by what amounted to a complete Music Hall programme. Although the play needed a licence, for some reason a MUSICAL play was exempt. By linking the incidental music to "Macbeth", it became a musical play! Some sixteen airs, solos and choruses were interpolated into the performance – numbers like "Many More, Murders More", "My Little Airy Spirit", "Here's the Blood of a Bat" and "Here's the Juice of a Toad" were no doubt considered appropriate!

The Corn Exchange on Market Hill, Luton, opened in 1869 and was demolished in 1951, long after it was used for concerts or other forms of entertainment. (LMS)

Entertainment in Nineteenth-Century Luton

In Luton, the Corn Exchange, the Plait Hall and the Town Hall were all popular venues for concerts and plays. During the latter part of the nineteenth-century, Lutonians established their strong taste for music – a taste incidentally which survives to this day. As well as music, the people of Luton liked the circus. On Bank Holiday Monday in 1879, for example, Batty's Great London Circus came to the town "with Great Equestrian Spectacle – THE AFGHAN WAR: Capture of the Khyber Pass introducing several natives of Cabul" (sic).

Roller Skating had also become a very popular pastime with the Alexandra Skating Rink re-opening on Saturday, 1st of November, 1879, with the Quadrille Band in attendance. It was not unusual for the Skating Rink, which was situated behind the Town Hall with its entrance in Manchester Street, to provide other forms of entertainment. In January 1880, a troupe of "bicycle equestrians" performing there for six days was just a taster of things to come. Meanwhile, the Town Hall continued to provide entertainment as well. Hoffman's celebrated

Town Hall, Luton, circa 1880; the venue was often used as both a theatre and a cinema before it burned down in 1919. (LMS/LN)

Boston Minstrels gave their popular "Negro Entertainment" on Saturday, 27th December, 1879.

In 1880, the Alexandra Palace Circus opened. As the press reported: "This is the title of the new place of entertainment in Waller Street which the proceedings before the magistrates have so well advertised and which is to be opened on Saturday, March 27th." The building was on the corner of Melson Street and Waller Street and was built without permission! To get round this problem, it was claimed to be a temporary building. Clowns headed by Chemah appeared there and the venue advertised in the local newspapers for a short period. Then it seems to have disappeared without trace, but it had given Luton a taste for stage entertainment – a taste which was about to be satisfied by conversion from one of the town's established entertainment centres. By now, Luton's Plait Hall in Waller Street had become a regular place for entertainment and concerts. To compete with the Alexandra Palace Circus, the Plait Hall presented the Court Minstrels accompanied by twenty "Great Artistes". They also laid claim to being the only troupe with a legitimate Military Band!

From Skating to Theatre

The Alexandra Skating Rink had established itself as a major venue for popular entertainment. In December 1880, it became the People's New Temperance Music Hall and Palace of Varieties. Great stress was placed on the "tasteful" nature of the acts on offer, clearly with a view not to offend the strong temperance lobby in Luton at that time. The first programme at the new Music Hall included "Barry and Grover, eccentric Negro Entertainers". A Mr. Harry Lenton, vocalist and comedian, was also on the crowded bill. Shortly after the Alexandra Skating Rink became a Music Hall, application was made for the Town Hall to have a theatrical licence. It was not long before plays were also presented at the newly opened music-hall. The name of the place was such a mouthful, folk continued to call it the Alexandra, so it was not too surprising that, when the management started offering dramatic entertainment, they also changed the name of the hall to the Alexandra Theatre.

NOTICE TO THE PUBLIC

– – –

Opening of the

People's New Temperance Music Hall

and

PALACE OF VARIETIES

(Late Alexandra Rink)

Proprietor....................Mr. C. J. RONSON

General Manager........Mr. **FRANK PIERCE**

T he above Hall having been comfortably seated, entirely re-decorated, and fitted with splendid new Stage and Magnificent Scenery, will open for the season on BOXING NIGHT, DECEMBER 27th, 1880, when the following array of talented Artistes will appear -

MR. HARRY LENTON

The popular Characteristic Vocalist and Comedian in new songs

Messrs. BARRY & GROVER,

Eccentric Negro entertainers and song and dance Artistes in their Burlesques and Knock-about Nigger Sketches, songs and dances.

Special Engagement of

Miss MARION RITTA,

Charming Ballet and Serio-Comic Vocalist and Dancer at this Hall only.

MR. FRANK PIERCE

Will recite the Pathetic poem, entitled LITTLE JIM, or the death of the **COLLIER'S CHILD** illustrated by a series of Tableaux Vivants, or

Living Pictures

First appearance of

Mr. GEO. LEONARD,

The Famous Character Vocalist and Comedian

Mr. J. G. GROVER,

Character Comedian.

MR. PAUL BARRY,

Patter Vocalist and Dancer.

MR. & MRS. FRANK PIERCE each evening in their new Sketches and Farcial Entertainments.

Leader of the Band.........Mr. H. **BRADLEY**

Admission-Front Seats (cushioned) 1/-; Second Seats (chairs) 6d.; Back Seats 3d.

Doors open at 7.15. Performance commencing at 7.45.

Left **Notice printed in the 24 December, 1880 edition of** *The Luton Times and Advertiser* **(reconstructed)**

Right **Luton's People's New Temperance Music Hall and Palace of Varieties, which opened in 1880, became the Alexandra Theatre from 1881. As this photograph shows, the building was later occupied by the Salvation Army who screened "animated pictures" (early films) in the building from 1907. (LMS/LN)**

ALEXANDRA THEATRE
(Late Music Hall)
MANCHESTER ST., LUTON
Licensed to the-

Proprietor .. .. Mr. C. J. ROSSON
General Manager .. .. .. Mr. FRANK PIERCE
GRAND OPENING NIGHT,
MONDAY, FEBRUARY 7th, 1881

**MONDAY and TUESDAY - Production of the great
Lyceum Drama**
THE CORSICAN BROTHERS,
With entirely new scenery and effects, by Mr. Charles
Ballenger.

WEDNESDAY- The Favourite Temperance Drama,
TEN NIGHTS IN A BAR ROOM.
THURSDAY - Grand Fashionable Night under Distinguished Patronage, production of an entirely

original Comedy entitled,
WORTH WINNING,
FRIDAY-The Romantic Drama,
I AM HERE, OR THE THRUST OF NEVERS,
SATURDAY-(The people's night) The Great
Sensation Drama, entitled,
DOOMED TO THE DIAMOND MINES.
Comic Songs (every evening) by Mr. Alf. Janes
Commencing each Evening at 7.45
With a **LAUGHABLE FARCE**; in which Mr. Chas.
Simpson Boote will appear.
Doors open at 7.15, commencing at 7.45.
Prices of Admission:- Front Seats (cushioned), 1s;
Second seats, 6d.; Back Seats, 3d
SATURDAY next Extra Performance. Production of
a New Farce, entitled, BOOTE AND PIERCE ON
THE SPREE, in which Messrs. Pierce and Boote
will appear, supported by the Company.

This notice in *The Luton Times and Advertiser* for 5 February 1881, announced the opening of the Alexandra Theatre in the premises formerly occupied by the People's New Temperance Music Hall (reconstructed).

What's in a Name?

Incidentally, it's interesting to note how frequently the name Alexandra was used during the latter part of the nineteenth-century. Then, as now, places of entertainment were keen to give the impression that they were special. At that time, the role of the Monarchy was unquestioned. Everyone was a Royalist and the use of the word 'Royal' was common. Equally common was the use of royal names. In 1863, the Prince of Wales (the future King Edward VII) married Princess Alexandra of Denmark. She was taken to the hearts of the British people in much the same way as the late Princess Diana was to be loved by the people more than a century later. That is why the name Alexandra was adopted by more than one of Luton's entertainment venues as well as an avenue! When the Alexandra Skating Rink became a music-hall, the word 'Palace' in the title was used for the same reasons. As will be seen, Palace was to become much used as a name for theatres and cinemas in South Bedfordshire. Then, in 1898, Luton – and indeed Bedfordshire – gained its first purpose-built theatre. It had to have a suitable name to convey its importance and to persuade folk in Luton, Dunstable and district to realise that this was a very special place to visit.

So they called it the Grand Theatre.

CHAPTER TWO

Bedfordshire's First Purpose-Built Theatre

Temperance was rife at the end of the nineteenth-century, and Luton seemed to have more than its fair share of those who sought to forbid the consumption of any intoxicating drink. Once the Grand Theatre had been erected, it was necessary for the owner, Reginald Frank Turner, to apply for a licence. As *The Luton News* was quick to point out, "theatres do not require a justices' licence to sell intoxicating liquors". As theatre licences for the performance of stage plays were granted by Bedfordshire County Council and, by definition, were allowed to sell intoxicating drink, the temperance lobby of Luton Town Council had a problem.

They had willingly permitted the building of the Grand Theatre, but it was clear that few if any had thought about the implications as far as selling alcohol was concerned. Nevertheless, the Grand Theatre duly opened its doors for a suitably grand preview on Saturday, 10th December, 1898. Luton could be justly proud of its new theatre, and there's little doubt that Reginald Turner had sited the building in a position convenient for the railway station. At that time, it was easy to reach Luton by rail from two stations in Dunstable, Leagrave (which was not yet a part of Luton), Harpenden and St. Albans (not to mention Chiltern Green and Luton Hoo, two small stations between Luton and Harpenden). It made a lot of sense, for Luton itself with a population of less than forty-thousand might have found it difficult to support such a magnificent theatre on its own.

Left **This early photograph of the Grand Theatre, Luton, which opened in 1898, shows the frontage with an early awning which did not remain. (LMS/H)**

A Grand Opening Ceremony

For the glittering opening ceremony, Turner entertained his friends, leading citizens and future patrons of the Theatre in grand style. The new building had been a hive of activity throughout that final week of construction but, by Saturday afternoon, the builders, the carpenters, painters and upholsterers had melted away to leave the completed theatre spick and span for the auspicious occasion. Another group of vital workers, the gas-fitters, would also have been found completing their task during that final week, for the whole building was lit by gas.

As someone pointed out as the guests began to arrive, more cabs could be seen in that one afternoon than would normally be seen all week in that part of town. The Theatre was situated in Waller Street, almost opposite the Plait Hall which, by then, served as a principal place of entertainment for Luton. Of course, only those with tickets could enter the building for the private view and members of Luton Constabulary were on duty to guard the entrance. As it was winter, it is unlikely they wore their straw helmets which would have put the final touch to a great Luton occasion.

The privileged few gasped with delight as they entered the building with its rich pile carpets on the stairs leading to the dress-circle. The fittings were truly luxurious and the decorations beautiful – a fine monument to the work of local builder Mr. Dunham. It was a splendid building which proved to be an asset to a flourishing manufacturing town which was on the brink of immense wealth, growth and influence. Everybody who was anybody in Luton and district was there – magistrates, county and town councillors, aldermen, doctors and, most influential of all, the plait merchants and straw hat manufacturers. Aldermen and councillors from St. Albans also came – and even the church was represented! Turner knew that his enterprise could only succeed if the venture was seen to be prestigious and totally respectable. The dignitaries, all men, were accompanied by their wives. The ladies took the opportunity to show off their beautiful hats, most of which would have been made within walking distance of Luton's magnificent new building.

The First Curtain-Up

The drop curtain was decorated with a scene depicting Why Axe Ye Cottage in Park Street. At 3.30pm, when all the distinguished guests were assembled in the plush auditorium, a hush descended as the curtain rose to reveal a full orchestra on the stage. The guests also saw long tables in the background groaning with

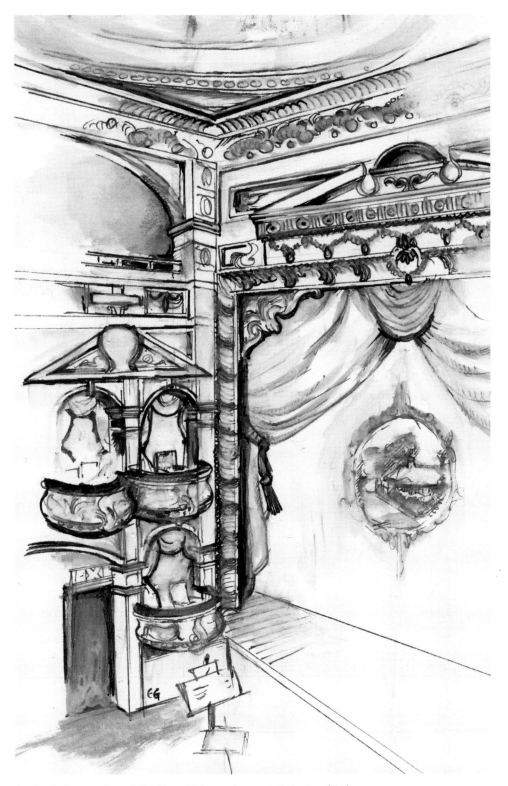

Author's impression of the Grand Theatre's ornate interior. (EG)

beautifully arranged refreshments. That afternoon, the audience would tread the boards!

In those far off days, no event of such importance would start without the national anthem and, at its close, the men cheered. The mood of the afternoon seemed to reflect the optimism of a wealthy town looking forward to a rewarding new century in little over a year's time. Then the moment everyone had been waiting for arrived. The architect, Charles Herbert Shoppee, escorted Mrs Lillie Langtry on to the stage. It must have been one of Luton's most magnificent moments. Actress Lillie Langtry was a theatrical giant in this country and America alike. Her beauty was legendary and here she was before the great and the good of Luton and district to open their brand-new theatre.

Mrs Langtry graciously accepted a bouquet as the audience held its breath. She opened the theatre with eloquence as she commented on the fact that not only was Luton the largest town in Bedfordshire, but it was the only town in the county to have the advantage of a theatre. She could not have known that although small auditoria were included in new civic buildings in Bedford, Leighton Buzzard and Luton during the latter half of the twentieth-century, it would remain the only purpose-built theatre in Bedfordshire until 2007 – but that's a later story. The Royal CountyTheatre in Bedford, which opened less than a year later, was an excellent conversion from an existing building. Other theatres (such as the Palace, the Alma and the Union in Luton) were built for cine-variety, with films as the main entertainment. Lillie Langtry went on to say that through the enterprise of Mr. Turner, the theatre "had been placed at the disposal of the inhabitants for their instruction and recreation". Touching a sensitive point, the lovely actress received loud applause from those present when she expressed the hope that "companies visiting it will produce such plays as will silence and remove any prejudices that may have existed against its erection".

The Absence and Subsequent Appearance of Reginald Turner

Sadly, the one man who should have enjoyed this triumphant occasion was not present to hear Mrs Langtry's address. Reginald Turner caught influenza and had to leave the arrangements to his able assistant J. Alban Newton. Turner would hand over the day-to-day running of the theatre to Newton within a year. Mrs Langtry nonetheless found room in her opening address to wish Mr. Turner every success in his "courageous venture". After referring to the opening performance, Lillie Langtry declared the Grand Theatre open "for the use and enjoyment of the inhabitants of Luton". She then broke the traditional bottle of champagne, which splashed on to her dress. With sheer professional aplomb, Lillie Langtry just smiled as though nothing had happened and made a gracious and dignified exit.

Following her exit, the visitors invaded the stage before exploring every corner of the theatre. Lillie Langtry attracted admiring glances as she sat in the orchestra stalls. Unable to stay away any longer – despite his weak condition – Reginald Turner put in an appearance and spoke to his distinguished guest before she became faint and needed medical attention. However, she did not leave before the ladies present had admired her elegant light fawn dress trimmed with gold. Her black hat was decorated with Neapolitan violets – though whether this was made in Luton is not recorded. Turner had employed a full orchestra for the theatre. Conductor Walter Scott composed a special inaugural overture for the occasion which he dedicated to the theatre's owner. Throughout the rest of that opening afternoon, a programme of popular items was played.

Programme of music for the Grand Theatre's Opening Ceremony on Saturday, 10th December, 1898. (LMS)

The Magnificent Building Itself

Meanwhile, the guests admired the building itself. It was constructed of red and glazed brick and the theatre had five public entrances. The Grand Central entrance had folding doors which led to a vestibule containing the box office. A wide staircase led to the boxes, the orchestra-pit stalls and the circles. The pit had its own entrance, vestibule and booking office, as did the gallery. There was a separate "Early Door" entrance; the "Early Door" and gallery booking offices were on the mezzanine floor. The theatre also had five emergency exits as well as a stage door and large "dock doors" for scenery. At the stage level, there were two stage boxes, while the ground floor, which had a good rake, had seating for three hundred and twenty-one in three separately priced areas. Nearest the stage, there was seating for fifty-five in the Orchestra Stalls, behind which were forty-three seats in the Reserved Pit Stalls. All these seats had finer upholstery than the remainder, called simply the Pit. There was also allowance for ninety standing (unheard of in today's theatres). A large refreshment bar served the stage level.

The wide staircase from the central entrance led to a promenade, buffet and lounge behind the Dress and Upper Circles, comprising some one hundred and seventy seats. These, together with four private boxes, were contained on the first tier. The arrangement of the Dress and Upper Circles was unusual in that they both occupied a single tier, but were on different levels. The Upper Circle was usually referred to as the Balcony. There was a further large refreshment bar at the rear of the Gallery which, with standing room, could hold at least four hundred; bench seating in this area meant that exact seating could not be determined; one or two small souls or children could usually be squeezed in. Because of this and the allowance for standing, most references give the theatre's audience accommodation as between nine hundred and one thousand. In later years, standing would have been abandoned and even the gallery was not used towards the end of the theatre's life, leaving just over five hundred seats. All the boxes were sold as Private Boxes. The proscenium arch, the boxes and balconies were upholstered in crimson plush. The stage itself, in front of which was a spacious orchestra well, was comprehensively fitted (tower, traps, machinery, etc). It was fifty feet wide and thirty-three feet deep with a proscenium opening of twenty-four feet.

The theatre had ten dressing rooms as well as a stage bar. There was ample storage under the stage itself; Mr. Turner also leased no 16 John Street, behind the theatre, for the making and storage of scenery, having reached agreement to lease these premises on 14th November, 1898, just weeks before the theatre opened. Having survived the misfortune of Mr Turner's ailment and Lillie Langtry's fainting spell, there was one incident which threatened to mar the opening. One of the firemen on duty was found to be drunk and was subsequently severely reprimanded by the Town Clerk.

The Grand Theatre Opens to the Public

The excitement didn't stop with the glittering opening ceremony. The Grand Theatre opened to an enthusiastic public on the following Monday, the 12th December, 1898. As Lillie Langtry had announced, the first production was "Sign of the Cross", a tried and true warhorse by Wilson Barrett. The sixty-strong cast was under the direction of William Greet. It played to a full house – but then, Reginald Turner had chosen his first play with great care. The choice could not possibly offend the dominant temperance lobby – and may even persuade the large number of non-conformists in the town that the theatre could be respectable. The play was also known to local audiences, for the well-established Ben Greet Company had performed the self-same play in Luton's Town Hall just over two years earlier on Friday and Saturday, 30th and 31st of October, 1896.

That first night in the Grand Theatre was a great success.

The Luton News summed it up thus:

Programme detail for "The Sign of the Cross", the first public presentation at the Grand Theatre, Luton. (LMS)

"If a crowded house and an enthusiastic audience could be taken as a guarantee for the future, then indeed would the success of the new theatre be assured. The building on Monday night was packed from top to bottom, and everybody was delighted with the magnificent decorations and appointments".

If the writer of those words had been able to see into the future, he would have realised that his comments erred on the side of optimism. The theatre did succeed and remained an essential part of Luton and district's cultural scene until the late nineteen-fifties, but the road was to prove hard and uneven. For now such optimistic words were in place, as the reporter noted that the choice of that first play was certain to appeal to the "sympathies of Luton". The theatre may have been new, appointed with all that was up-to-date, but Reginald Turner did not trust a new play for his opening.

Before the curtain went up at 7.30pm on that opening Monday, Reginald Turner went on to the stage and was greeted with cheers and applause. He expressed his appreciation of the welcome he had received and the way in which he had been supported. He didn't forget those who had paid just six-pence to sit in the "Gods" – he called upon the "good old gallery boys" to help him keep order, not to whistle and not to smoke. Those in the stalls and circles applauded loudly.

First Night Performance

After a solo rendition of the National Anthem, the audience joined in the chorus. At last, the curtain went up on that first performance and the audience was transported back to ancient Rome as Nero persecuted the Christians in 65 AD. The city's prefect, Marcus Superbus, charged with the task of exterminating Christians, falls in love with Mercia, a beautiful Christian girl. Recognising that the play would be "pretty familiar to most of our readers", *The Luton News* nevertheless reported that, while the audience followed the story with great interest, "occasionally some of the inexperienced playgoers gave vent to feelings which were slightly out of harmony with the scenes portrayed". Generally speaking, the writer concluded, the audience applauded at the right moments! There was loud applause when Marcus exclaimed: "What this Christianity is I know not; but this I know, that if it makes many such women as Mercia, Rome – nay, the whole world – will be all the purer for it". Reginald Turner had judged his audience well.

As was the custom at that time, the play was accompanied by music and a song was included. At the end of the piece, there were loud calls for Mr. Turner who was forced to make another appearance. He took the opportunity to introduce his acting manager J. Alban Newton. "Good old Newton!" called out the audience, while architect Charles Shoppee was so pleased to hear William Greet (whose company performed the play) describe the Grand as the "handsomest, prettiest and most comfortable theatre in the provinces", he was compelled to admit it had been the proudest evening of his life. It was the first theatre he had designed; when one remembers that many mistakenly believed the theatre to have been designed by leading theatre architect Frank Matcham, it is easy to guess where his inspiration and example came from. However, it has to be noted that, though the Grand was beautifully decorated, it did not really achieve the opulence which was (and indeed, still is) the hallmark of a Matcham theatre.

Euphoric Response

Everything had gone according to plan. "The theatre must certainly take rank as the handsomest of our public buildings," commented the editor of *The Luton News*, but he warned that the uniform enthusiasm expressed on that memorable evening would not necessarily prevail when the licence came up for renewal in a couple of weeks' time. There were councillors who were still concerned that,

The superior design of the Grand's front stall seats is clearly evident in this view of a later pantomime audience. (LN)

in granting a stage-play licence, they had no control over the sale of intoxicating drink in the bars. Meanwhile, Reginald Turner had booked "The Days of Cromwell" to follow the first play and proudly announced that his first annual pantomime, "Little Red Riding Hood", would open on Boxing Day.

Arrangements were made for advance tickets to be purchased during the day at Staddon's Library in Bute Street, an arrangement which lasted many years. Private Boxes cost a guinea, while seats in the Dress Circle and the Orchestra Stalls were three shillings . Seats in the Balcony and the Pit Stalls cost two shillings, the Pit cost one shilling and the Gallery ("The Gods"), sixpence. The doors opened at 7 o'clock for a seven-thirty start but an extra sixpence (or threepence for the Gallery) enabled members to enter during the "early doors" period from quarter to seven, thus enabling them to select the best seats in their part of the theatre.

Above **From its earliest days, the Grand Theatre presented pantomime at Christmastime. This view of a later production shows Buttons with some of his young audience outside the theatre. (LN)**

Left **The ornate design of the Grand's interior is still clearly evident in this photograph taken during the theatre's demolition. (LMS/LN)**

Immediate Competition for the Grand

With all the excitement of the Grand Theatre's opening, Lutonians hardly noticed the entertainment revolution taking place across the road. On the very Saturday the theatre opened, the Plait Hall was offering "Dioramic Entertainment" together with "good animated pictures". A diorama was a huge pictorial roll which gradually unfurled to reveal a panorama of continously changing scenery. The evening was presented in entertaining style by a Mr A. Meager who chose Derbyshire and the Peak District as his subject. For good measure, the evening started with one hundred pictures depicting a tour of Scotland.

Late nineteenth-century audiences were used to magic lantern slide shows, dioramas and the Gloucestershire-based "Poole's Myriorama", which was an imaginatively-lit dioramic travelling show. However, before the century finally petered out, it was animated pictures which began to attract bigger and bigger audiences. It wasn't the first time that Luton audiences had witnessed the new-fangled moving pictures as they flickered across a white screen. In fact, Luton's first film show took place in the Plait Hall in December, 1896, the very year in which cinema was born in Great Britain. The true birth of cinema had taken place in Paris at the very end of 1895; one year later, only a few cities and towns in Britain had the privilege of seeing "The Cinematographe". It was sheer chance that Luton should have been one of those select towns to see animated pictures in that first year, but more of that in Chapter Three.

The Grand was clearly going to have competition, and not only from moving pictures. The indefatigable Mr E. Hyde, a well-known "character comedian" who often presented variety concerts at the Plait Hall, was determined to compete with Reginald Turner's first pantomime. He arranged three days of Christmas Concerts at the Plait Hall from Boxing Day –

> "to be followed each night by a Dance, for which he has gone to enormous expense in engaging the largest variety of first-class artistes ever placed before a Luton audience, and to make this a most unique performance. Important starring engagement of Rice, Rose, Davis and The Half, the great Negro Sketch Artistes in their screaming sketches entitled 'Under the Gaslight' and 'Nick of the Woods'".

Other acts from the London Music Halls were also engaged and E. Hyde made his usual appearance. Perhaps the most significant item was the engagement of:

"Temple Somerset and Alberto's Perfected and Marvellous Cinematographe

Towards the end of the nineteenth century, crowds would turn out to see the first lantern lecture at Luton's Plait Hall, which became the first venue in the town to show "animated pictures" in December, 1896. (LN)

Animated Pictures. Clear, steady and powerful life-sized Pictures. In all new and up-to-date war scenes".

As in other towns, the Cinematographe was just a turn on a variety bill, but who in 1898 could have foretold a time when theatres dedicated to showing "animated pictures" would arrive in South Bedfordshire?

Early Problems at the Grand

It wasn't only competition from other halls which gave the theatre cause for concern, even in those earliest of days. Many years later, the owner of the Grand, Mrs Newton, would explain how difficult it was to keep a regular audience for weekly "rep". Mr. Turner engaged touring companies during the early years of the century, but he soon experienced a similar phenomenon common to theatres throughout the land. To start with, a large, enthusiastic audience would give unswerving support. Gradually, audiences would tail off and the theatre would rely upon a smaller, hard-core audience. It wasn't that the rest of the town was indifferent to the theatre or that they didn't treasure it. When something they fancied came along, audiences would turn out in droves, but everyone came to expect that the theatre would always be there whether or not they supported its programmes on a regular basis. It was ever thus and continues to be so.

When the licence came up for renewal just three weeks after the opening, the Grand faced considerable opposition. When they realised they could not stop the bars from selling intoxicating liquor, many members of the Council regretted ever granting a licence in the first place. The Mayor, Councillor G. Warren, and the whole Council was present to deliberate; the Town Clerk and other officials were joined by a deputation from the clergy and the temperance lobby as well as the Chief Constable. Reginald Turner came to face the music in the company of a barrister, the architect Charles Shoppee and the theatre manager, Alban Newton. The battle lines were drawn.

The town's Free Church Ministers had written a letter to "beg that when application for the theatrical licence be renewed, the permission to retain liquor be expressly withheld". It was the first of a number of letters from various temperance bodies in the district. Bringing some balance to the argument, Councillor Attwood thought that "if they had the Women's Temperance Federation and the whole crew speaking, the others ought to have a chance of replying". Such an outspoken remark met with instant disapproval and the good councillor was obliged to withdraw his description of "respectable ratepayers as a crew"! Clearly, the concept of "political correctness" is not as new as we thought.

Audience of Fifteen Thousand in Three Weeks

Mr. Dodd, the barrister appearing on Mr. Turner's behalf, then stood up to put the case for the management of the Grand, pointing out that some fifteen thousand people had gone to the theatre since it had opened and not one case of drunkenness or disorder had been reported. This, he contended, was all the more remarkable since the three-week period included Christmas. He went on to explain that the bars were only available to patrons when the theatre was giving a performance and, furthermore, could only be used during intervals as the stage was not in view from any of the refreshment areas.

Mr Dodd also pointed out that the arrangements made with touring companies visiting the theatre during the forthcoming year included a percentage of the box-office sales and it was unreasonable if the theatre could not attract the largest possible audiences. Needless to say, these arguments had not occurred to most members of the Council – one can only wonder how many of them were among the fifteen thousand who had flocked to the brand new theatre in Waller Street. The discussion was heated and lasted a long time. In the end, however, the original motion granting the full licence was carried by fifteen to eight. Mr. Turner could breathe a sigh of relief, though he knew that he would have to face them all again when he applied for the renewal of his licence twelve months hence.

An Early Critic

Nevertheless, the theatre remained the focus of attention. One letter to *The Luton News* complained at the length of the four intervals for a play called "The Lights O' London" performed during November, 1900. It has to be said that the whole performance lasted three hours. Apparently, one of the intervals was 'well over twenty minutes'. No doubt the patrons were pleased that the Council had allowed the bars to stay open during the intervals! The company presenting the play replied to the letter (which had implied that the intervals were for the actors to rest!) pointing out that the intervals were long on the first night as the theatre staff were handling a large quantity of scenery for the first time.

Change of Conductor

The theatre's first conductor, Walter Scott, retired not long after the opening and his place was taken by Ernest Kent. Music was something of a family affair; Mr Kent's father played in the orchestra and his daughter Greta was a singer who, on one occasion at least, crossed the road to sing in a Plait Hall concert. To complete the credentials of a very musical family, Kent's wife was a pianist who accompanied singers in the Plait Hall concerts. Daughter Greta clearly enjoyed life as a child in the world of the theatre. Many years later, she wrote her memoirs and recalled the importance of the orchestra at a time when music was integral to the performance of a play.

The theatre presented a diverse programme which included Shakespearean plays, opera and musical comedy, with pantomime a special treat at Christmas time. The young Greta, who entertained never-to-be-realised ambitions to be an actress, sometimes appeared in crowd scenes when children were required. She recalled the bleakness of the theatre on a Monday morning when the music and cues were sorted out. What a contrast to the warmth of a full theatre with an expectant audience chattering excitedly before the lights went down!. The orchestra would strike up and, as the curtain was raised, a hush fell upon the auditorium. Those of us who remember the Grand many years later would experience that self-same thrill. The theatre was full of atmosphere and, by the time I had the great pleasure of entering that wonderful auditorium – sometimes in the "gods", occasionally in the stalls – there were many ghosts. They were eventually laid to rest never to return when the theatre was finally dismantled but, as we shall learn, the theatre was to have a very eventful career during its fifty-nine year life.

The theatre saw the old century out and was well established as a part of Luton's life by 1900. J. Alban Newton now managed the theatre, though it was still licensed to Reginald Turner. Towards the end of the first year of the new century, a week-long run of "Uncle Tom's Cabin" was supplemented by a day-time performance for children. "School-children admitted at reduced prices to all parts" read the advertisement, "All parents should bring their children to see this magnificent production."

An Important New Name

A name new to the Grand began to appear. In February 1901, a large cast of "speciality artistes" were drawn together for "The Forty Thieves" – Mr. Edward Graham Falcon's Pantomime. It would not be long before the name E. Graham Falcon would be more closely associated with the Grand. He was a well-established theatre owner who ran the Royal County Theatre in Bedford. As well as devising pantomimes, he was already known in Luton for the productions he presented at the Town Hall before the Grand opened; in November 1896 for example, his company presented a two-day run of "Gentleman Joe" ("the most successful musical comedy ever produced" claimed the advertisement). Graham Falcon would soon dominate theatre in Luton; meanwhile, the varied programme continued.

The Popularity of Shakespeare

Rawson-Buckley's Shakespearean Company brought their repertoire to Luton, presenting a different play each night. Shakespeare was to prove eternally popular at the Grand; companies presenting several plays during one week became a regular feature down the years, giving Luton audiences an opportunity to see the works of our greatest playwright on a regular basis. Shakespeare remains popular in Luton and South Bedfordshire to this day. Similarly, opera would be presented in repertory on occasion. During Easter week in 1901, for example, the

Grand English Opera presented no less than seven operas in six days. It had been preceded by a Sacred Concert at the theatre on Good Friday, which had already become an annual event.

Variety Comes to the Grand

In the meantime, the Plait Hall continued to offer healthy competition. E. Hyde had not been put off by the opening of the Grand. On Whit Monday 1901, he again presented "Rice, Rose, Davis and the Half" as the top-billed attraction for his variety show. The act performed in "all the principal Theatres and Music Halls". Hyde's variety show also included Mr Arthur Flitton, "The Rising Luton Comedian". Within a few years, Mr. Flitton would be presenting variety in Luton.

The Grand did not stand by and let Mr. Hyde have it all his own way. Hyde's show was presented for just one day, so the Grand started a week of "Anglo-American Vaudeville" on the same day. The show comprised "the most expensive array of Refined and Artistic Variety Talent". By December, Reginald Turner set up his own "Grand Vaudeville Company". The bill included the "Tourbillon Troupe of Trick and Acrobatic Cyclists" direct from the Pavilion, London, as well as Miss Maud Esmeralda – "a second Jenny Lind".

Luton's Town Hall was also still pressed into service for concerts, often performed to benefit a local charity. One presented by Estelle M. Hawson in 1901 was in aid of the Children's Home and Bute Hospital, a popular local charity.

Sherlock Holmes at the Grand

Reginald Turner continued to present a wide range of quality fare. Everyone was talking about Sherlock Holmes at Sir Henry Irving's Lyceum Theatre in London. Turner rightly considered this to be a "must" for Luton, so April 1902 saw the

"Important and Expensive Engagement of the Ben Greet Company for the production of the World-Renowned Success – SHERLOCK HOLMES, THE FAMOUS DETECTIVE by A. Conan Doyle and William Gillette. The most thrilling Drama ever produced".

At the Lyceum, a young Charles Chaplin was playing the boy Billy in the same play, though there is no evidence that he was in the production which reached the Luton stage. *The Luton News* critic was very impressed: "Mr Bliss, who undertakes the title role, affects a deliberate, cool and decisive demeanour which is admirable". Having given audiences the doyen of sleuths, Mr Turner presented "The King of Crime" the following week. Nothing like a balanced programme! In October, the Grand presented a play called "A Man in a Thousand". It needed to be a play in a thousand, for the newest form of entertainment was offering a real challenge at the Town Hall.

Competition From the Town Hall

"Enormous Attractions" screamed the huge advertisement in *The Luton News*. "For One Week only, commencing Monday 6th October – First Visit of the New Edisonograph". The programme had been presented at the London Hippodrome and included "magnificent scenes of Animated Pictures depicting King Edward VII's Coronation". Because they knew the good folk of Luton would be impressed, the advertisement also informed readers that the film was "As shown before the Shah of Persia, by Special Command of King Edward". The programme also included:

"THE SEASON'S SENSATION
– A FANTASTICAL TRIP TO THE MOON".

The film, made by Georges Melies, is still regarded as a masterpiece of cinema fantasy. The complete show promised over 10,000 animated pictures new to the public of Luton. It was accompanied by the Famous Luton Red Cross Silver Band and, with prices at two shillings, one shilling, and sixpence – children half price – the Grand had real competition on its hands. Crowded audiences enjoyed the animated pictures and were particularly impressed when they saw the previous Saturday's Luton Town football match on the screen. The programme even included "coloured views of Ali Baba and the Forty Thieves".

Continuing Competition for the Grand

By 1903, Luton's "Rising Comedian" Arthur Flitton was presenting his own concerts at the Plait Hall featuring performers like Knight and Day – "sketch artists and comedians from principal music halls". 1903 was also the year Buffalo Bill's Wild West Show came to Luton. In September, they set up their show on Powdrill's Meadow opposite Wardown Park in New Bedford Road. As various performances were held in the Town Hall, the Corn Exchange on Market Hill and the Plait Hall, the Grand was never short of competition. Perhaps that is why the Waller Street theatre came up for sale and was auctioned in London on 20th October, 1903.

New Owners for the Grand

Until the theatre was taken over by the new owner, it stayed open into the early months of 1904; in March, there was even a week of Grand Opera with a different opera each day. The theatre was in the news that month for another reason. George Benson had presented a play at the Grand called "The Crimson Club" and had hired hoardings to advertise his production through Luton's well-known bill-poster, Charles Irons. However, when Mr. Irons asked for payment, he was put off several nights before losing patience – and his temper! There was clearly a bit of a to-do, for the police had to be called and Charles Irons had to sue for his money. In court, he was asked if he saw the play. "I had no time," he said, "I was simply following this man about trying to get my money."

During his final weeks at the Grand, Reginald Turner was determined to present a popular programme. In May, he brought back "Sherlock Holmes", which he followed with F.S. Gilbert's Opera Company. The theatre closed for a short period while the new owner, Edward Graham Falcon, redecorated the theatre and installed electric lighting. The licence had to be transferred and Mr. Falcon rapidly came face to face with Luton Town Council's antagonism towards the liquor licence. Reginald Turner had agreed to certain restrictions, mainly to do with the opening of the bars during actual performances. Mr. Falcon wanted this restriction lifted and applied for a new licence to be granted. He planned a different kind of programme to that presented by Mr. Turner and intended to offer an initial seven-week season of variety which was known at that time as "A Hippodrome". Alderman Hucklesby had heard this, but admitted that he was not familiar with the term "Hippodrome" and asked for an explanation. In replying to this query, the Alderman was told that the original meaning had "something to do with horses", but it now had a wider meaning. *The Luton News* reported: "It was not their intention, he believed, to bring horses there".

Licence Transferred and the Opening of the "Hippodrome Season"

In the event, the Council voted unanimously to transfer the licence rather than renew it. This was at the end of July and Lutonians did not have to wait long for their theatre to re-open. Or, indeed, to discover what was meant by "Hippodrome". There was a "Grand Opening" on Monday, 1st August, 1904 and, as that was a Bank Holiday, the first performance under the new regime was a matinee. The "Hippodrome Season" promised a change of artistes twice weekly and *The Luton News* gave the theatre's re-opening a welcome review:

"To the large audience of first-nighters, it was patent that the new management had not been idle between the close of the old and the commencement of the new regime. Every part of the building appeared to have been refurbished and on the stage the substitution of electrical for gas illuminating was not one of the least notable alterations".

The report added that with the new management came an entire change of staff; the marked improvement in the orchestra was also noted. The first "Hippodrome" programme included wire-walkers, tricksters and a hand-cuff act! The programme included Dainez's Comedy Circus which, with its well-trained dogs, donkey and pony was counted the hit of the evening. As predicted, there were no horses! The programme of acts was completed with singers, jugglers, eccentric dancers, comediennes and "burlesque novelties". The reporter noted that all the acts were excellent; he also remarked that the programme was long. Edward Graham Falcon, who made a brief speech during the interval on the opening night, had got off to a good start with his "new regime".

The Falcon Era

Throughout August, the new programming continued to be popular. The mixture of Music-Hall and circus acts (which included a performing bear) was complemented with the "Hippodrome Bioscope" which featured, among other filmed events, a popular wrestling match in the Albert Hall. These films, known as "actualities", were the forerunner to the newsreels which would become such a popular feature when the cinemas eventually came to stay. Mr. Falcon never lacked imagination. To the long list of varied acts already featured he added swordsmen, skate-dancers and conjurers. He did not rely on variety alone, for he also presented a wide range of theatrical productions. Even before 1905 was out, he presented plays and musicals, including a production of the ever-popular "Floradora" which, with its hit song "Tell Me Pretty Maiden, Do, Are There Any More At Home Like You?", had been a big hit in London five years earlier. In that same year, 1900, it became the first British musical to take Broadway by storm and set a trend for many years to come.

Though he continued to run his Bedford theatre,which had opened in 1899, Edward Graham Falcon now brought his long experience to Luton on a permanent basis. (He had already presented his pantomimes at the Grand during Reginald Turner's tenure). By the time he took over the Grand, he had held theatre licences for a total of twenty-one years. That experience was to prove invaluable, for the Grand Theatre prospered and served Luton and the surrounding district for many years under his guidance.

Falcon soon experienced the competition which had dogged Turner. In

September, 1905, the Town Hall presented a whole week of "Joseph Poole's Latest Myriorama, Myrio-Graph and Variety Amusement Amalgamation"! At that time, "actualities" were very popular and Mr. Poole's programme didn't disappoint as Luton audiences witnessed "War in the Far East" which included "The Great Battle of the Japan Sea". Audiences genuinely believed they were witnessing animated pictures of the actual events, though they were often re-created in England! Other animated pictures in Joseph Poole's sensational programme included the St. Louis Exhibition (which, forty years later, was celebrated by Judy Garland and a sparkling MGM cast in "Meet Me In St. Louis"). These early films were accompanied by a full programme of variety and an orchestral band, anticipating the cine-variety which would become a permanent part of Luton life for more than two decades. Joseph Poole's Myriorama was a regular visitor to Luton's Town Hall.

Audiences soon began taking the Grand for granted again. As early as January 1905, *The Luton News* reviewer gave the musical "My Lady Molly" a good notice, but was moved to comment: "It is a rather remarkable thing that it did not attract bigger houses".

Entertainment in Early Twentieth-Century Dunstable and Leighton Buzzard

Entertainment in South Bedfordshire at this time was not confined to Luton. Both Dunstable and Leighton Buzzard enjoyed productions by "travelling theatres" and travelling theatre companies. One such group, the Lyric Travelling Theatre, visited Linslade in the summer of 1904, but the drama extended beyond the stage. The proprietor of the Lyric was sued by actor J.O. Stevenson who claimed that he had not received payment in lieu of notice when he and his wife had worked for a joint salary of £2.5.0 per week. Mr and Mrs Stevenson had travelled from Sunderland to take up positions to play "responsibles" and "leading lady" roles respectively. The Leighton Buzzard court heard that, during "Sherlock Holmes", some of Mrs Stevenson's lines had to be spoken by the leading actor as she didn't seem to know them!

Working in such theatres was not easy. They often had to perform three or four different plays in a week and the actors were obviously expected to know all their parts. As the actress concerned had not learnt all her lines or stage directions, it would seem reasonable for the owner of the Lyric Travelling Theatre to dismiss her. In the event, the court found in favour of the Stevensons who, it was stated, were entitled to a week's pay in lieu of notice. All this took place many years before legislation protected employees, so it undoubtedly indicates a sense of fair play on the part of the Leighton Buzzard court.

In Dunstable, a visiting portable theatre in January, 1910, advertised itself as "Palace Theatre, Union Street" with a different play every night. *The Dunstable Borough Gazette* reported that Mr F. Langley, the proprietor and manager of the theatre was a regular and welcome visitor. The previous January, they had occupied Bull Close Field.

The Circus and Other Entertainments Come to Luton

Even though more and more entertainment was provided in various halls in the area, not to mention the Grand itself, the Circus was still very popular and remained so well after the Second World War. Even today, the circus still visits South Bedfordshire, but animals no longer perform under the Big Top. Sir Robert Fossett's London Circus came to Dunstable and then to "The Old Football Ground" in Luton's Dunstable Road in September, 1905, their first visit to the area for ten years! Swimmers were also thrilled that September when Australian champion Annette Kellerman (famous for the "One-piece Bathing Suit") visited the Luton Baths; early booking was advised!

Various organisations presented variety shows to benefit local organisations and charities. For their Christmas, 1906 concert, Luton Red Cross Band hired Walter Sutton's celebrated company of "talented artistes". The performances took place at the Plait Hall, still a leading place of entertainment in the town. Proceeds from the concert were in aid of the New Uniform Fund. Meanwhile, Philip Bone, who ran a music shop and warehouse in Manchester Street, gave lessons in mandolin, guitar and banjo. His popular Mandolin Orchestra gave regular concerts at Dunstable Town Hall and would eventually perform in Luton theatres yet to be built. On Christmas Day, 1906, 'A Grand Concert' with popular artistes engaged at "enormous expense" was presented at the Plait Hall by the Red Cross.

Luton's Love of Music

A fine Choral Society was formed in 1866, followed by their first concert in the Waller Street Wesleyan Chapel on 26th June, 1867. The venue was also used for concerts by their own choir under the direction of James Congreve. Well over a hundred years later, Luton Choral Society remains a strong part of Luton's arts scene. Musical talents could spread their wings now that Luton had such a beautiful and well-equipped theatre. The Luton Amateur Operatic and Dramatic Society was formed and, in January, 1907, they hired the Grand to perform Gilbert and Sullivan's "The Pirates of Penzance" with a one-act comedy called "A

BEDFORDSHIRE'S FIRST PURPOSE-BUILT THEATRE

Privy Council" as a curtain-raiser. The proceeds, after paying their expenses, were given to local charities. Sometimes, the Society dropped the word "Dramatic" and called itself the Luton Operatic Society, but it should not be confused with the modern-day society which was not formed until 1923. It is only speculation, but one suspects that the original society came to an end with the First World War.

Not to be outdone by all the musical and other performances in the town, the Grand was always prepared to try something new. At the end of May, 1907, the Pierrot Serenaders offered refined "al fresco" afternoon entertainment in Wardown Park and then presented a further concert in the Grand Theatre itself in the evening. The afternoon performances in the park proved to be very popular, but the evening concerts, though different, were not so well patronised. However, the Theatre made up for any lessening of their Box Office take when they presented "Kennedy's Komiks" the following week. There was a far bigger threat on the horizon however. More and more film shows, called "animated pictures" during the early years of the century, were being presented at Luton's Town Hall, the Plait Hall and the Corn Exchange.

Then, to prove the point, Bedfordshire's first purpose-built cinema opened in Luton in 1909.

Grand Xmas
ENTERTAINMENT.

WHERE ??

AT THE . . .

WALLER STREET
PLAIT HALL,

ON

BOXING-NIGHT,

DECEMBER 26th.

Monday Afternoon & Evening,

DECEMBER 28th.

Don't fail to see the latest Wonder of the XIX
Century, the

ANIMATOGRAPHE

(From the Polytechnic, London).

SPECIAL ENGAGEMENT OR

Mr. WALTER BANKS

(The Up-to-date Corney Grain),

IN HIS HUMOROUS AND MUSICAL SKETCHES.

GRAND VENTRILOQUIAL AND CONJURING
ENTERTAINMENT,

BY PROFESSOR DARVILLE (Of London).

Mr. H. A. GENTLE'S ORCHESTRAL BAND.

Change of Programme each Performance.

ADMISSION SIXPENCE. Reserved Seats 6d. extra.
Children half-price to all performances. On Boxing-Day
doors open at 7 p.m. On Monday doors open at 2.30 & 7 p.m.

Proceeds in Aid of the New Athletic Ground.

CHAPTER THREE

Early Flicks

ome two years before the Grand Theatre even opened, Luton experienced
its first public cinema show. It turned out to be an unexpected
bonus, for a late cancellation had given Luton Town Football Club an
opportunity to present a fund-raiser at the Waller Street Plait Hall. They
organised a variety show and, at very short notice, were able to present
the "Animatographe from the Polytechnic" on Boxing Day, 1896.

Variety shows were not new to the hall, by now a regular venue for entertainment.
It was an irony that the beautiful Plait Halls, built for the trading of straw plaits so
vital to the local hat trade, came too late. The declining trade needed the halls for
but a few years before the Cheapside building became a storage area. The larger
Waller Street Hall became a centre for concerts, meetings and variety shows. So it
was that the Plait Hall took its place in cinema history with a touring programme
of animated pictures screened in that very first year of cinema in England.

Lumiere's Cinematographe had come to London in February, 1896, having
caused a sensation in Paris just a few months earlier. The Cinematographe made
its debut at the Polytechnic in Regent Street, but competition was at hand. W.S.
Paul and Birt Acres had been making films on the roof of the Alhambra Theatre
in Leicester Square and had already filmed the 1895 Derby. Initially such films
were not projected on to a screen, but were seen as peep shows. It wasn't long
before Paul rivalled Lumiere's Cinematographe with his Animatographe at the
Alhambra. Paul's original name for his film show was the "Theatregraph", but the
Alhambra preferred "Animatographe". When Paul toured his show, both names
were used.

Left **Advertisement in *The Luton Reporter* announcing the "Animatographe" at Luton's Plait Hall
on Boxing Night, 1896, South Bedfordshire's very first film show.**

A Conundrum

The way in which Luton's (and Bedfordshire's) first film show was announced therefore poses a conundrum. If it was Paul's Animatographe, it should have come from the Alhambra, not the Polytechnic. If Luton's first film show did indeed come from the Polytechnic, it would have been Lumiere's Cinematographe. Even a hint of the films screened on that historic occasion would offer a clue to identify whether it was the Animatographe or the Cinematographe, but no real evidence exists to solve this puzzle. The newspaper reports were scant in the extreme, being more concerned to report that the first few films were shaky. When they stopped shaking, they scored a hit with the Luton audience, but the reporter did not think to give any description whatsoever of the content of the films shown.

It should be pointed out that films were not titled at that early stage but, as the content of both the Cinematographe and the Animatographe are known, even the slightest detail would probably be enough to say which it was. Sadly, it seems that a footnote in Luton's history is lost in the mists of time. Unless a programme or old diary entry of that evening comes to light, we are destined not to know which show was screened on that Boxing Night so long ago.

Turns and Tours

Animated pictures gained almost immediate popularity. Variety shows which visited the town on a regular basis began to include animated pictures as one of the "turns" on the bill. At that stage, no one thought that a complete cinema show would attract an audience, for the "flickers" were considered little more than a novelty. It wasn't long before that situation changed, however, for travelling "Biographs" visited the towns of Bedfordshire and various operators became known in each town. In Dunstable, Freddie Marchant became fascinated by the moving pictures and soon began presenting film shows in the Town Hall (already established as the town's entertainment venue with touring plays and shows). In Luton, Jury's Imperial Pictures became a regular feature of the entertainment programmes presented at both the Town Hall and the Plait Hall. William Jury, one of the first large-scale film renters in Britain, had a wide range of films under his control and was able to hire out his "Imperial Pictures" throughout the country.

It was inevitable that someone would risk showing films on a regular basis. Purpose-built cinemas as well as permanent conversions began to appear in London and the big cities from 1904. The first to be built in the area came in 1908 when the Alpha Cinema opened in London Road, St Albans. The later Capitol/ Odeon stood on the same site.

Town Hall, Dunstable, the town's principal venue for stage shows during the 19th century and early 20th century, was also used to screen early film shows before the town had its own cinema; by the time this photograph was taken, it was the home of the Dunstable Repertory Company and remained so until it was demolished. (DG)

The First Purpose-Built Cinema in Bedfordshire

The first permanent cinema in Bedfordshire opened in October, 1909. Called the Anglo-American Electric Picture Palace, it was converted from an existing building owned by local builders T & E Neville who leased it out for use as a cinema. The plans, submitted by Frederick Percy Aulton, were passed just over a month earlier at Luton's Council meeting held on the 7th of September; by all accounts, other business-men in the town thought he and the operators, Luton Electric Theatre Ltd.,were taking an enormous risk. Film shows were undoubtedly popular in the town, but few could envisage that a hall built or adapted for the specific and only purpose of showing films every night of the week could possibly succeed. As far as they were concerned, the suitability of animated pictures was restricted to either "penny gaffs" – make-shift entertainment halls fitted into converted shops – or visiting showmen who set up their equipment in the Town Hall, the Plait Hall or a Church Hall.

Having opened on Saturday, 16th October, the operators of the Gordon Street hall applied for a temporary music and dancing licence the following Wednesday. Mr Aulton could not apply for a full licence until two weeks hence, but this initial application caused some confusion. There were those who thought that no licence was necessary and a discussion on that very point occupied the magistrates for

Right **Staff pose outside Bedfordshire's first purpose-built cinema, the Anglo American Electric Picture Palace, which opened in Gordon Street, Luton in 1909. (LMS)**

Left **Interior of Anglo American Picture Palace in Gordon Street taken from a contemporary newspaper article in 1912. (LCL/LN)**

some little while. To press his case for Sunday opening, Mr Aulton assured the magistrates that the films shown on the Sabbath would depict Bible stories and would convey a moral message "such as might be preached in a sermon". They were also assured that the music, to be played on a piano or an organ, would only be played in the intervals between the films. To make the point, the magistrates were invited to attend the cinema with the promise that he would not open on the following Sunday if they witnessed anything they found distasteful. They declined the offer and issued a licence to open only from Mondays to Saturdays.

Even at that stage, the Anglo-American Electric Theatre in Luton was not without competition. Jury's Imperial Pictures started a special two-week season at the Plait Hall on 11th of October. To meet the challenge of the new Gordon Street cinema, Jury presented

"All the Latest Events and Picture Gems, including – A Marvellous Series of Arctic Pictures A DASH FOR THE NORTH POLE".

The Paragon Picture Palace

Even earlier, on Saturday 25th September, The Paragon Picture Palace opened in Castle Street

"For a Short Season, with High Class VARIETY AND CINEMATOGRAPH ENTERTAINMENTS Under the direction of Mr Frank Blythe late Manager for Catlin's Royal Pierrots".

The Paragon Picture Palace operated as a full-time cinema for a short period. Ultimately however, it could not compete with the Gordon Street venture and did not succeed. Similarly, Jury's Imperial Pictures would fade from the scene within a few years. The admission prices for all these shows were similar; all had a top price of one shilling, though there was some variation in the cheaper prices. The Paragon, which probably occupied a church hall, offered reserved and numbered seats for a shilling, ninepence and sixpence. Unreserved seating was also offered for threepence. Jury's "popular" prices were one shilling, sixpence, fourpence and twopence with special "scholar's" prices for the Saturday Children's matinee. The Anglo-American Electric Picture Palace charged one shilling, sixpence and threepence, with sixpenny, threepenny and twopenny tickets for children on Saturday afternoon.

The Success of the Gordon Street Electric

It wasn't long before Lutonians referred to the Anglo-American Electric Picture Palace as the Gordon Street Electric. Realising that the official name was rather long, the owners initially dropped the word "Electric" and then restored it when they finally settled for the Gordon Street Electric Pavilion. It was a very small cinema which occupied a site less than thirty feet wide. In those far-off days, regulations regarding seating were less stringent than they are today and standing was permitted. Even so, the hall would have been very crowded and cramped with an audience of up to four hundred, the capacity reported in *The Luton News*. Like many cinemas built at that time, seating was variable and an exact number is impossible to ascertain. One thing is certain – the cinema was very popular despite prophecies of gloom and doom. In 1912, some three years after its opening, it was reported that the hall had been so successful that it had only closed on one week-night since its opening. That was when King Edward VII died in May, 1910, but then all places of entertainment closed on that sad Saturday as a mark of respect. Mr. Graham Falcon actually closed the Grand Theatre for a whole week.

The success of the Gordon Street Electric was due to good management and programming which included "the best films of leading English and foreign makers and some of the most notable pictures put on the market have been exhibited". As a result, people had come back again and again to form a regular cinema-going habit. That habit was to dominate the entertainment scene in South Bedfordshire until television finally took its toll – though, as we shall learn, it did return in the mid-eighties.

A Popular Range of Films

The Gordon Street cinema was described as "cosy" and the educational value of travelogues and films depicting the latest scientific discoveries was not lost on audiences. It has to be said however that the following description of screen entertainment was probably what filled the seats:

"Visitors may also find themselves led into a state of almost uncontrollable merriment over some droll or farcical representation of every day life".

Even at that early stage, cinemas presented a very wide variety of cinema fare – historical dramas, stirring adventures and "grand plays of olden days" were all included in the programmes. By November, 1912, the Gordon Street Electric was reported to have shown some 3,500 films! These included newsreels which were sent to the cinema by the fastest possible means. Film recording the death of General Booth was rushed into the London studio for processing by 6pm – it was on the Gordon Street screen at 7.55 that same evening. Newsreel footage of the opening of Luton's new Carnegie Library on the 1st of October, 1910, built by T & E Neville, had also been screened at the cinema on the evening of the event.

Up-to-Date Equipment in Gordon Street

When it opened in 1909, the Gordon Street cinema was equipped with the latest projector. At the end of each reel (which lasted about ten minutes) shaded lights would come up while the next reel was mounted on to the only machine. The pianist of course kept on playing! The cinema was also fitted with an early organ and a "cinephone", a type of gramophone which was supposed to play recordings to match singing performances on screen. In 1909, this really was a novelty!

The projector, or "bioscope machine" as it was called, was made by Pathe Freres and was housed in a fire-proof operating room ten feet above the entrance. Before the opening, *The Luton News* assured readers that the cinema would be fitted with the latest "improved flicker-less projector" – but that didn't stop folk calling them "the flicks"! The cinema itself was built by local men for Luton builder A. Attwood. The floor was raked and rose two feet from front to back. The best seats (and therefore the most expensive) were at the back. Programmes changed twice a week and matinees were provided on Wednesday (early closing day in Luton) and Saturday.

The Grand Fights Back

The Grand Theatre had already included the "Bioscope" within its variety programmes. In June 1910, the following announcement appeared in the local press:

GRAND THEATRE, LUTON   MONDAY, JUNE 6th
The Above THEATRE will be Opened as a PICTURE PALACE
One House Nightly at 8.30   SUBJECTS COMPRISING
DRAMATIC   HUMOROUS   INDUSTRIAL   HUNTING and TRAVEL
TOGETHER WITH THE LATEST PICTURES of UP-TO-DATE EVENTS
POPULAR PRICES   Gallery 3d Pit 6d Balcony and Stalls 9d Circle 1/-
Children Half-Price to all parts except Gallery
MATINEE, SATURDAY, at 3 Doors Open at 2.30

Not that the Grand ever closed. The week before it turned itself into a cinema, the Grand had presented "the Celebrated London Actress Miss Grace Warner from the Lyceum, Princess, Drury Lane, Lyric and Prince of Wales Theatres" in a series of plays. "The Wages of Sin" – a drama – was presented on Monday and Tuesday, the farcical comedy "My Artful Valet" on Wednesday and Thursday, "Lady Audley's Secret" was the choice for Friday and the week-long season came to a close with "The Secret Clue" on Saturday. No doubt, the back-stage staff welcomed a less strenuous time when the movies came along!

Unfortunately, the screen was too small for the size of the Theatre and, after a couple of months, regular screenings were abandoned in favour of a return to variety. Occasional screenings of prestigious films were presented until 1930 – the very end of the so-called "silent" era. It should be rememberd that films were rarely if ever actually shown in silence, for they were accompanied by a piano, an organ or, in the bigger halls, an orchestra. Albert Leigh, whom Mr. Graham Falcon employed as his general manager, announced that the Grand would become a "First Class Variety Theatre" with performances twice nightly at 6.45 pm and 9 pm from Monday, 1st August, 1910. Seat prices ranged from 1/6 in the circle to just 3d in the gallery. An extra 3d was charged for "Early Doors".

The attempt to turn the Grand into a cinema may not have succeeded, but the Gordon Street cinema still had competition. The visiting Jury's Imperial Pictures, which had established themselves as regular exhibitors in Luton, had not been put off when the permanent Gordon Street cinema opened. In fact, they were still showing their films in the Town Hall in 1911. "At enormous expense", they brought "The Great Shooting Affair at Hounsditch" in January and announced that "Jury's Orchestra" would be coming the following week. The Grand was back in its familiar stride with E. Graham Falcon's pantomime "Dick Whittington".

Meanwhile, in Leighton Buzzard . . .

Theatre also continued to be popular in Leighton Buzzard. The Corn Exchange had already established itself as a popular venue for professional and amateur shows as well as films. In the twenties, the Corn Exchange would become the Exchange Theatre – but that's a later story. Throughout South Bedfordshire, however, it was the Cinematograph and its many rivals which proved most popular during those years leading up to the First World war.

. . . and Back in Luton

The Chapel Street Wesley Guild in Luton announced a Grand Cinematograph

Luton's second purpose-built cinema, The Picturedrome, opened in 1911. By the time
this photograph was taken in 1937, it had become part of the Union circuit. (CTA)

Travelogue in February, 1911. Various church and chapel halls in the area had already established regular film shows but, apart from the Paragon's brief spell as a full-time cinema, the movies were but one activity in a full programme of events. In the meantime, more permanent film shows were being planned. In March 1911, the Luton American Roller Skating Rink in Dunstable Road announced that they were going to install "Pictures". The venue changed its name to "American Rink and Picture Hall" with a complicated mixture of film shows and skating sessions. For 3d or 6d, Lutonians could see Pictures between 5.30 and 7.30 on Mondays, Wednesdays and Saturdays, while two houses nightly were presented on Tuesdays, Thursdays and Fridays. Skating was fitted around these shows each day. Whether it was the complex programming or the opening of a brand new cinema in Park Street – or perhaps both – the arrangement seems to have lasted for only a short while. There was a link between cinemas and skating rinks at that time. Both were very popular and the management of both was clearly regarded as compatible, as the manager of another Luton skating rink in Park Street left to manage the new picture house.

Luton's Second Purpose-Built Cinema

The Park Street cinema in Luton opened with a great flourish on Saturday, 8th April, 1911. Called the Picturedrome, the opening programme was made up of the following ten shorts:

Lea Finds a Way Out
In Perfect Harmony
Happy Go Lucky Tim
Glimpses of China
The Knife
The Bonanza King
Nat Pinkerton's Jewel Mystery
Mission of the Dessert (sic)
Tontolini Automobilist
When Lovers Part

A completely new programme was presented the following Monday and, thereafter, a complete change of programme was made twice weekly on Mondays and Thursdays. Seats in the stalls were priced at 3d and 6d, while the better-off could sit in the cosy balcony for 9d. Advance booking was offered for the numbered seats in the balcony; the films were accompanied by an orchestra under the leadership of M.A. Laidlaw.

Inside The Picturedrome looking towards the stage and screen following extensions and improvements made in 1928. Note the "stamped steel" ceiling, often installed into older cinemas built during the "silent" period to improve sound quality in readiness for the talkies. (CTA)

Gordon Street Fights Back

Not to be outdone by such strong competition, the Gordon Street Electric presented Sir Herbert Tree in "King Henry VIII" as produced at His Majesty's Theatre. The film was so popular, it was also shown at the Town Hall (which still served as one of Luton's part-time cinemas). Another gimmick offered at Gordon Street was the hiring of a soloist to supplement the films which anticipated the cine-variety soon to come.

Comfort a Priority at the Picturedrome

Like the Gordon Street cinema, Luton's Picturedrome was built by Mr Attwood, now an Alderman of the Borough. The cinema contained some six-hundred "plush" seats, with comfort as a key factor in the overall design. *The Luton News* enthused over the new picture palace:

The Picturedrome auditorium showing the "pretty balcony" following the 1928 extensions. (CTA)

"There is a very handsome entrance hall leading to the ground floor seats through swing doors, whilst on the left is a fire-proof stone staircase leading to a very pretty balcony. The interior is of a light colour set off with green window frames, whilst the floor gently slopes from the rear seats to the curtain, so that everyone can get an admirable view of the pictures. All the seats are comfortable and of red plush. The building is lighted by electricity from the ceiling, whilst down the side are small red-cased gaslights, which are so shaded that they do not interfere with the pictures. All the appointments are of first class character and the result must be gratifying to the builders, architects and owners. Alderman A. Attwood was the builder, and he is also the lessor. The lessees are the Luton Picturedrome, Ltd of which Mr. Anson V. Squire is the managing director. The Picturedrome is in the Lion Circuit".

During the jollifications which took place after the opening, reference was made to the fact that the cost of operating the Picturedrome was almost one eighth of a skating rink and that they must therefore be more profitable. It proved to be fair comment. Though skating was popular, it was soon overtaken by "The Pictures". The site of the Picturedrome had been chosen with care. Park Street was a bustling thoroughfare in a thickly populated part of the town. Trams passed the door every few minutes as they trundled to and from the tram depot further down Park Street. It's interesting to note that, during the "silent" era, further cinemas were generally built in different parts of the town to attract very localised audiences. However, as we shall learn in the next chapter, a super town-centre cinema would soon be built which would put all the others in the shade.

Lutonians Offered a Stake in the Picturedrome

Before the Picturedrome was built, a magnificent specification was prepared, giving the people of Luton the opportunity to invest in their new cinema. Within a few months of opening, the Picturedrome experienced drama both on and off the screen. In August, a fire drama called "The Still Alarm" was being screened when the film itself burst into flames and caused the alarm to ring! It was not unusual for the highly flammable nitrate film to catch fire in those days, but in this case, members of the audience were in no danger. The operation room at the back of the hall was fire-proofed, the only connection with the audience being the small aperture through which the film was projected.

On January 1st, 1910, the first Cinematograph Films Act (1909) came into force. As several serious cinema fires had occurred in this country and in Europe, this first Films Act was concerned principally with safety. It became compulsory for operating boxes to be fire-proofed; had this Act not been passed, the Picturedrome fire could have been far more serious. Passers-by in the street outside saw smoke escaping into the street and called the fire brigade; *The Luton News* reported that the audience was speedily reassured!

The Cinema Bug Hits Dunstable and Leighton Buzzard

Needless to say, the cinemas in Luton attracted audiences from beyond the borough boundaries. Train services from Dunstable, Leagrave and even Leighton Buzzard brought South Bedfordshire's film-goers to swell the audiences at the Picturedrome, the Gordon Street Electric and, of course, the Grand Theatre. It was inevitable that both Dunstable and Leighton Buzzard would demand their own cinemas and neither town was short of entrepreneurs ready to meet that demand. Local histories tell us that the townsfolk of Leighton Buzzard enjoyed a day-trip to Luton – not only to visit the palaces of entertainment, but also to travel on the trams! As trams passed the door of the Picturedrome every four minutes or so, that cinema did particularly well.

Leighton Buzzard's First Cinema

In 1910, the Purrett family in Leighton Buzzard had built a piano and organ store in Hartwell Grove. The corrugated iron building, which had a steel span roof and brick walls, seems to have been converted to a skating rink shortly after it was built, but it began to serve a rather more popular form of entertainment in 1911. Taken over by Captain Webb and Mr. Trigg, it was announced in May that the building was to be converted into an "Electric Picture Palace". Seats were installed in the main part of the small building with three steps at the back leading to four raised rows (which commanded a higher seat price). Recalling visits to the cinema many years later, pensioner Fred Groom (who, as a well known local musician, was later employed by Captain Webb) estimated that the cinema could hold about three hundred. Other estimates were considerably lower, but the higher figure probably included standing customers.

Known initially as the Victoria Electric Palace, it is reputed to have had a screen which measured 18 feet by 16 feet. The films were accompanied by a grand piano, played by Captain Webb's wife Sybil, which was placed conveniently at the front of the auditorium to allow her to see the action as she played appropriate music. The little cinema was operated by Captain Webb and his family; his son Larry operated the hand-cranked projector, while daughter Frederica ran the Box Office. The little family-run cinema gained immediate popularity with local audiences. Opening on Whit Monday, 1911 (12 June), the new cinema boasted a three-hour continuous programme which allowed patrons to come in at any point in the programme and leave when the picture they had seen came round again. As the programme comprised eight shorts (the normal type of cinema programme at that time), it was an entirely practicable method of operation. Interestingly, the concept of "continuous programmes" lasted well into the sixties, long after such a policy suited the length or style of films shown. The practice was lampooned by Danny Kaye in his 1944 film "Up In Arms" during his frantic "lobby number". Facing a huge queue waiting to get into the cinema after the film had started, Danny Kaye explained in his inimitable zany style that they should not be concerned, for the film was designed for people who came in – in the middle! The practice is unheard of today, but many older film-goers will remember continous performances with a mixture of nostalgia and irritation. There was nothing more annoying than having to get up to let someone go by just as the exciting bit had started.

Ticket prices at the Victoria Electric Palace were very much in line with those charged at the Luton cinemas – 3d, 6d and 1/-. The shilling seats could be reserved. There was a matinee on Saturday for children, with another on Tuesday (Market Day) for "farmers and their wives". By 1913, newspaper ads were headed just "Picture Palace", with "Webb and Trigg – Sole Proprietors" prominently displayed at the bottom. The mid-week matinee changed to Thursday at 3pm; programmes changed twice a week on Mondays and Thursdays. Like other cinemas of that period, it had only one projector when it opened. Music was provided by a pianist both during and between the films. As we shall learn, cinemas would introduce a second projector to avoid frequent breaks in the programme for reel changes. Nowadays, of course, there is only one projector per auditorium, but it can take up to four hours of film on one of its "platters".

Grand Schemes for Dunstable

Three schemes for cinemas in Dunstable were proposed. The grandest was for a site between Clifton Road and Waterlow Road with an entrance from High Street North. It was clearly favoured, for two separate plans for substantial developments which included a cinema were submitted. The first was passed in June, 1911, and, had it been built, would have been a tremendous asset to the town. The plans revealed an attractive frontage with a fine arch flanked by tastefully designed shops on either side. The arch, topped by a bell-tower, was designed to lead directly into the vestibule and pay-box. Beyond that, a hall and an inner hall were linked by a wide corridor leading to the auditorium. The plans show that the theatre itself was to be set diagonally. It had a stage, an orchestra pit – and even a fly-tower! Had it declined as a cinema, it would have provided the perfect venue for future societies such as the Three Arts, the Dunstable Repertory Company and the Dunstable Operatic Society. It could also have accommodated touring companies.

A balcony with 171 seats was planned to overlook stalls with two blocks of 209 seats each. In addition, two insets on the left and right side of the auditorium would have provided 50 and 49 seats respectively. With a total seating of 688 arranged ideally for live performances, it was nevertheless intended to be a cinema, as a screen measuring 20 feet by 15 feet was envisaged. As if that wasn't splendid enough, a dance hall opening into Clifton Road was also part of the planned development. The beautiful plans by London architect Max Zimmerman have been preserved by the Bedfordshire & Luton Archives & Records Service in Bedford, as have alternative plans for the same site.

In December, 1911, Mill Street Development Syndicate Ltd of Luton submitted their plans for the same Clifton Road/High Street North/Waterlow Road site. Architects F. Taperell and Haase of London envisaged a more conventionally angled theatre with a much shorter entrance into the auditorium. The Dance Hall had become an Assembly Hall with a platform. Once again, the attractive frontage on to High Street North was dominated by an arch crowned with a bell-tower. As with the earlier plans, two shops would have flanked the arch on either side. The auditorium itself was to have been larger, with 729 seats on a single level. This version would also have had a stage and two dressing rooms. The plans clearly didn't meet with full approval when they were first submitted, for a follow-up letter was sent on the 19th of December overcoming Borough Surveyor John Stewart's objections. Why the earlier, passed plans should have been superseded by this later scheme is anyone's guess, but in the event, neither development took place. It is possible that the second plan didn't take place because another development pipped it to the post.

Fred Marchant's Intervention Brings Dunstable's First Cinema

Dunstable builder George S. Wood prepared plans for businessman Fred Marchant and submitted them on 1st November, 1911. Described on the plans as "Marchant's Picturedrome", the rather smaller building was also planned for High Street North (destined, incidentally, to be the street which contained all Dunstable's cinemas). The site was near the Unionist Club (now the Conservative Club), thirty to forty feet north of Manchester Place. The small cinema, only some 29 feet wide and 65 feet deep was built next to the Manor House Garden (long since gone). Because the plans were not totally satisfactory, Fred Marchant had to agree to a temporary building which could be removed at six month's notice. It was a very basic cinema containing a total of 375 seats on a single floor arranged as twenty-five rows of fifteen seats each. Aisles on either side of the seats led to the screen on the back wall of the building. There were no toilet facilities for the ladies and only one urinal at the back for men. There was one exit beside the screen, with two further exits on the south side of the building. These led into an open passage some 4 feet 6 inches wide. The pitched roof was hidden behind a facade designed like many a cinema of its day. On the first floor a circular window gave light to the operator's box which was reached from a set of iron steps just inside the entrance. As one entered the double doors from the street, the meagre vestibule contained a paybox with entrances on either side leading into the auditorium.

By the time he opened his cinema, Fred Marchant had been exhibiting films in Dunstable Town Hall and was to dominate the showing of films in the town for some time to come – though not without competition, as we shall see. When it opened in 1912, Marchant's Picturedrome was called the Palace and it was the first of four cinemas to open in Dunstable.

Author's impression of the first Palace, Dunstable, referred to as "Marchant's Picturedrome" before it opened; it was built for Fred Marchant, a well-known film exhibitor in the town before permanent cinemas were built. (EG)

CHAPTER FOUR

South Bedfordshire Goes Movie Crazy

A new cinema for Luton proposed in June, 1911, was refused planning permission. St. George's Picture Palace planned for Bute Street was not approved in June and, when the plans were re-submitted in July, they were turned down again. No more was heard of the proposed Bute Street cinema – more than seventy years would pass before folk in Luton could claim to have seen a film at St. George's!

By 1912, Luton had given the thumbs up to the cinematograph. With the success of the Picturedrome, Jury's Imperial Pictures had faded away and the American Skating Rink in Dunstable Road was no longer operating as a picture hall. None-the-less, no fewer than three new cinemas opened to make it the town's best year for new cinema buildings, until two luxury cinema palaces with a total of nearly four thousand seats between them opened within a week of each other in 1938. For now, cinemas tended to be built on a more modest scale. Messrs Jeffs and Bennett had proposed cinematograph exhibitions in Wardown Park, but the Electricity Committee were so concerned at the cost of laying a cable to supply electric current (£120), the scheme never went ahead. An attempt to use a petrol-driven dynamo was not successful and the couple ended up in the courts when they couldn't pay their debts. It is perhaps interesting to note that, by 1912, Lutonians were rapidly turning to electricity for lighting and, with an increase in the use of electric motors as well, the supply of electricity in the town rose by 28% in just one year.

The Wellington

On 2nd May, the first of the 1912 cinemas opened in Wellington Street. The required music and dancing licence was applied for and granted on the previous day. At the Borough Sessions, the new cinema was referred to as the "New Hall, Wellington Street", but it was advertised from the start as the New Wellington Street Picture Palace. The cinema was a conversion from an existing building which had opened as the Temperance Hall in 1875, but the front of the building was completely rebuilt in a style popular for cinema frontages at that time. The Wellington was owned under lease by Walter Frederick Goodwin and Charles Stanley Smith and managed by Bert E. Major who had run a picture palace in Crewe. Amazingly, the cinema was allowed to be opened with temporary chairs.

There were large numbers at the early shows which *The Luton News* described as "excellent". The newspaper also praised the hall itself, which measured 80 feet by 25 feet. Temporary chairs notwithstanding, the reporter found the hall "comfortable". It was well fitted up and "an even temperature is always maintained". The programme, comprising some seven films, during the first week included two which were coloured – "Sumeria" and "The Witch's Kiss". The colouring would have been produced by one of the early, primitive methods employed at that period. Very early films were tinted, initially by hand and then by using stencils for staining the colours on to the film. By 1912, a two-colour system called Kinemacolor was in existence and it is likely that this or a similar system would have been used to produce these films. The most popular item of all in

Interior of the Wellington Cinema, Luton, a few years before it closed. (LMS/LN)

Author's impression of the Wellington Picture Palace, Luton; opening in 1912, this little cinema outlived most of the other cinemas built during the "silent" era. (EG)

that opening week was a film about the sinking of the Titanic. In their inaugural advertisement, the Wellington picked this film for special mention:

> "At enormous expense a film has been secured depicting various incidents in THE TITANIC DISASTER and a big programme of up-to-date films".

They also claimed that the theatre was

> "magnificently appointed, and the ventilation is perfect. The pictures are absolutely <u>rock steady</u>".

Clearly the flickering of early films had been noted and cinemas were keen to cure this problem. Programmes were changed every Monday and Thursday, a practice followed by the Wellington for most of its long life. In fact, it wasn't until the cinema became the Coronet in the early fifties that films were shown for a whole week. In 1912, that was very far into the future. Very much in line with other halls in the area, admission prices were 3d, 6d and 1/-. Children were admitted for 2d and 3d on Saturday afternoons when the continuous programmes ran from 2.30 pm. During the week, continuous programmes ran from 6 pm to 11 pm each evening. So pleased were the management with the response to the Titanic film, they presented "The Naval Review at Weymouth" for three days from Thursday, 9th May. For their second week, the Wellington also secured the

"Exclusive Rights for the Town of ST. GEORGE AND THE DRAGON".

In December, G.A. Brown took over the management of the Wellington and an orchestra and organ were added to enhance the programmes.

When the Wellington got its fixed seating it probably accommodated nearly four hundred. Early plans no longer exist, as they were destroyed in the Town Hall fire. However, plans were drawn up in the forties when the seating was 377 arranged as two blocks on either side of a central aisle. Each block had a width of six seats. Four steps led up to the cinema's entrance which was gained through a single set of double doors leading to a central pay box set within a small lobby. Doors on either side of the pay-box led directly into the auditorium. It would appear that only gentlemen were afforded wash-room facilities, for a ladies room was not added until 1944! (hence the need to redraw the plans). Like the Picturedrome, the Wellington was situated in a densely populated area which was thus served by its own local cinema. It was clearly successful for, at the outbreak of World War II, it was the only small cinema still open.

The High Town Electric Picture Theatre

Lutonians had just got used to the new cinema in Wellington Street when another picture theatre opened, this time in High Town. Describing their new venture as

"The Finest Picture Hall in Bedfordshire",

the management opened their High Town Electric Picture Theatre at 2.30 pm on Saturday, 24th August, 1912. In *The Luton News*, a lengthy article declared:

"At last the High Town district is to have its own place of public entertainment, and having regard to the manner in which the population in that quarter of the town has grown of late years there should be a very good field for this enterprise".

Author's impression of the High Town Electric Picture Theatre, Luton, which opened in 1912. The name was later changed to Plaza. Closed in 1937, the Plaza re-opened for a few years from 1952. The cinema never screened films in 'scope. (EG)

Just to be sure that everyone was welcome, however, the advertisement for the opening gave the address as High Town Road, Luton – "Just over the railway bridge".

Designed by local architect W. H. Guest Hubbard and erected by local builder T. Day of Smart Street, the cinema was originally in local hands. Heating was provided by gas radiators supplied by the local Diamond Foundry. For its time, the auditorium was lofty and fans were installed to aid ventilation. There were 259 single and 24 triple seats in the stalls with a further 84 seats in the balcony, providing seating for a total of 415. The local press reported that the management was proud of the tip-up seats upholstered in "saxe blue plush, the colour chosen being a welcome change from the crimson usually adopted in places of entertainment". Saxe blue was also used for the carpets and "heavy drapings" of all the doors. The most expensive seats were to be found in the balcony (or "Grand Circle" as it was described in the inaugural advertisement). But then the seats upstairs had arms, a feature singularly lacking in the stalls. Circle seats cost 9d and 1/- and could be reserved. On the ground floor, seats cost 3d and 6d. There was a children's matinee on Saturday afternoons at 2 pm with admission at just 1d, 2d and 3d. "Picture Play Chocolates" – so called because each packet contained a "Popular Picture Artist" – were on sale in the hall.

The cinema had a bold electric sign, PICTURES, above the entrance, while an impressive portico fronting the building allowed waiting patrons to shelter from the rain. Once inside the vestibule, the simple but effective decoration and mosaic floor could be appreciated. Clearly, designer and owners had gone to great lengths to make their picture palace attractive to the eye. Even more impressive, great care had also been taken in other, more technical aspects of the theatre. The screen was built out from the wall in order to avoid the sweating which had proved to be such a problem in earlier cinemas. Following a practice which had proved effective in other cinemas, a current of air was constantly passed behind the screen to keep it completely dry. It should be remembered that, at this time, picture exhibitors were still learning about the buildings in which films were to be screened. The proprietors of Luton's latest cinema were also keen to point out that *two* Pathe machines had been installed in the projection box. The point they wished to make was that the use of two projectors would obviate the need to wait between the ten-minute reels. Many earlier cinemas would have installed only one projector and audiences would have had a brief interval between each film. This was not as bad as it sounds, for most films were only one reel in length and the interlude would have been filled with piano music.

Special Opening Programme at High Town

The High Town Electric had a special programme for its opening day, with a completely new programme starting a three-day run on the following Monday. The cinema clearly wanted to ensure that their patrons would have every inducement to attend as frequently as possible. The opening programme included "The Picture Idol" starring Maurice Costello, a popular silent screen star. There were two dramas – "The Convict's Parole" and "Nick Winter and the Banker". The Nick Winter series had already proved popular with cinemagoers. "Chauffeur's Dream", "A Dash Through the Hills" and "Amorous Arthur" ensured a merry dose of comedy, while "The Triumph of Right" was the already obligatory cowboy picture. The High Town Electric Picture Theatre secured the local rights to "Pathe's Animated Gazette" which changed every Wednesday and Saturday. To press home the point, the initial advertisement promised

"No Flash in the Pan, but a High Quality of Programme, which will be maintained at all times".

The first manager was Stephen Slinger, late of the Picturedrome and Park Street Skating Rink. Clearly, with so many new cinemas being built, cinema managers could pick their jobs. In September, a "co-operative competition" with £5,000 in cash prizes was offered. The film associated with this competition, "The Great Anarchist Mystery", based on a story by Silas B. Hocking, played for the whole week from Monday, 2nd September. It was far more usual for programmes to play for just three days.

The Truly Palatial Palace Theatre

The third cinema to open in Luton in 1912 was to outclass all the rest. However, the Palace Theatre's development was not without its problems. Richard George Irving Byers, of Lansdowne Road in Luton, originally intended to build a small cinema in Mill Street, very much along the lines of those already existing in the town. As he got under way, he seems to have had more ambitious ideas, but he went broke before the building was completed. Plans for the new cinema had been passed in 1911, but further plans were submitted by D.A. Wheeler in February, 1912. These were not passed without modification. The "little" cinema had become a theatre suitable for films and variety with seating for 702 in the stalls and a further 416 in the circle. There were also four boxes, each of which could seat two. Altogether, the Palace had seating for a total of 1,126, larger than the Grand Theatre or any other cinema in town.

Mrs Millie Williams bought the Palace before it was completed towards the end of 1912 and she applied for the necessary music and dancing licence in early December. Due to the bankruptcy, the building had become notorious, but Mrs Williams was determined to open a first-class theatre with high-class entertainment. Mrs Williams' husband, an experieced cinematograph theatre manager who had run the Imperial Cinema in London's Edgware Road, was put in charge of the theatre's operation. It was proposed to show pictures interspersed with operatic singing, with a full symphony orchestra of ladies to accompany the films and the performers (including two who had been singers at Covent Garden). Mr and Mrs Williams would allow nothing "suggestive or vulgar", though it was proposed that future live entertainment would include "high-class music-hall turns". In addition to the price she paid for the hall itself, Mrs Williams spent a further £10,000 to bring the theatre up to the right standard. £10,000 was an enormous amount in 1912.

When this picture was taken, trams still passed the Palace Theatre. (LN)

Licencing Concerns

Having spent such a large sum, Mrs Williams was keen to open her new theatre on Boxing Day in order to take advantage of the Christmas holiday season. The problem was that the magistrates charged with the task of inspecting the building in order to grant a licence were unable to do so until Christmas Eve. As a result, the opening of the Palace could not be advertised in the local papers. It was touch and go, but the new theatre did open on December 26th, 1912. A great deal of interest in the hall had been generated and, despite the lack of newspaper advertising, word of mouth ensured full houses on opening day. Before the theatre opened, the magistrates had been concerned about a garage next door as there was general concern about fires in cinemas at that time. Several bad fires had been caused due to the extreme flammability of film stock ("safety" film was not introduced until the early fifties and strict rules to ensure that reels of film were contained in fire-proof metal containers did not come into force until 1922.) It was the flammability of petrol which exercised the minds of the authorities on this occasion. They were assured that that side of the theatre would be fire-proofed. The owners of the Palace wanted to purchase the offending building, but could not persuade the owner to sell. As a result, the wall at the back on the left hand side of the theatre as one faced the screen veered inwards and affected the symmetry of the auditorium when viewed from the stage.

Luton's Most Expensive Picture Show

Seats could be booked in advance at no extra charge, with no "early doors" fee imposed. Boxes cost 5/- (for two) while seats in the front row of the Dress Circle cost 2/-. The next two rows cost 1/6 while the rest of the circle seats could be bought for 1/-. In the stalls, called "Fauteuils" in the impressive programme produced each week, seats could be purchased for 9d and 6d. As can be seen, it was significantly more expensive than other cinemas in town. The weekly

The magnificent auditorium of the Palace Theatre, Luton, seen from the stage. (LN)

programme gave details and summaries of the films shown during both halves of the week, together with a listing of the acts to be seen on stage. There were seating plans and the programme proudly proclaimed that "In the interest of Public Health this Theatre is disinfected throughout with Jeye's Fluid". This indispensable publication cost just one penny.

The programme included a note – "A Few Words About Ourselves". It claimed to be one of the most luxurious Cinematograph Theatres in England and promised exclusive films "... though the cost of such pictures is necessarily very high, we are convinced that our patrons will duly appreciate them". The note also introduced the resident Royal Cremona Band under the direction of Miss D. A. Vincent. As we shall see in a later chapter, the Palace always held its orchestra in high esteem, and it paid off! Like other new establishments, the Palace sought to assure audiences that the pictures would be "rock-steady" and clear due to the excellence of their projection equipment.

A Magnificent Building

The building was truly magnificent. The imposing frontage had balconies on the first and second floors and the structure was topped by tasteful statues and a large dome. Three arches into a recessed entrance area led to three double doors. These led into the marbled foyer area with separate pay-boxes for the stalls and the circle. The two staircases up to the circle had polished brass handrails and seemed to carry on beyond the balcony. It has been suggested that an upper circle may have been planned before the building had become engulfed in bankruptcy. Two boxes flanked each side of the stage, while an illuminated board indicated the number of the act performing on stage. There was an orchestra pit in front of the 17 feet deep stage which had red velvet "tabs" or front curtains. The stage "turns" shared five dressing rooms and living accommodation was provided for the manager. When compared to other cinemas already operating in South Bedfordshire, it was very impressive and held its own as Luton's leading cinema until its pre-eminence was challenged by the Alma – but that's a story yet to come.

The Palace had been granted a temporary licence while some minor work was completed. A proper licence was finally granted at the Council's licensing committee held on February 5th, less than a week before the theatre's first really important film presentation. For one week from February 10th, 1913, the Palace screened Albert Capellani's version of "Les Miserables" – in eleven acts! The programme lasted four hours. In 1914, the theatre, already operating as a cine-variety hall, became owned by Palace Theatre (Luton) Ltd.; shortly afterwards, a young man joined the orchestra to play cornet for such artistes as Marie Lloyd and Harry Tate. That young man went on to achieve fame equal to these legends of the Music Hall as the leader of championship brass bands. His name was Harry Mortimer.

Increasing Popularity of Cinema Causes Concern in Dunstable

The increasing popularity of cinema clearly caused concern among some. The Reverend H. Merchant of Dunstable's Congregational Church predicted that "people would grow into a brainless generation without thought, and altogether a giddy people". He came to this conclusion in 1913 because he believed "pictures were too rapid and one could often return after spending an hour watching the Cinematograph and testify seeing nothing except the movement or jumble of incidents". His remarks were made shortly after a second cinema for Dunstable was planned.

Dunstable's Second Cinema

The success of Fred Marchant's Palace attracted competition from Charles Abrahams when he submitted plans for a "Proposed Picture Palace" opposite the Town Hall on the 10th of June, 1913. The town's main Post Office had moved to new premises to the north of the Manor House (not far from Marchant's Palace) and Abrahams proposed to convert the vacated building opposite the Town Hall into a cinema. It was a long, narrow building with a twenty-four foot frontage. It went back more than ninety feet, affording a depth of seventy-five feet for the auditorium. However, the major part of the building narrowed to only sixteen feet and could only accommodate two banks of seats with a central aisle. There were just four seats on either side, with a total of thirty-three rows. This should have afforded a total of 264 seats but, as two exits were required on the north side of the building, the number of seats was reduced to 256. Toilet accommodation was provided behind the screen which was suspended in front of the back wall. The floor was raked with a fall of one inch in ten feet.

The operator's box together with a w.c. was on the upper floor which was reached by an iron staircase towards the back of the auditorium. On the outside, a glass-covered wrought-iron canopy adorned the top of the entrance. Five steps led up into the small entrance hall. A pay-box faced the entrance, with doors on either side leading into the auditorium. The plan for this small cinema was drawn up by Luton architect A. Wilkinson. In December, 1913, plans were submitted to add an extension to the back of the building, thus providing a small stage. The theatre was electrically lit. The owner quickly put his theatre on to the market, for it was auctioned at the Sugar Loaf on 29th July, 1914. The particulars were described thus:

> "All that Valuable and Commanding block of Freehold Property well situate in the centre of the HIGH STREET, DUNSTABLE and known as THE CINEMA THEATRE together with the DWELLING HOUSE adjoining".

"The Cinema Theatre", also known as the Electric Kinema, offered a few years' competition to the Palace, but it was remembered by older Dunstablians until the latter years of the twentieth century. As no advertisements seemed to be included in *The Dunstable Borough Gazette* until July, 1915 (and then only briefly), exact opening and closing dates are not known. The advertisements pointed out that the cinema was opposite the Town Hall, Dunstable. A special war-time matinee on Monday, 12th July, 1915, was held to benefit the Mayor's local distress relief fund.

Cinema Habit Grows in Leighton Buzzard

To start with, the Victoria Electric Palace in Leighton Buzzard could not sustain film shows on every day. The venue was also used for dances and, in 1913, the men of the town used the "Vic" to give the town's children a "Christmas Treat". However, the popularity of films ensured that the Victoria Electric Palace became a full-time cinema. During the twenties, it became known as Ye Olde Vic and, hoping to claw back some of the cinema audience which travelled to Luton by train, Captain Webb looked for return business by advertising in the Luton papers! For some reason, the cinema did not open on Mondays, though this notice outside Ye Olde Vic could have given the wrong impression –

> "Good clean entertainment all the week except Monday"!

It was a very small cinema and, bearing in mind the competition to come, the fact that it remained open so long is a great tribute to the cinema's management and staff.

Wartime Luton

The Grand Theatre in Luton continued its policy of presenting a very varied programme. Edward Graham Falcon presented his annual pantomime, travelling companies presented popular contemporary plays such as "The Headmaster", the occasional revue came along and the projection equipment was occasionally brought into use. In December, 1914, the Grand offered:

"With Capt. Scott in the Antarctic
Mr Herbert C. Ponting's
CINEMA LECTURE
Illustrated throughout by the most wonderful
MOVING PICTURES".

Another intriguing show presented early on during the War was "Maskelyne & Devant's Mysteries" which included The Yogi's Star & Disappearing Donkey! The modern mind doth surely boggle! In 1915, wartime audiences were entertained by famous music hall stars like Harry Tate and his company. The Grand was redecorated in 1916 and, from 1st January, 1917, the Grand Theatre screened "The Birth of a Nation", still regarded as one of the cinema's greatest achievements even though its blatantly racialist stance would never be tolerated today. It is none-the-less such an important film, it is still occasionally screened, but is now preceded by a message putting the film into its context in the history of cinema in order to avoid giving offence.

GRAND
LUTON.

Proprietor   -   -   -   Mr. GRAHAM FALCON

MONDAY, JULY 19, 1915.

6.45 | **TWICE NIGHTLY** | **9.0**
FIRST-CLASS VAUDEVILLE

Expensive Engagement of

HARRY TATE'S No. 1 Co.
In the Famous **"FISHING."**
The most laughable playlet ever produced.

10 DIXIE GIRLS 10
In Charming Scena **"OLYMPIC REVELS."**

ROSIE GASTON
Dainty Soubrette

ALFONZO A wonderful Equilibrist

PHIL KAUFFMAN
The British Coon Delineator from London Pavilion.

PHOEBE FIELD A Soprano Vocalist of rare range.

The World-Famous

FRANCO MIDGETS
Smallest Illusionists in existence
Direct from tour round the Globe
A Truly Remarkable Performance.

For Prices of Admission see other Bills.

The Grand Theatre in Luton offered "First Class Vaudeville" during WWI. Harry Tate was a very popular Music Hall star of the period. (LMS)

The Palace Theatre in Luton applied for and got a Stage Play Licence in 1914, though they continued with cine-variety. Luton's first permanent cinema – now officially known as the Gordon Street County Electric Pavilion – was still popular. Their normal twice-weekly change of programme was suspended in favour of week-long runs for notable films like "Tilly's Punctured Romance", the first feature-length comedy which starred Charlie Chaplin and Marie Dressler, and "Antony and Cleopatra", a five-reel epic from Rome. Early in 1914, the Picturedrome and High Town cinemas amalgamated to show the same films. Luton's High Town cinema was destined to have more changes of ownership than the majority of the area's cinemas; as will be seen in a later chapter, most were eventually drawn into the big chains.

Apart from a short-lived amalgamation, the Wellington remained resolutely independent to the very end. In 1914, they offered a top price of 4d when the normal top price was 9d (it was even higher at the Palace). Determined to compete, the Wellington adopted an aggressive stance by declaring in their weekly ads:

"Still On Top – The Leading Picture Theatre".

All places of entertainment in Luton benefited from an influx of some twenty-five thousand troops based in and around the town. Under the auspices of the Soldiers' Entertainment Fund, the Plait Hall offered concert parties to entertain "The Tommies".

Wartime Dunstable

Since its opening, Fred Marchant's Palace in Dunstable had been a big success. His small cinema outflanked the even smaller Cinema Theatre, even though that hall introduced variety turns to accompany films. Not to be outdone, Marchant beefed up his programme with live acts and the Cinema Theatre did not survive for very long after the end of the Great War. Fred Marchant, undoubtedly the father of cinema in Dunstable, was destined to play a leading role in the film exhibition industry. He was also set to give Dunstable a far grander Picture Palace after the war.

Wartime Leighton Buzzard

Leighton Buzzard only had the Victoria Electric Picture Palace during World War I, though cinema shows were also occasionally given at the Corn Exchange. When the war was over, the scene for Leighton Buzzard's cinemagoers was to improve enormously. Places of entertainment may have had rich pickings during the war, but one war-time innovation was not welcomed. The Finance (New Duties) Act of 1916 caused Entertainment Tax to be introduced from 20th August, 1917, with the inevitable result that seat prices went up, but it didn't stop a post-war boom for theatres and cinemas.

Dunstable's second Palace Cinema was far grander than the first. Like its predecessor it was built for Freddie Marchant. The cinema was taken over by the fledgling Southan Morris Circuit before being absorbed into the far larger Union chain. (CTA)

CHAPTER FIVE

Post-War Boom

The population as a whole took some time to recover after hostilities ended with Germany in November, 1918. By the early twenties, just about everybody decided to let their hair down and have some fun. Jazz had invaded Britain and dance music became immensely popular. The big West End hotels and restaurants in London employed the leading dance bands to perform nightly. Various halls and hotels in South Bedfordshire held regular dances, though usually only on a Saturday night. In Luton, the Corn Exchange, the Plait Hall and the Winter Assembly Hall (a winter venue which became the indoor swimming pool during the summer) all had music and dancing licences. Before it was burned down, there was also dancing in the Town Hall.

Having fun also meant going to the theatre and the cinema. Light, tuneful musical comedies dominated the West End theatres and soon found their way to Luton's Grand Theatre. Variety at the Palace was very strong; theatregoers could see a movie feature as well as a variety bill which included the likes of Max Miller, singer Elsie Carlisle as well as less well remembered acts like the "Delightfully Dainty Duo Zoe and Zona". Everyone was wild about the movies. Going to the pictures no longer meant watching a string of shorts, for the feature film had come to stay. That is, films which lasted fifty minutes or more, though there were still plenty of shorts to fill the programme.

This growing interest led to new cinemas in the South Bedfordshire area, with brand new cinemas in Dunstable, Luton and Leighton Buzzard. In 1919, Freddie Marchant deposited plans for a new cinema in Dunstable. The beautiful plans were prepared by architects Franklin and Deacon. They depicted a magnificent "Cinema Theatre" for High Street, Dunstable. The thirty-seven feet frontage was set back from the road, with four steps leading to an arched entrance with a pay-box on either side. Two sets of double doors led into a foyer and a staircase leading to the balcony. The ground floor contained a block of four hundred seats with aisles on either side.

The gallery contained a block of one hundred and twelve seats with aisles on each side. The "Lantern Room" sat atop the high entrance area and had a vent in the ceiling which allowed the hot air to rise out of what looked like a small bell-tower. This tower was a feature of the well-proportioned, attractive frontage rendered in brick. The lantern room had an oval window looking out on to High Street North. Inside the auditorium, the ceiling was barrelled, which was not uncommon in cinemas at that time. The building was just over one hundred feet deep; much larger than the old Palace Cinema. In fact, this elegant new cinema was built virtually next next door to Marchant's first cinema and he called it – The Palace! It opened in 1919/20 (the exact date is not recorded) and quickly became a favourite haunt for Dunstablians. When Freddie Marchant opened his new Palace, he closed the old one, though the front seemed to form a wall which remained in place for some years.

Off-stage Drama for Travelling Players in Dunstable

Notwithstanding the opening of their beautiful new cinema, the people of Dunstable still enjoyed live shows. Touring companies still presented occasional plays at the Town Hall and one such visit early in 1920 created as much drama off stage as on. The company concerned brought their production of "Jack and the Beanstalk" and, following the final performance on the Saturday night, the scenery and effects were taken to the station and loaded into a box van in readiness for its Monday morning departure for Aylesbury. Unfortunately, the van caught fire in the early hours of Sunday morning; it became so fierce, one of the coaches for the Leighton Buzzard train, sharing the siding, also caught fire. Both the passenger carriage and the box van with all its contents were destroyed and the unfortunate theatrical company (which was not insured) found themselves stranded in Dunstable. The town's mayor, Councillor J.T. Dales, came to their aid. He arranged for them to give a concert for their own benefit at the Town Hall. He also opened a subscription list with £5 and arranged for an appeal through the theatrical press. The company missed their Aylesbury date, but Dunstablians responded magnificently to the impromptu concert and added a further £29.1s to the Mayor's fund.

Charlie Chaplin a Big Hit in Luton

As if to underline the growing popularity of films in Luton, Charlie Chaplin's huge hit "The Kid" was shown at two cinemas in the town during the same week in September, 1921. Still leading the way with a mixture of films and variety,

Above The auditorium of Dunstable's new Palace.   Note the traditional barrelled ceiling which was a common feature of earlier cinemas. (CTA)

Below The attractive screen area of the new Palace, Dunstable seen from the balcony. The cinema was also used as a theatre on occasion. (CTA)

the Palace offered its usual bill of four variety turns to accompany the Chaplin film. There was even a one-reel short – "Ghost of Slumber Mountain" – to complete the programme. The Palace also offered matinees on Wednesday and Saturday so, not to be outdone, the Gordon Street County Electric Pavilion (as the Gordon Street cinema was now called) offered continuous performances of "The Kid" (described in their advertisements as "6 Reels of Joy") from 2 pm every day. There was also a special children's matinee on Saturday morning. Interest in these screenings was no doubt boosted by news of Charlie Chaplin's recent visit to London, the city of his birth.

Another New Cinema for Luton

With so much interest in the cinema, it was little wonder that a certain Mr Barber was confident of success with his Bury Park Road conversion in Luton. His new cinema, the Empire, opened on 29th November, 1921. Operated by Luton Cinemas Ltd., music and dancing licences had been granted the previous Wednesday. After the Mayor and other dignitaries attended a private view of the new cinema in the afternoon, this new, well appointed cinema flung wide its doors to Luton's cinemagoers at 6pm. *The Luton Reporter* was unstinting in its praise:

> "Admirably situated for the district it is designed to serve, the Empire Cinema cannot lay claim to be the largest picture theatre in the town, but for its size there is certainly nothing to surpass it in cosiness, airiness, picturesqeness and general arrangement in all Bedfordshire. The magistrates who inspected it were unqualified in their praise of its many excellent features, some of them quite unique; in fact, it is claimed to be a West End cinema out of London".

As we'll soon learn, references to West End grandeur would also be applied to another South Bedfordshire cinema due to open just one year later. Edgar L. Barber adapted his propeller factory from plans drawn up by architects Brown and Parrott who had their offices in Castle Street, Luton. Mr. Barber had established the propeller factory in response to Air Ministry requirements during World War I, but the building had become idle. It stood in a "central position in the crescent-shaped sweep at the Dunstable Road end of Bury Park Road". It was considered to be an architectural asset to the neighbourhood and it certainly had a commanding site. The building still stands to this day and its small-scale grandeur can still be appreciated.

Luton's Empire Cinema in Bury Park Road opened as an independent cinema in 1921. It was taken over by Southan Morris before becoming part of the Union circuit in 1933. (CTA)

The building is open to the pavement now, but in 1921 the Empire stood behind iron railings. Half-timbering added to the attractiveness of the red brick frontage, while circular steps led to a portico with stone columns. The entrance doors were of polished walnut, while the foyer was oak-panelled. Several busts were among the decorations inside the foyer which included carved heads to represent comedy and tragedy. There were also busts of Punch, John Bull, Royal heads – and Charlie Chaplin! Perhaps Mr Barber included the little tramp because "The Kid" had been so popular in the local halls with which he was about to compete. Inside the foyer, there was one paybox with separate windows for the stalls and balcony. Upon entering the well-appointed auditorium, the stunning proscenium

The magnificent interior of the Empire Cinema, Luton with its distinctive Oriental decoration had been considerably enlaged by the time this photograph was taken. (CTA)

was in full view. English gold-leaf was included in the design for which the general motif was otherwise oriental – principally Japanese. Coloured glass depicting a Japanese garden bordered the proscenium arch, beyond which could be seen the curtain which, when opened, revealed the orchestra sitting below the 16ft by 12ft screen. The effect of the glass decoration was heightened by hidden lighting, while the walls of the stalls were oak-panelled. Even the ceiling was ornamental and the upper wall had the pilasters with cornices and friezes we now firmly associate with the twenties.

The small cinema had three hundred and twenty seats in the stalls, with a further one hundred and twenty in the balcony. During the late twenties, the size of the auditorium was almost doubled when a wall between the cinema and a large area on the left of the building was removed. It was also necessary to extend the tiled roof to cover the new area. The spacious, fire-proofed operating room contained two Simplex projectors driven by a Crompton generator, with a winding-room next door. Before the introduction of modern "cake-stand" projectors in the sixties, the winding-room would have been in constant use as the reels had to be rewound after screening in readiness for the next performance.

Ten minute reels would pass through one projector while the second machine was loaded. When the projectionist spotted the tell-tale cue-dots on the film, he would switch manually from one machine to the other and the unwound reel would be taken into the winding room.

Programme Policy at the Empire

The programme policy at the Empire was to show a big feature film with a supporting programme of comedy, drama and travel shorts. A Gaumont Graphic newsreel was also included in each programme. The policy did not include serials which were still a popular feature in other local cinemas. The opening feature was the film version of Jerome K. Jerome's "Three Men in a Boat" with "The White Dove" following three days later. The Empire's first manager was Mr. W. Austin who had some fourteen years experience of cinema exhibition. The projectionist

Though it was first seen at the Alma in October, 1932, "Tarzan The Ape Man" returned to the Empire in September, 1934. The enterprising cinema enlisted the aid of an elephant to promote the film, and then rubbed salt in the wounds by parading the magnificent creature past the rival Palace Theatre on its way from the station. (LN)

After WWII, the Empire was acquired by the local Jewish community to become the town's synagogue. (CG)

was Mr. A. Smith, while the three-piece orchestra (piano, violin and 'cello) was under the direction of local musician Reginald Clarke.

The building stands to this day and is still recognisable as the former Empire Cinema. For many years after World War II, it served as Luton's synagogue and is now used as an Islamic centre.

Another Warning on the Bad Effects of Cinema

With new cinemas in Luton and Dunstable (not to mention a couple more soon to open in Leighton Buzzard), alarm signals about the bad effects of cinemagoing were once again being sounded. Mr P. Lymbery, headmaster of Pulford's School, talked about the good and bad effects of the cinema to the Church of England Men's Society in Leighton Buzzard. While recognising the educational and entertainment value of pictures, Mr Lymbery warned of eye strain. He also complained of the "trashy stuff shown", believing it to be harmful to young minds. He claimed that hanging scenes, picking pockets, robberies and murders had been emulated by children with "disastrous results". He believed the opulent life-style of certain characters depicted on screen created more class distinction than ever and that scenes showing how crooks evaded the police led to "disobedience of the law". Mr Lymbery was also concerned with morals both on and off the screen and made a point of criticizing "the orgies such as had recently been disclosed". Such orgies, he felt, were made possible because of the "enormous salaries paid to cinema actors". Nice to know some things never change! Notwithstanding Mr Lymbery's dark vision of cinemagoing and its consequences, the population of Leighton Buzzard was about to have far greater opportunities for cinemagoing on their own doorstep.

Ideally situated for the local Muslim population, the former Empire Cinema is now known as The Islamic Centre. (LN)

Leighton Buzzard's First Purpose-Built Cinema

Leighton Buzzard's first purpose-built cinema was known variously as the Hippodrome, the Empire and the Grand. It was actually just over the bridge and was therefore situated in Linslade. However, it drew audiences from both towns. The building stood until destroyed by fire in 1999 having spent many years as a car showroom. Run by George Henry Blackburn, the film announcements on the front page of *The Leighton Buzzard Observer* were comprehensive indeed! In his "Special Announcement" for the Empire Cinema, Bridge Street, Leighton Buzzard (sic), Mr Blackburn included the author's appreciation of "Mrs Erricker's Reputation", the film he was showing at the end of February, 1922:

> "I hope that I may express my warm appreciation of Mr Cecil Hepworth's production of "Mrs Erricker's Reputation" as a picture play, without appearing to venture an opinion of my own" he began. He then went on to praise the star, Alma Taylor, and others associated with the piece. The author, Thomas Cobb, clearly believed that everybody would have read his book, for he made no attempt to offer any description of the content of the film itself!

Unfortunately, such extravagant advertising took its toll on Managing Director Blackburn, for the Empire (in which he had a third share) ran at a loss. The cinema closed only a few months after opening and Mr Blackburn was in the bankruptcy court by June. His association with film exhibition in Leighton Buzzard went back to the War years. The cinema itself was built by Thomas Yirrel, a local stonemason and builder, and it proved to be popular when it re-opened as the Grand Cinema on Thursday, 3rd August, 1922. It was then under the general management of Harry J. Benjamin who had been the resident manager for Mr. Blackburn. With continuous performances from 6pm nightly, tickets cost 1/3, 1/-, 9d and 6d. The cinema could seat about five hundred. The re-opening programme included Viola Dana in "The Chorus Girl's Romance" based on F. Scott Fitzgerald's "Head and Shoulders". The supporting programme included a two-reel comedy, an "interest" film and the Gaumont Graphic newsreel. The Grand Cinema now settled down to a run of success, but strong competition came at the end of that very same year.

Right above **Author's impression of the Grand Cinema, which served both Leighton Buzzard and Linslade, opened as the Empire. (EG)** *Right below* **The former Grand Cinema was converted into a car showroom; this photograph was taken before it was destroyed by fire in 1999. (TL)**

Competition for the Grand Cinema

There was already competition from Fred Webb and his Victoria Picture Palace. Mr Webb had also signed a lease giving him control of the Corn Exchange, Leighton Buzzard's only public hall. The signing of the lease had alarmed some in the town, for they feared that it would be confined to cinema shows, though Mr Webb promised that he would equip the hall for theatrical purposes. Indeed, he renamed it the Exchange Theatre. Before he took control, the Leighton Buzzard Amateur Operatic and Dramatic Society pre-empted this name change when they presented their production of "Miss Hook of Holland" (The Dutch Musical Comedy) in November, 1922. They advertised the venue as the "Corn Exchange Theatre".

Soon after the Armistice in 1919, a seventeenth-century house with splendid oriel windows was sold to Ben Brown for conversion into a cinema. Strict conditions were applied to the house in Lake Street which meant that the frontage of the old building must remain intact. The rear of the building was to be torn down to make room for the auditorium. The cost of the scheme proved to be much higher than anticipated. Work started on the ambitious project, but lack of funds forced work to stop. As more capital could not be raised, the scheme

When it opened, the Oriel Cinema in Leighton Buzzard retained the frontage of the original building, noted for its oriel windows, but this attractive art deco frontage was added in the thirties. This view was taken at the end of 1963. (CTA)

remained in suspension until November, 1921. The company owning the site was "reconstructed" with Thomas Keens of Luton as secretary and the necessary capital was raised to complete the project.

After almost two years of on-and-off construction by local builder A. E. Dawson, the magnificent Oriel Picture Theatre opened on Boxing Day, 1922. Cinemagoers entered through swing doors built into what was the front wall of Oriel House. *The Leighton Buzzard Observer* noted that, having entered the new cinema:

> "The visitor finds himself in a large, well-decorated vestibule, which would do credit to a West End Theatre, and mounting half a dozen steps, enters the theatre by swing doors to the right or left".

The newspaper went on to say that "probably the finest picture hall in the county" had been built to the design of a well-known West End Theatre (though which one

Left **The Oriel, Leighton Buzzard, spent its final days as a Bingo Hall. (TL)**

The Oriel Cinema was almost opposite the Corn Exchange, later the Exchange Theatre. Both can be seen in this 1966 photograph of Lake Street. (BLARS)

was not named). More praise flowed from the enthusiastic pen of the Observer reporter, claiming the Oriel to be "the last word in comfort and convenience". The screen could be seen without interruption, for the auditorium had a rake of some three or four feet from front to back. The comfortable seats were of the "plush, tip-up type, with arms, and are well sprung". We may now take such comfort as standard in modern cinemas, but in 1922 memories of bench seats in the smaller halls built less than a decade before would still have been fresh in the memories of film-goers. A further comparison with the West End could be made with the gas-operated heating system which used hot air to maintain a constant temperature and kept the atmosphere free from "impurities". Cigarette smoking was very common at that time and was not restricted in places of entertainment.

The stalls area contained a total of 550 seats arranged in three blocks. Although the new cinema had a gallery, it did not contain seats when it first opened. As audiences grew, so the Oriel would be able to (and indeed did) accommodate a further 326 cinemagoers in the upstairs area. Two modern projectors were installed in a chamber just above what would become the last row of the circle. The theatre was lit by electricity – in 1922, there were still theatres lit by gas. Commenting on the pleasing design of the cinema, *The Leighton Buzzard Observer* commented:

"There may be differences of opinion as to the need for three picture halls in Leighton Buzzard, but there can be no disagreement on this point – that the Oriel Theatre – which is the largest public hall in the town – is a welcome addition to local public buildings".

Clearly, the reporter's views were echoed by audiences who still remember the Oriel as a very comfortable, pleasing place to see films. Needless to say, it outlived its competitors (the Exchange, the Grand and the Old Vic) by many years. It should of course be remembered that the Grand was actually just inside Linslade which, at that time, was not only a different town but was also in Buckinghamshire. Sadly, the old Oriel House frontage did not remain. For the first decade or so of its life, the cinema remained in complete sympathy with the fine architectural line of Lake Street. Not only the upper windows, but three magnificent chimneys could be seen. The cinema was virtually opposite the old Corn Exchange, now known as the Exchange Theatre, but changes were on the way. In 1932, the magnificent tower, which stood atop the grand entrance to the Exchange, was removed and a well known land-mark had disappeared. Not long afterwards, the frontage of the Oriel no longer seemed appropriate for a modern cinema and a thirties facade was installed with a delightfully typical art-deco pay-box in the foyer. The face of Lake Street had changed forever.

The Oriel's Opening Programme

The opening programme at the Oriel included Norma Talmadge in the film version of the famous stage play, "Smiling Through". The sentimental weepie also starred a certain Harrison Ford! The supporting programme included a "Pathe Gazette" and a comedy-short featuring Chaplin-clone Billy West. This programme lasted just two days, with a 3-day run of the British film "Tilly of Bloomsbury" following on Thursday, 28th December, 1922. This film starred the popular British actress Edna Best, some years before she defected to Hollywood. "Tilly" was supported by "a unique film depicting the dangers and thrills of Elephant Hunting". Called "The Great Elephant Kraal", it is difficult to imagine that any cinema, let alone one in Leighton Buzzard, would show such a film today. Indeed, I can find no evidence of a passion for elephant hunting in any part of Bedfordshire during 1922 either!

A 1929 advertisement in *The Leighton Buzzard Observer* for a D.W. Griffith picture at the Oriel Picture Theatre.

> **ORIEL** Picture Theatre, Tel.
> Leighton Buzzard. No. 160
> Manager: MR. R. BARRIE.
>
> MONDAY, JULY 8th, for 3 days.
> JEAN HERSHOLT in D. W. Griffith's
> **" The Battle of the Sexes."**
> Also CHESTER CONKLIN, in " A NINE DAYS' WONDER."

The Celluloid and Cinematograph Film Act, 1922

One thing that affected all the cinemas in South Bedfordshire – and, indeed, the whole of Britain – was the introduction of the Celluloid and Cinematograph Film Act, 1922. From 1st October that year, Local Authorities were made responsible for ensuring that proper provision be made to prevent fire through raw celluloid or cinematograph film. This was achieved through regular inspections by the Chief Officer of the appropriate Fire Brigade. The cinemas were required to keep film in metal boxes and were also required to pay £2 each year to help defray the cost of Fire Brigade inspections.

Dunstable Amateurs and the Palace Cinema

In December, 1922, The Dunstable Amateur Operatic and Dramatic Society had been successfully launched. The following year, they convinced Fred Marchant to erect a stage and "other accommodation" in his Palace Cinema for their first production, "The Geisha Girl", in May. The production had some sixty performers and was the first of many amateur productions to be performed at Dunstable's cinema. Incidentally, 1923 was the year the new Luton Amateur Operatic and Dramatic Society was formed. They were fortunate enough to have the Grand Theatre for their performances (as had the Society's predecessor before the World War) and, in 1924, they presented "The Gondoliers", the first in a series of shows which continues to this day – though, sadly, not in the Grand Theatre.

Live Theatre in Leighton Buzzard

Live theatre was also getting a boost in Leighton Buzzard. The townsfolk had feared that they would lose the live shows presented on occasion at the Corn Exchange. In changing the name of the building to the "Exchange Theatre" it may have been Captain Webb's intention to allay such fears. It was indeed fitted out as a cinema; his little Picture Palace in Hartwell Grove could no longer compete with the Oriel and the Grand and he was determined to stay in business. He used the ground floor hall for his cinema shows. It had an un-raked flat floor, but there was a small balcony. He also took advantage of the larger venue to offer a trio to play music during and between the films. Indeed, for really important films like "The Four Horsemen Of The Apocalypse" (which brought instant fame for Rudolph Valentino when he danced a steamy tango) and Douglas Fairbanks' lavish version of "Robin Hood", the trio was bolstered with the talents of trumpeter Fred Groom and trombonist Fred Branton. It did not become a full-time cinema, for live shows were also a prominent part of his programme. The Exchange Theatre was never "wired for sound" and ceased showing films when the talkies arrived.

More Live Theatre in Leighton Buzzard

Live theatre came to Leighton Buzzard and Linslade with a vengeance when it was decided to convert the Grand Cinema into the Hippodrome, Linslade. The building came into the hands of Walter Leitch and he shared a generally-held view. With three cinemas open each night, he said "Leighton Buzzard and Linslade had rather an excess of entertainment of that class". Having changed the name, he decided to abolish cinema shows altogether and, with the Countess of Orkney in attendance to perform the opening ceremony, the Hippodrome had its "Grand Opening" as a theatre on Monday, 3rd September, 1923. Mr Leitch promised musical comedy, revue, variety and drama. For those used to taking the train to Luton, the only unique attraction left in the larger town was the tram service! A stage was fitted with a proscenium in white and gold. It was planned to offer one show nightly from Monday to Friday, with two shows on Saturday. Ticket prices ranged from 6d to 1/10.

The first presentation at the new Hippodrome was

"JINGLES AND SMILES
the great musical comedy success in twelve scenes
supported by
Full London Cast and Beauty Chorus,
including the
Twelve Musical Comedy Kids".

Proceeds of the opening night went to two local nursing associations.

Opening a live theatre in Leighton Buzzard/Linslade proved to be a very successful move – to start with anyway. Crowds turned up for the opening night and many had to be turned away. After the Countess had officially opened the theatre, Mr Leitch invited the audience to let him know if they didn't like the shows he presented. He also hoped they would let him know if they DID like them as well! The Countess was then presented with a casket of flowers and chocolates by Miss Fairy Dale, one of the dancers in the show. Theatre historians and buffs may like to know that the stars were Mamie Soutter and Partner. The Hippodrome operated successfully for just a few years before changing its name back to Grand Cinema – and film shows.

Dunstable's "Theatre"

In Dunstable, Fred Marchant wasn't averse to his Palace being called a "Theatre" on special occasions – and not only when the local amateurs presented their popular shows. In fact, he was clearly determined to make his cinema the focus of local attention. During the General Election of 1923, the "Palace Theatre, Dunstable" was used for a meeting in support of the candidature of the Hon. Geoffrey Howard, the Liberal Candidate for the Luton Parliamentary Division which, at that time, included Dunstable.

Assembly Hall Planned for Luton

In Luton, it was proposed to spend £8,000 in altering and improving the Waller Street Plait Hall. A span roof would allow the central pillars to be removed; a stage and artistes rooms would be built. There would be a gallery holding 300 in addition to 700 in the main part of the hall. It was also proposed that a smaller hall be included in the Cheapside Plait Hall. The population of the town had risen from 36,404 in 1901 to an estimated 59,220 by 1924. Luton desperately needed an assembly hall and the Waller Street Plait Hall had served the town well as an entertainment and concert venue over the years. It seemed like a perfect solution; Luton would get a good hall and an historically significant building would be preserved in a useful capacity.

There's no doubt that such an investment in the building would have been very welcome, but it was not to be. It was considered that a covered market was a more urgent need and both the Waller Street and Cheapside Halls were converted for that use. The site of so many Music Hall entertainments and the site of Bedfordshire's first cinema performance would see no more concerts. The outside of the Halls would now be shop-fronts; that wonderful space would be filled with market stalls. One of the reasons given for not going ahead with the Plait Hall conversion was that a large Assembly Hall would be incorporated into the new Town Hall which would replace the old building burned down in the 1919 riots. Although the plans were drawn up and can still be seen, the Assembly Hall was never built.

There was still the Winter Assembly Hall of course. Used as indoor baths during the summer, this Waller Street venue was virtually next door to the Plait Hall and was offered for concert use. Luton Choral Society, with nowhere else to go, took up the offer, but were less than impressed by the hard, wooden chairs provided by the council. In fact, they wrote to the Council in October expressing the complaints they had received from members of their audience, asking that some 200 comfortable seats be installed at once. The Council delayed their discussion until the next estimates were considered in February, 1925.

Notwithstanding the disappointment over the loss of the Plait Halls as assembly rooms, going to the "pictures" went from strength to strength. Throughout the twenties, audiences flocked to see the non-talking movies accompanied by anything from a piano to a full orchestra. As early as 1924, there were signs that the ownership of local cinemas would be consolidated. In April, 1924, the Picturedrome and the Wellington were brought under the same management. William Southan Morris of Selbourne Road, Luton, would soon become a very important player in the world of cinema. For the present, he owned the Picturedrome and, in 1925, Southan Morris bought the Wellington for £1,980. He retained his ownership for less than a year, however, selling the little cinema to Joseph Angel in 1926. Angel leased the Wellington to Herbert William Mead who ran it until his death in 1946. Bearing in mind the number of cinemas he was to control in the years to come, it is not clear why Southan Morris did not retain control of the Wellington. In many ways, it proved to be to the advantage of the cinema as, unlike all the other surviving early cinemas in the area, it remained independent of the major circuits.

Growing Popularity of "The Pictures" Brings a Cinema to Toddington

Even Toddington got its own cinema when the Guides Hall in Gas Street was converted into the Picturedrome in September, 1925. With only about 140 seats it was very small, which may well have prompted an early name change to The Cozy. To start with, it did not open every day, but performances increased as its

Toddington's Picturedrome Cinema opened in 1925; the original building is currently maintained and operated by the Toddington Amateur Dramatic Society as the TADS Theatre. (EG)

popularity grew. The rural edition of *The Luton News* rarely if ever carried details of the films on show. It seems that the local population of Toddington kept in touch by strolling down Gas Lane to find out what was on! The hall also had a stage some 18 feet square, together with a dressing room for occasional live performers. It is gratifying indeed that the building is still in use by TADS (The Toddington Amateur Dramatic Society), but more of that anon.

Growing Popularity of Cinema in Luton Gives Empire Opportunity to Expand

In Luton, soon to incorporate the outlying villages of Leagrave, Limbury and Stopsley (though proposed, both Caddington and Hyde escaped such incorporation), the cinemas wished they had rubber walls so that they could accommodate the crowds. Not that oft-full houses stopped cinemas trying to attract the biggest audience possible. For ten days in July, 1926, programmes at Luton's Palace included special film of Luton Jubilee Day Celebrations to give as many people as possible the opportunity to see their town, and possibly themselves, on the big screen.

In order to accommodate this growing audience, Luton Cinemas Ltd. applied for permission to make alterations and additions to the Empire Cinema. Initially, these plans were not approved, but the Empire was soon extended. Adjoining buildings were incorporated into the cinema, giving it almost twice the width of the original cinema. A dressing room was also built behind the screen and the orchestra pit widened. Now the auditorium had two aisles between the seats. The two side blocks contained 22 rows in the stalls, while the middle block had nineteen rows. There were now 553 seats downstairs, with a further 228 in the extended balcony. The Empire now had a total of 781 seats, a considerable uplift from its original planned seating for 494, let alone the 440 it had when it opened in 1921.

High Town Electric Changes Hands and is Improved

The High Town Electric was taken over by Palace Theatre (Luton) Ltd. and became the next Luton cinema due for a face-lift. Plans for alterations were approved in September, 1927, and the cinema closed for a few months before re-opening on Boxing Day with new seats and a new central heating system. The theatre was also enlarged, allowing the number of seats to increase. The balcony now had thirty-seven double seats plus one single seat. The total seating in the upstairs area was now seventy-five mahogany-backed iron-frame tip-up seats with stuffed backing covered in maroon corduroy velvet finished with brass studs.

The ground floor contained a total of 370 single seats in three different styles plus 16X4 ft iron frame tip-up triple seats. The seats and backs were stuffed and covered in leatherette. Triple seats brought the seating in the stalls up to 418. The improvements meant that the capacity of the refurbished cinema had increased by about one hundred.

Redecoration to go with these improvements had a colour scheme of blue and gold with white panels. There were new projectors in the operating box and an enlarged screen. As *The Luton News* noted:

"High Town has now one of the most up-to-date and cosy places of entertainment in town".

Even so, it became a second-run theatre, playing films which had already been seen at its parent cinema, the Palace. However, although it had already been screened in Luton, "Ben Hur" offered a very prestigious film for the refurbished cinema's second week. It was noted especially for the magnificent chariot race which was not matched until the film was remade in 1959. It also included a colour sequence which proved to be very static due to the clumsiness of the colour cameras used in the twenties. At High Town, it was announced that the film was accompanied by

"special music played by an augmented orchestra, and there will be performances nightly at 6 and 8.30, and matinees on Monday, Wednesday and Saturday at 2.30. For this week only the prices of admission are fixed at 1s 6d upstairs, and 1s and 6d downstairs, and there will be no advance booking".

The Palace and the High Town Electric both became the property of the General Theatre Corporation (GTC) in March 1928, just over a year before that organisation was absorbed into Gaumont British. The new owners retained the Palace, but sold the High Town Electric to William Southan Morris. It was full circle – the High Town Electric Picture Theatre and Picturedrome (also owned by Southan Morris) had been linked for a while during the First World War. The next chapter will reveal that it was Southan Morris who was responsible for the next major cinema developments in Luton.

Meanwhile, in Leighton Buzzard . . .

In the meantime, Leighton's "Old Vic" re-opened. It had been a victim of the plush

Oriel but, in the hands of new lessee G. Crickett, it was brought back to life as "Ye Olde Vic". The small cinema was totally redecorated for the occasion. New seating and heating were installed and two new, up-to-date projectors ensured that films were shown "without the slightest vibration". The special opening programme on Saturday, 31 March, 1928 was for the benefit of the Hospital Association and included live performances to accompany the film.

The refurbished cinema opened to the public the week before Easter with "Surrender" and the latest Empire News Bulletin. From Maundy Thursday, "Nelson" was the main attraction, while Lon Chaney in "The Hunchback of Notre Dame" was presented from Easter Monday. The advertisement for these re-opening films said:

"Rally round the "Old Vic", the first Picture Palace in Leighton to give REAL SHOWS".

Proud to the last, it also proclaimed "Always was and always will be the favourite Entertainment House".

Bedfordshire Bans "Dawn"

In *The Saturday Telegraph* of 9 June 1928, this intriguing advertisement appeared:

"DAWN"

Picturegoers of Luton and District at last have the unique opportunity of seeing this remarkable and controversial film, which has not been passed by the Beds. County Council.
On WEDNESDAY JUNE 13th at 1.25 pm, THURSDAY, JUNE 14th, and FRIDAY, JUNE 15th, at 5.15 pm., char-a-banc will leave Albert Edwards' tobacco shop for the AERO KINEMA, HEMEL HEMPSTEAD, where the film is being shown. Fare 2s 6d return. Book early. 'Phone 31 (ADVT)

Sybil Thorndike played World War I nurse Edith Cavell with dignity and to critical acclaim. Nurse Cavell had been executed by the Germans for helping British soldiers to escape. This topic met with criticism from the German Ambassador and, even though he had not seen the film, the British Foreign Secretary. It is thought that such high-powered disapproval may have influenced the British Board of Film Censors (BBFC) in denying the film a certificate, which meant that it was up to individual local County Councils to decide whether or not it should be shown in their areas. Most, including Hertfordshire, did pass the film, but Bedfordshire accepted the judgment of the BBFC. Thus a marketing opportunity opened up for the enterprising Aero Kinema; one cannot help but wonder how many responded to *The Saturday Telegraph* advertisement.

Cinemas Make the News

The Luton News carried another item which must have sent a chill down the spines of the small cinema operators. In October, 1928, it was announced that planning permission had been granted for the building of a magnificent cinema and variety theatre which was to be the largest yet built in Bedfordshire. Called the Alma, it was destined to be at the centre of a drama which saw out the twenties in Luton. No wonder so many cinemas invested so heavily to improve their theatres!

In December that year, the Gordon Street County Electric Pavilion secured – "at Enormous expense" – a special attraction called "Fire". It proved to be prophetic.

This Luton News advertisement announces the "Commencement of the Talkie Season" at the Palace Theatre, Luton.

CHAPTER SIX

The Cinemas Make Themselves Heard

During the late twenties, it was the cinema industry itself which provided the drama.

The first English language "talkie" feature, "The Jazz Singer", had caused a sensation when it was premiered in New York on October 6th, 1927. The Warner Brothers had taken a terrific gamble and it seemed to come off. To start with, the other studios didn't know which way to turn. Developments in film stock and in production technique had brought the so-called "silent" movie to the peak of perfection. Week after week, cinemagoers were treated to beautifully produced films; by the late twenties, the cinema had established itself as the art-form of the twentieth-century. Now, when the movies were as good as they had ever been, film-makers had to start all over again as they tried to come to terms with an entirely new dimension. The actors had to be heard speaking their lines.

Apart from Warner Bros., Hollywood's film studios had hoped that "The Jazz Singer" was nothing more than a nine-day wonder, but when Al Jolson made a second film in 1928, they knew they had to compete. Jolson had scored a massive hit as the Jazz Singer but, when he sang a maudlin song called "Sonny Boy" in "The Singing Fool", audiences queued around the block to see and hear him in every city which had a cinema wired for sound. Talkies didn't arrive in South Bedfordshire until 1929 – the very year in which two Luton cinemas were locked in a sensational drama. However, before all that happened, other developments began to mature.

The "New" Picturedrome

The Picturedrome in Luton's Park Street had closed for extensive alterations in

1928 and, before it re-opened on September 29th that year, expectations were raised with this announcement in *The Luton News*:

> "The magnificent new Picturedrome will be devoted entirely to the presentation of modern motion picture entertainment. The new balcony will contain luxurious tub seats, and there will be powerful searchlight projection on a stereoscopic screen without eye-strain, and ventilation and deodorisation by modern scientific methods. The orchestra, always an important feature at the Picturedrome, will be bigger and better. It may not be too premature to announce that such successes as "Uncle Tom's Cabin" from the London Pavilion, "Four Sons" from the Capitol, "Speedy" from the Plaza, and "Wings" from the Carlton are to receive their exclusive premier presentations at the new Picturedrome".

On January 10th, 1929, a large display advertisement in *The Luton News* announced the completion of the Picturedrome's rebuilding. Headed "The Old and the New", the advert proudly confirmed that the "New" Picturedrome was "Owned and Conducted by a Luton Resident whose entire Interests are in the Town" (William Southan Morris). The advert went on to describe the re-built Picturedrome as "Luton's most Up-To-Date Cine-Variety Theatre with luxurious accommodation for 1,000 patrons". It seems unlikely that the enlarged building actually held as many as 1,000 patrons, even though the Cinema Buyers Guide for 1937 gave the seating as 985. Unfortunately, the plans submitted to the Council in June 1928 oulined the seating configuration in the balcony (176), but not in the stalls. The extension was certainly considerable; in addition to more seating, a new orchestra-pit had been built in front of the screen and stage, with accommodation behind the screen for a music library and storage. No doubt, there were also facilities for artistes to change their costumes. The advertisement also announced:

> "Synchronised Music on the Exclusive Electric Panatrope"
> "Full Orchestra under the direction of Alfred Bailey"
> "First Class Variety from the Principal London Theatres"

The extensions to the Picturedrome had actually been promised in the prospectus issued before the cinema first opened its doors in 1911. When they were at last incorporated into the building, they proved very popular and the Park Street cinema retained a faithful audience to the very end of its days. The New Picturedrome was quick to use the new facilities – the first cine-variety presentation, "Master of the Ventriloqual Art" Benson Gray on stage, was retained for the whole week. As the film still changed, as usual, on Thursday, audiences had the chance to see him twice!

The Grand Hits Back

Meanwhile, the Grand Theatre hit back at the end of January with a welcome return of Edward Dunstan and his Shakespearean Company. Dunstan was very popular in Luton; most people who remember going to the Grand at that time recall fond memories of these forays into the works of Shakespeare. During that early week in 1929, the company presented a different play each night, with a matinee of "As You Like It" on Saturday – and the audience clearly liked it very much.

The Continuing Strength of Luton's Palace

The Palace in Luton continued to present a strong programme of cine-variety, with the "Cheeky Chappy" Max Miller heading the bill for one week from 8th April, 1929. He was one of four "Special Varieties" booked to support the silent film version of the famous musical play "Rose Marie" with Joan Crawford in the title role. MGM were to eventually make two sound versions (with the songs intact) during a period when they were regarded as the leading producer of screen musicals. At this period, however, they seemed keen to produce famous musicals as silent features; the Empire in Luton played MGM's silent version of "The Merry Widow" the following month. Curiously enough, MGM also made two talkie versions of that musical in the coming years. To compete with the Empire's presentation of "The Merry Widow", the Palace included Jack Payne, "The Wonder Boy Whistler as discovered in the streets of Coventry", among their "special varieties". To counter "The Merry Widow" and a whistling Jack Payne, the extended Picturedrome, keen to fill its new seats, offered a three-feature bill which included the popular Tim McCoy in "Riders of the Dark", screen comic Chester Conklin in "Fools For Luck" and the first episode of an Edgar Wallace serial, "Mark of the Frog".

Talkies Come to South Bedfordshire

In July, the Gordon Street Electric Pavilion, which had opened as the Anglo American Electric Picture Palace in 1909 as the first permanent cinema in Bedfordshire, now became the first cinema in the area to introduce the talkies. Advertising themselves as the "Most Up-To-Date Entertainment in Luton", they presented their first "100 per cent ALL TALKING PROGRAMME" from Monday, July 1st, 1929. The programme included "Her New Chauffeur" and "Mr. Smith Wakes Up". The programme, despite its claim to be 100% All Talking, also included the silent "Undressed". Not for the first time, the Gordon Street Cinema made the news. It wasn't the last time either. Within a matter of months, the cinema was destined to fill the columns of the local press for weeks and weeks.

Birth of New Cinema Circuit in Luton

Former General Manager of the Palace, Fred V. Morris, was in the news. In recognition of his services as secretary of the South Midlands branch of the Cinematograph Exhibitors' Association, he received a special presentation. Vice-chairman of the Association was William Southan Morris who operated the Picturedrome and the High Town Electric cinemas in Luton. Mr Southan Morris was to become even more influential in the cinema world of South Bedfordshire before setting foot on the national scene. He acquired Luton's Empire Cinema and, on 25th July, 1929, Southan Morris Circuit, Limited was registered as a new company, with Mr W. Southan Morris listed among the directors. Advertisements in the local press promised "The Pick of the Pictures at Popular Prices".

More Luton Cinemas are Wired for Sound

In September, a second Luton hall installed sound equipment. Announcing the "Commencement of the Talkie Season", the Palace screened the now legendary Al Jolson talkie, "The Singing Fool", throughout the week commencing September 23rd. It proved so popular, it was retained for a second week. Now owned by the General Theatre Corporation, the Palace was managed by Gaumont British; it had become the practice of this company to introduce talkies with this film. They also changed their matinee arrangements; hitherto, a matinee was offered only on Wednesday afternoon (early closing day in Luton). Now, matinees were presented daily at 2.30 pm at special prices of 6d in the stalls and 1/- in the circle. As before, continuous performances were presented in the evenings from 6 pm to 10.45 pm. It was not long before the Palace presented continuous performances from 2.30 pm. The cheap matinee seat prices were retained provided members of the audience bought their tickets before 4 pm.

Just one week after the Palace introduced talkies, the Picturedrome advertised the "Miracle of the Talking Screen". Their first talkie, presented from Monday, September 30th, was the "Sensational Luton Premiere" of the 100% All Talking, All Singing, All Dancing "The Broadway Melody". Giving a little support to their sister cinema on the other side of town, the still silent Empire advertised the week before that the Empire Symphony Orchestra would play "The Broadway Melody". This "Brilliant Orchestral Presentation" accompanied the now famous King Vidor film "The Crowd".

Fire!

Then it happened. On Tuesday October 15th, 1929, the Fire Brigade received a call at 2.07 pm – Luton's Gordon Street cinema was in flames. As they returned to their offices after lunch, passers-by saw smoke pouring out of the cinema. Within minutes of receiving the phone call that raised the alarm, Chief Fire Officer Andrew and his crews had turned up with two fire engines. In the meantime, volunteers had tried to quench the flames. One man ran into the cinema with a chemical fire-extinguisher and was confronted by burning curtains just inside the entrance. As it became clear the fire was too big for the volunteers to handle, they found themselves being choked by acrid flames.

Crowds soon gathered in Gordon Street where they saw the roof lift as though

When Luton's Gordon Street Electric Theatre caught fire, it drew a large lunch-time crowd. (LN/CG)

by an explosion. The fire made the back wall in Lancret's Path unsafe and it had to be closed. The fire engines got to work, though several officers had a narrow escape when it seemed as though a minor explosion set another part of the cinema alight. The Fire Brigade worked swiftly and the first fire-engine was able to leave by 2.30 pm. The second left at 3 pm. On the lighter side, *The Luton News* reported that, as the floor was ripped up to check the fire, a mouse walked sedately out! The last films to be shown at Luton's pioneer cinema were "The Valiant", "Sing Me Baby Song", "The Burglar and the Girl" and a silent film, "Fangs of Fate".

Arson Alleged

The cinema was insured for £6,000 against fire and £1,000 for lost profits, but the cinema's current operator was never to benefit. Just over five weeks after the blaze, he was in the dock at Luton Borough Court charged with maliciously setting fire to the cinema. He was remanded until the following Wednesday, without bail being granted. The following week, the magistrates decided to commit him for trial at Bedfordshire Quarter Sessions. On this occasion, bail was allowed, with the cinema's manager becoming surety. The court heard how two petrol drums had been found in the cinema. Winesses had smelled the petrol in the building and, just before the fire was detected, a man was seen hurrying away from the scene. It was alleged that a man had been paid £150 in £1 notes to set fire to the premises. The cinema had been sold to the current owner some time after its opening and was mortgaged to the Westminster Bank for £4,000.

On December 18th, witnesses, lawyers and police officers went to the Quarter Sessions at Bedford's Shire Hall, but they were not there for long. It was agreed that the case should be tried at the Bedfordshire Assizes in January and bail in £50 was granted. As the story unfolded in court and in the local press, interest in the case began to grow. The report of the Quarter Sessions appeared in the very same issue of *The Luton News* which reported the imminent opening of the new Alma Kinema. The following week, the opening of the Alma was reported – and so were more sensational facts surrounding the Gordon Street fire. Another man had been arrested; the story was to become even more sensational when it was alleged that the fire was linked with the owner of the new Alma. As we will learn, there were sensational statements in the new year.

In the meantime, every effort was made to attract Luton's cinemagoers to the new Alma Kinema.

Bedfordshire's First Super Cinema

By the time 1929 dawned, the corner of Alma Street and New Bedford Road was being cleared. It was already known that the site was to be used for the new Alma Kinema, for sketch plans had been made public during the previous November. The new cinema had been put out to tender and the contract was won by Douglas Halse and Company of Woolwich who promised to complete the ambitious project in twenty-nine weeks at a cost of £53,650. The cinema was designed by renowned cinema architect George Coles. As in other towns up and down the land, the small cinema operators steeled themselves for competition from a "super cinema".

The Alma Kinema – which was also fully equipped for stage performances – was officially opened on Saturday, December 21st, 1929. It had taken longer than the anticipated twenty-nine weeks to complete and the final cost was more than double the original estimate. As those selected to attend the official opening on

Opened at the end of 1929, the Alma Kinema was the area's first cinema to be built in the talkie era. It was considered by some to be the finest "super cinema" ever to be built in Bedfordshire and was always intended to be a "cine-variety" hall. This view was taken after conversion to a full time theatre in 1948. (LMS/LN)

After dark, the Alma's lights were bright and cheerful, even on a rainy night! (LMS/LN)

that Saturday night gathered to view the magnificent building, final touches were still being made. The opening went ahead anyway, for owner Sydney Dillingham desperately wanted to open his brand new cine-variety hall before Christmas. He succeeded with just two days to spare as the general public crowded into their new place of entertainment on Monday, December 23rd. The white frontage glistened and was flood-lit at night to highlight the theatre's prominence in such a central position in the town. It was indeed very well situated, for buses and trams passed the door, while other nearby routes were well within walking distance.

The facing of the Alma came from the Hathern Station Brick and Terra Cotta Company based in Loughborough. Architect George Coles favoured the facings, known as "faience tilings", having first used them for the Broadway Super in Stratford which had opened two years before in December, 1927. Coles used this company more than twenty times for cinemas in various parts of the country, though mainly in the London area. In fact, he used Hathern tiles on arguably his finest cinema, the Commodore in Hammersmith, which opend just two months before the Alma. Both the Commodore and the Alma made use of "Ivory Hathernware".

The Alma Stops a Train

Apart from flood-lighting the front of the new cinema (and there's no doubt Hathernware lent itself magnificently to flood-lighting), the name "Alma" shone like fire in red Neon lights, while the front of the building was crowned with an illuminated ball. The ball was originally lit in red, but this could be seen from the main railway line and had to be changed to blue after a train had mistaken it for a "stop" light! The side of the building visible in Alma Street was not faced with Hathernware. Instead, over one-hundred-thousand "G.P." Luton facing bricks were used. These had been supplied by George Powdrill and Son, along with many other materials used in the construction of the cinema. While some thought the side of the building was plain compared to the ivory-coloured facing of the frontage, it was actually very elegant and was commended as the best brick-work Luton had seen for a long time.

Inside the Alma Kinema

The initial seating was for a total of 1,664, though this number was reduced slightly during the forties. About six hundred of the seats were in the balcony which was constructed on to a single-span girder weighing some twenty tons. The rake of the seating ensured a good view from every seat. The seats in the stalls were also

Taken from the balcony, or circle, this interior of the Alma Kinema shows the ornate ceiling and gives an idea of the theatre's size. The balcony level gangway, leading towards the stage, was a safety requirement for evacuation in case of an emergency; the size of the circle made this necessary. (CTA)

arranged to give as good a view as possible, even at the sides. This was achieved by placing the rows of seats in an arc – a fairly new concept in 1929. All seats were of the tip-up variety and were upholstered in blue. The huge circle needed a suitably large girder to hold it up.

It was always intended that the new building should be used for live as well as screened entertainment. The fully equipped stage was 36-feet wide and 25-feet 6-inches deep. A total of seven dressing-rooms were available, though not all on the same floor. Golden curtains with blue fringes matched the gold carpet. Soft browns and gilt were used in the rest of the interior decoration. A chandelier hung from the ornamental ceiling; other lighting was mainly indirect, though there were also shaded side lamps. Ventilation and heating came from an attractive grille over the proscenium which was a feature of the theatre's design. Air was drawn in through this grille, then "washed" and warmed before being distributed throughout the auditorium. The grille also had a safety function as air could be

NORTONS (TIVIDALE) LTD. LONDON & TIPTON   A 5200

Above This fascinating construction photograph shows the huge girders required to hold up the Alma's balcony. (CTA)   *Below* The size of the Alma's circle can be seen in this somewhat sad photograph taken during the theatre's demolition. (LMS/LN)

drawn into the system to avoid smoke getting into the audience area should a fire occur on stage. This was but one of the safety features built into what was at that time South Bedfordshire's largest theatre or cinema.

The large projection room actually had three sets of Western Electric equipment, which included Magnascope – a wide-screen system installed well over twenty years before CinemaScope came to Luton! Few films were made using the system, however, and it was removed after only a few years. In the Box-Office, "Automaticket" machines were installed to speed up the sale of tickets. The vestibule was attractively decorated with a marble floor. Because the land sloped down Alma Street towards New Bedford Road, the stage was situated at the same end of the building as the entrance. Though far from unique, it was more usual to find the stage at the far end, away from the entrance. The Alma also had its own "tea lounge" and a small ballroom which could accomodate a hundred couples. In many ways, it anticipated modern "entertainment centres". It was these facilities which caused some to consider this Bedfordshire's only super cinema though, with more magnificent cinemas to come, the point is at the very least arguable.

Luton Cinemagoers Experience their New Theatre

Following an opening ceremony by the Mayor, Alderman Murray Barford, on Saturday, December 21st, the public was admitted to the continuous performances for the first time at 2 o'clock on Monday, December 23rd. The first film to be shown was "The Divine Lady", described as a "Colossal Sea Epic" including "Trafalgar re-fought with the crash of cannon and the clash of steel". In fact, this sequence was filmed in Magnascope; as the film reached its action climax, the curtains were drawn back to reveal the wide screen. The "divine lady" of the title was Lady Hamilton, played by Corinne Griffith. Although the Alma had its own "Ladies' Orchestra", a recording of the "Tannhauser" Overture by the New York Symphony Orchestra was also included in a crowded programme which had a "singing cartoon", a comedy, a "talking" magazine film and "Gaumont Sound News". The Alma was the first cinema in the area to be built as a sound cinema; silent films were never shown there. Tickets for the Alma at its opening cost three shillings and two shillings in the balcony and two shillings and one shilling in the stalls. Not surprisingly, the smaller halls in the town were cheaper. The Alma's second programme, which commenced on Monday, December 30th, included "Innocents in Paris" starring the very popular Maurice Chevalier.

The Gordon Street Cinema Fire Affair Concludes

Once the excitement of the Alma opening had died down, a new decade saw the resumption of the Gordon Street cinema fire affair. On January 1st, 1930, several men found themselves in Luton Borough Court on a charge of conspiracy. They all had to answer the charge that they maliciously set fire to the cinema.

One of the charged men had prepared a preposterous statement alleging that Sydney Charles Dillingham, owner of the recently opened Alma, invented the idea of "abolishing the cinema property by fire and that the destroying of the cinema business was done for the sole benefit of the new Alma cinema". Needless to say, these allegations were repudiated as wild and baseless. Indeed, such an allegation beggars belief; the Alma was in an altogether different league to the little Gordon Street Electric Pavilion and no one could possibly consider it to be a threat to the magnificent new venture, even if it was only in the next street. The court handed down custodial sentences.

Talkie Theatre and a Change of Ownership in Dunstable

It was reported that Fred Marchant, owner of Dunstable's Palace Cinema and, by now, a councillor as well, was to retire from the cinema world. Ownership of his Palace passed into the hands of William Southan Morris, owner of the growing Southan Morris Circuit which included the Picturedrome, High Town Electric and Empire cinemas in Luton. Marchant and Southan Morris had been closely associated since about 1924 as both were heavily involved in the South Midlands branch of the influential Cinematograph Exhibitor's Association. Fred Marchant had held the chair for three years and William Southan Morris was the current vice-chairman at the time of the Dunstable takeover. The change of ownership brought immediate improvements to the Dunstable cinema. The seating capacity was increased and sound equipment was installed. "The Broadway Melody" gave Dunstablians their first talking picture on Monday, February 3rd, 1930.

New Owner for Luton's Alma

The Alma, Bedfordshire's first Super Cinema, changed hands just a few months after its opening. It was taken over by Walter Bentley who already controlled super-cinemas in Nottingham, Middlesborough, Twickenham and other places. When he set eyes on the Alma Kinema, Bentley considered it to be "one of the finest buildings of its kind in this part of the country". He promised a big orchestra, the biggest variety stars on stage and a "suitable dance band in the

Above This fine view inside Luton's Alma shows the stage area and disguised organ chamber after installation of the Compton Organ. (CTA) *Below* The Alma was fitted with a Compton organ shortly after opening, still in the building when it was demolished. (LN)

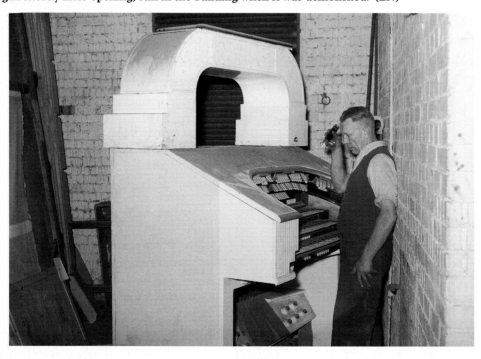

ball-room". Day to day management of the cine-variety hall was in the hands of J.B. Cooper-Reade from February 3rd. By the end of the year, he had wooed popular Sydney Phasey from Gaumont-British, operators of the Palace, to lead the "Alma Symphony Orchestra". He had also installed a new "Wonder Compton Organ". The original design allowed for an organ, but it was not installed for the opening.

This was the period of strong competition between the orchestra leaders. Girls queued up on Saturday night to ensure their places on the front row in either the Alma or the Palace, depending on which was their favourite leader. The reason? The conductor threw his carnation into the audience on a Saturday night and it was easier to catch it if you were in the front! At that time, dance bands and orchestras playing popular melodies were extremely popular. The bandleaders were the stars in those days, not the singers. This was reflected locally, for audiences were attracted as much by a good orchestra as they were by the films being screened. Both the Alma and the Palace competed very strongly for this audience; both devoted a large portion of their newspaper advertisements to

Theatres above small-scale size were required to show their safety curtain once during every performance. This delightful, if cluttered, curtain greeted Alma audiences during the interval. (LN)

their orchestras and leaders. As a result, there were queues around the block to see the latest films and the live performances that went with them.

Mr Cooper-Reade also devoted a lot of attention to the Alma Cafe; with films and stage shows as well as the cafe and ballroom, the Alma was a comprehensive entertainment centre which needed to be sold as such. No other theatre in South Bedfordshire ever had such a wide range of services and facilities, though an entirely different concept was introduced in the 1990s – but that really is a later story.

Talkie Crazy

Talkies were all the craze during those early sound years. Cinemas in the area couldn't "wire for sound" fast enough. Advertisements carried phrases like:

"Sound or Silent, the Southan Morris Circuit Gives You the Best".

But William Southan Morris knew the silents were doomed and hastened to equip all his theatres. He quickly fitted Luton's Empire for sound, offering a special pre-release presentation of "The Co-Optimists" from Monday, March 3rd. He even persuaded famous theatrical designer Sir Gordon Craig to attend this notable performance. Many years later, Gordon Craig (who was the son of stage legend Ellen Terry) gave his name to a theatre in nearby Stevenage which was to be used by Luton companies unable to find adequate facilities in their own town.

The Talkies Come to Leighton Buzzard

Leighton Buzzard and Linslade audiences had their first taste of the talkies two days before Luton's Empire. The Hippodrome was no more; it had been re-opened by London and County Cinemas under its former name of The Grand on Saturday, March 1st announcing "the First Talkies in the District". The Grand chose the first film version of "Show Boat" to introduce Leighton Buzzard and Linslade to talking pictures. Two further film versions of this famous musical were made in 1936 and 1951 but, for now, audiences in the two towns could see Laura La Plante as Magnolia.

The film has an interesting history. Universal bought the rights of Edna Ferber's novel before it was turned into a musical by Jerome Kern and Oscar Hammerstein II in 1927. Not only that, but the talkies were introduced while it was being made. Clearly, the producers could not ignore these two facts, so they added sound to their silent feature. Miss La Plante, it is reputed, did not have a

In 1933, when this photograph was taken, popular films attracted huge queues - though "I'll Stick To You", a British comedy featuring Louis Hayward before he went to Hollywood, is barely remembered today. (LN)

suitable singing voice, so her singing voice was "doubled" by Eva Olivotti, though it is unlikely that either the film company or Miss Olivotti wanted this fact to be known. It was probably the first example of what we now call "dubbing" in the cinema. Universal also added a sound prologue to the film featuring stars from the Broadway version. Thus, Helen Morgan and Jules Bledsoe (the original Joe) could be heard on a primitive sound track in Linslade!

London and County Cinemas refurbished the Grand in readiness for its re-opening. It had a reputation for draughts; crooked gangways meant that members of the audience were known to bump into protruding seats. The new owners corrected these faults by installing a new heating system and the gangway was straightened. The cinema was also re-decorated and carpeted throughout. The curtains were made to operate electrically, which was quite a novelty at that time. One of London and County's directors, C.E. Le Grice, supervised the improvements and assured patrons that only the best equipment was installed.

The Oriel Fights Back

Leighton Buzzard's Oriel Cinema was now part of the Shipman and King Circuit and they had no intention of allowing the Grand too big a lead. The Oriel's operating box was doubled in size in order to fit the latest sound projectors from Western Electric. It was admitted that the larger cinema was late in getting the talkies, but the proprietors stressed the fact that the Leighton Buzzard cinema would benefit from Shipman and King's experience in their other halls. One area in which that experience paid off was in the regulation of the speed of operation. In the "silent" days, it did not matter if the speed of the film passing through the projector varied a little. Indeed, when the projectors were hand-cranked, variations in speed were inevitable – and not only because the operator would sometimes go faster than necessary in order to get home early! Hand operation for sound films was impossible. It was imperative that the speed should be as constant as possible, for a variation could be detected in the quality of the sound during projection. This was only one of many problems presented by the introduction of sound-on-film.

The Oriel fitted a new screen for the talkies and the loud-speaker horns were placed at the right height for the best sound quality. The cinema's manager, R. Barrie, had expressed hesitancy towards the talkies, but the care with which all the equipment was installed set his mind at rest. He stood outside his cinema with confidence when the Oriel's first talkie, "The Broadway Melody", was presented on Monday, March 17th. The programme changed on Thursday and Leighton Buzzard audiences were given the opportunity to hear Ronald Colman in "Bulldog Drummond". Both programmes in that first "talkie" week included Mickey Mouse cartoons.

Luton's Wellington and High Town Electric are Wired for Sound

Back in Luton, the Wellington Cinema presented their first talkie – Maurice Chevalier in "Innocents in Paris" on Monday, April 28th, 1930, leaving the High Town Cinema as the only picture house in the whole area still screening "silent" films. Indeed, they held out until September. The final silent film to be shown as part of Luton's regular cinema scene was the British drama "White Roses". When the curtain came down at the High Town Electric on Saturday, September 6th, 1930, it was the end of an era. From then on, every cinema in the area offered sound films. The first talkie for High Town audiences was also filmed in "natural-colour" (a two-colour system which would look far from natural to modern audiences). The film was, appropriately enough, "On With the Show". The cinema industry had undergone its most dramatic change but, in the true tradition of show business, the show went on – and on.

Shifting Ownership and an Early Closure

Less than a year after installing sound, the Southan Morris circuit released control of their High Town cinema. Opening under new management in May, 1931, the cinema was now known as the Plaza. At least the new owners kept it open – for a few more years anyway. In Leighton Buzzard, a change of ownership at the Grand spelled its early closure. It was bought out by the Shipman and King circuit who made their Oriel Leighton Buzzard's only cinema in 1932.

Consolidation of Film Exhibition in Luton

By 1935, Southan Morris was showing the same feature at both the Empire and the Picturedrome in Luton. It was a logical decision – the cinemas were at the opposite ends of the town and tended to serve entirely different audiences.

The doorman outside Luton's Empire Cinema in Bury Park Road in 1936 advertised "Forced Landing", a largely forgotten film which was also shown at sister cinema, The Picturedrome. From 1935, the Empire and Picturedrome usually, but not always, screened the same programme. Both cinemas were part of the Southan Morris Circuit until it was taken over by Union. (LCL/LN)

Many big names visited the Grand Theatre in Luton throughout the thirties. These girls were selling roses for Alexandra Day; behind them can be seen a poster for Hughie Green and his BBC Gang. Hughie Green became well known as a television game-show personality. (LN)

There was something of an irony in the fact that the Plaza in High Town, which had enjoyed a similar relationship with the Picturedrome during World War I, stopped advertising shortly after this new arrangement came into operation.

Of course, it wasn't only the cinemas which provided entertainment for Luton audiences during the mid-thirties. The Grand Theatre was still going strong as it presented a varied programme of plays and variety. The young Hughie Green and his "Famous All-Star B.B.C. Gang" appeared in June, 1935. Earlier that year, the famous Bertram Mills Circus set up business at Stockwood Park. It was the sixth time they had visited the town and their four-day visit was as popular as ever.

At the Alma, popular stars like Elsie and Doris Waters ("Gert and Daisy") came to entertain Luton audiences. When Maurice Chevalier visited Luton in 1935, he made a personal visit to the Alma. Traffic was brought to a standstill as hundreds of fans crowded Manchester Street to see their idol. Apart from being a huge star at that time, Lutonians felt a kinship with Chevalier because he bought his trade-mark straw hats from Olney's Hat Factory in the town. Needless to say, he was presented with a few locally-made straw boaters.

Within a few years, modern cinema palaces opened in both Dunstable and Luton and a new era was ushered in.

Elsie and Doris Waters ("Gert and Daisy"), household names during WWII, pictured in their dressing room at Luton's Alma in 1937. Many stars performed to support films at the theatre. (LCL/LN)

Above **Crowds surge round Maurice Chevalier when he arrives outside the Alma Theatre in 1935. (LMS/LN)** . *Below* **Inside the Alma, Maurice Chevalier tries on a few new boaters presented to him by Olney's (LMS/LN)**

CHAPTER SEVEN

The Big Circuits Dominate

The cinema scene changed out of all recognition during the thirties. Throughout the twenties, picture palaces provided work for a vast army of musicians – though they began to feel the pinch as early as 1929. During the very early thirties, larger halls still offered a variety show to accompany the film, and the orchestra played a major part in a night out at the pictures. Cinemas which remained open in 1930 were now wired for sound. It wasn't long before variety as support for films was abandoned in favour of a "second feature", though some cine-variety persisted well into the talkie era, with bigger halls like the Alma offering variety as well as two feature films! In the main, however, if live music remained a part of the programme, it was now played on a magnificent, illuminated organ which rose up in front of the screen. These were very fine instruments which provided the audience with considerable enjoyment, but they required just one organist – not a full orchestra.

Cinemas built during the thirties reflected this change and the tremendous boost the talkies gave to audience figures; all the new cinemas were built by the fast-growing circuits. The Alma in Luton certainly anticipated the huge cinema buildings to come, but it was the last independently-built theatre in the area.

The Union Chain

Meanwhile, the Alma joined four other local cinemas to become part of the rapidly growing Union Cinema chain. A few years before in 1933, the Southan Morris circuit was absorbed into Union, with William Southan Morris becoming a senior executive within the group. As a result, the Empire, Picturedrome and Plaza cinemas in Luton, together with the Palace in Dunstable, became part of National Provincial Cinemas, a subsidiary of Union. It was Union's policy to buy up as many cinemas as possible in any one town. If they could acquire all the cinemas, they had far more negotiating power with the film distributors.

119

In 1937, The Palace clearly saw the advantage of advertising in Luton Town Football Club's grounds! (LN)

They didn't succeed in buying all the cinemas in Luton, however. Although they now controlled four halls, including the prestigious Alma, the little Wellington Cinema remained resolutely independent as it continued to show continuous performances with a change of programme every Monday and Thursday. The Palace was also prospering under the wing of Union's arch rival, the Gaumont-British circuit, and it kept up the competitive pressure by offering Sunday concerts (their cine-variety policy had declined).

Sunday Variety Concerts in Luton

In fact, Luton had a choice of Sunday concerts in the mid-thirties. Early in 1936, for example, the Alma offered strong competition with Sunday appearances by such stars as the very popular Elsie Carlisle and, not yet quite top of the bill, Cyril Fletcher ("Jest Different"). Unbelievably, Luton had Sunday concerts at a third cinema early in 1936. High Town's Plaza was the host, though their humbler offerings could not compete with the starry programmes at the Palace and the Alma.

With such a diversity of live performances on offer, the other Luton cinemas were content to show just films. As one small experience at the Empire showed, just showing films was not without incident. *The Luton News* reported that, during the screening of "Smilin' Through" in September, 1936, the Empire discovered a sharp increase in lost pipes in the auditorium. Manager Francis Garrett was puzzled – until he saw the end of the film in which the star, Leslie Howard, dies and slumps forward in his chair. As he does so, he drops his pipe from his lips. Mr. Garrett could only assume that certain pipe-smoking members of the audience were so spellbound by the performance that they dropped their pipes and the emotion engendered by the moment made them forget to pick them up! Incidentally, the film was originally released in 1932, but was often revived due to its considerable popularity. The Empire booked it on three separate occasions.

Big New Cinemas Planned

In addition to taking over existing cinemas, Union also had a programme of building grand new palaces of entertainment. Plans were submitted for two in the area – a huge cinema in Luton's Gordon Street and another smaller, but no less grand cinema in Dunstable. Both were planned with the Union "house" name of Ritz but, as things turned out, neither opened with that name. In fact, the major

With three cinemas in Luton and one in Dunstable, the Union circuit issued a card listing their films in August, 1937, not long before they opened major new cinemas in both Dunstable and Luton. (CTA)

Following their expansion, the Union circuit built many new cinemas, often called Ritz. Their palatial hall in Dunstable was their first new cinema to be called just Union. When this photograph was taken in the late thirties, the Palace next door was still open. The Union is Grade 2 listed. (CTA)

circuits built three huge cinemas in Luton during the second half of the thirties. They all had about two thousand seats each, offered unparalleled comfort and an excellent view of the screen. Before any of these opened, however, work began on the first thirties-built cinema in the area. It was in Dunstable.

Dunstable's New Cinema

Plans were first submitted on January 31st, 1935, but the cinema which eventually opened was rather different to the proposed "Regal". With the Southan Morris circuit now a part of the huge Union circuit, Mr. Southan Morris himself became an important member of the fast-growing company and often submitted plans on their behalf. The plans for Dunstable's Regal envisaged a large cinema embracing land which contained both the old and the new Palace cinemas – a plan, incidentally, which would have deprived Dunstable of its only cinema while the new one was being built. Designed by architects Leslie H. Kemp & Tasker, organ pit and chambers were included in the design for the 1,432 seat cinema

(1,048 in the stalls; 384 in the circle), though revised plans in 1935 reduced the seating to 1,361. The develoment also envisaged a cafe.

Yet another set of plans was drawn up and submitted by Leslie H. Kemp and Tasker on May 26th, 1936. This changed the orientation and proposed a smaller cinema; it was no longer side-on to High Street North, but now ran parallel with Manchester Place. The entrance was still in the High Street but was no longer flanked by shops. It occupied the site next to the Palace Cinema which was now retained. This third version of the proposed Regal had 803 seats in the stalls plus 278 in the circle; the cafe on the first floor was still in the plan, as was an organ to rise in front of the screen. The basic shape and size of the cinema remained the same for the fourth and final set of plans which resulted in the building which stands in Dunstable to this day. The name had changed from "Regal" to "Ritz", though, in order to identify ownership, its full name was "Union Cinemas Ritz". Union as a company went out of its way to identify ownership outside its cinemas. The local cinemas formerly owned by Southan Morris were all clearly identified as "Union Cinemas".

Early in 1937, *The Dunstable Borough Gazette* reported:

> "The towering building which so quickly made its appearance in High Street North, dwarfing the Palace Cinema standing beside it, gives point to the statement of the directors of Union Cinemas, the owners of the "Ritz" – the name of the new entertainment house – that an extensive building programme is in progress".

The report in the January 22nd, 1937 edition of the Gazette was optimistic and a photograph of the cinema "growing up" appeared two weeks later (February 5th). As things turned out, such optimism ultimately proved to be unfounded; Union chairman David Bernhard died in mid-September, less than two weeks before Dunstable's new cinema opened. Although Bernhard's death was to prove catastrophic for the Union cinema chain, the Dunstable opening itself offered nothing but optimism.

Dunstable's New Cinema Opens as the Union

By the time the new cinema in Dunstable opened on Monday, September 27th, 1937, the company had decided to call it simply "Union", even though the sky-sign erected on the buildings roof displayed the Ritz name almost up to the opening date. It was the first new cinema in the chain to be called simply "Union". As the audience entered the foyer, they were greeted by ornamental mirrors and chandeliers. The decoration throughout was designed to give cinemagoers the feeling of tasteful opulence. Comfort was a key-note; the latest "semi-tub seats" were installed and the auditorium was heavily carpeted. The walls were decorated in terra-cotta, peach and gold.

The *Dunstable Borough Gazette* reporter commented on the use of electricity in the cinema:

> "Electricity plays an outstanding part in the new Union Cinema. It serves the patron from the moment he enters until the moment he leaves. It lights, warms and ventilates the building, works the clocks, operates the curtains in front of the wonderful stage, projects the films, reproduces the sound, and is responsible for hundreds of other services".

If this paragraph seems strange, it should be remembered that electricity was still something of a novelty in 1937 with many homes in the district served only by gas. Much was made of the fact that local labour was used and that, wherever possible, the materials used were local too. As the thirties were marked with depression, the point was well made.

The beautiful interior of Dunstable's Union cinema shows the circle and the decorated ceiling. (CTA)

More of the interior design of Dunstable's Union can be seen in this view from the circle. (CTA)

Opening Night Competed with the Statty Fair

Interestingly, the Union opened on the night of Dunstable's "Statty" Fair, but more than one thousand Dunstablians preferred the new cinema – well, to start with anyway. Apparently, many went to the "Statty" after the show! The new cinema was managed by W.D.G. Grant, who was also manager of the Palace next door. He attended the opening in the company of Mr F. Chandler, assistant managing director of builders H.C. Janes, Ltd., Mrs Chandler, Union Cinemas' general manager Mr J.H. Lundy and the cinema chain's Controller, Mr E.P. Adams. The cinema was formally opened by the Mayor, after which well-known broadcasting organist Harold Ramsay took the stage to host a local version of the popular radio show "In Town Tonight". Ramsay was Union's Director of Entertainment and he had a lot of fun with the local personalities taking part. He particularly enjoyed talking on stage to Mrs Violet Turvey from Totternhoe who kept a huge number of pet mice in her home! "They do like cheese," she told Mr Ramsay, "but it isn't good for them!"

Telegrams from screen personalities Jessie Matthews, Jack Buchanan, Maureen O'Sullivan, Shirley Temple, Gracie Fields and Clark Gable were flashed

UNION CINEMA

PHONE 480 — DUNSTABLE

GRAND OPENING

MONDAY NEXT

AT 7·30 P.M (DOORS OPEN 7.PM)

BY

HIS WORSHIP the MAYOR OF DUNSTABLE

COUNCILLOR FRANK KENWORTHY & THE MAYORESS

ALL SEATS BOOKABLE

FROM **TODAY (FRI.)** AT 10·0 A.M.

SPECIAL OPENING NIGHT PRICES

1/-   1/3   1/6   1/10   2/4

CAPT. DRUMMOND RETURNS IN 6z the **SCREEN**

A WHIRL OF THRILLS & ACTION! MON. 3 DAYS

'BULL DOG DRUMMOND at BAY'

WITH JOHN LODGE .U.

ALSO 'MIND YOUR OWN BUSINESS'

WITH CHARLIE RUGGLES .U.

THURS. NEXT

TOGETHER AGAIN IN THEIR GREATEST LAUGHTER HIT !

JACK **HULBERT**· CICELY **COURTNEIDGE**

in **TAKE MY TIP** u.

ALSO **CONFLICT** WITH JOHN WAYNE

UNION CINEMA CAFE

OPENS TO THE PUBLIC & THEATRE

PATRONS ON TUES. NEXT AT 10·0 A.M.

& DAILY 10 AM. — 10·30 P.M.

SUNDAYS 3 P.M. — 10 P.M.

The Dunstable Borough Gazette **advertisement for the opening of the Union Cinema, Dunstable.**

on to the screen before the opening programme of films, John Lodge in "Bulldog Drummond at Bay" and Charles Ruggles in "Mind Your Own Business", got under way. There were special opening prices – 1/-,1/3,1/6,1/10 and 2/4. The cafe on the first floor opened to the general public the next day. Like the Palace Cinema next door, the programme changed each Monday and Thursday (the second programme starting from Thursday of that first week was headed by the popular husband and wife team of Jack Hulbert and Cicely Courtneidge in "Take My Tip". The second feature, "Conflict", starred John Wayne, just over a year before he was propelled from "B" pictures to top films when he starred in John Ford's "Stagecoach" in 1939).

Meanwhile, the Palace remained open and proved to be as popular as ever despite very strong competition next door! In fact, at 2.30 pm on Saturday October 2nd, the "Chums Club" was inaugurated at the Palace. Saturday films were screened especially for "Chums" for just 3d and 6d; mums and dads could also attend – for 6d and 1/- ! Gradually, however, the audience deserted for the far grander Union.

More Cinemas Planned for Luton

Not long after the opening of the Union in Dunstable, the biggest single-screen cinema ever built in South Bedfordshire opened in Luton's Gordon Street. By now, the Picturedrome and the Empire usually screened the same programme, though there were exceptions, but the days of both these cinemas were numbered. By the end of 1938, the number of cinema seats in Luton would rise to well over nine thousand, not including three smaller cinemas which closed well before the outbreak of World War II. The Union circuit already controlled four cinemas in Luton, but if they thought they were going to have it all their own way, they were mistaken. Two other major circuits were breathing down the necks of Union chiefs David and Fred Bernhard. The company was especially concerned by the competition from Oscar Deutch's Odeon chain; rumour has it that the Bernhards encouraged their staff to report Odeon activity so that they could counter it as soon as possible. In George Streeet, the ABC circuit had plans which would also concern the Bernhards.

In September 1936, *The Luton News* readers mulled over this tantalising paragraph:

> "There is a probability that besides the Gordon-street cinema (the Ritz, going up soon) and the George-street cinema (lease taken and detailed plans being prepared), Luton will have yet a third new cinema.
>
> Yesterday the "News" was told that plans were in existence for a cinema (the Odeon), seating 2,500, to be built in Castle-street on land between Holly-street and New Town-street."

Odeon Cinemas apparently were keeping quiet, for *The Luton News* reporter could get no one to admit that such plans had even been submitted. "You see, dear old boy, there are so many of these cinemas" was all he was told. That was fair, if quaint comment; modern picture palaces were being built by the circuits all over the country as cinemagoers made going to the pictures an ever more popular pastime. They now demanded more than was offered by the small halls they had patronised before the talkies came to stay. In fact, the plans for a new cinema, petrol station and car park in Castle Street had been submitted by a certain K. McLaglan and these were passed by Luton Town Council in November, 1936. The plans did not include any name for the cinema designed by architect Edwin Westerman and the cinema was never built.

Plans for yet another cinema, this time in Dunstable Road, were submitted by Stanley E. Leighton who had acquired the freehold for land formerly occupied by Luton Town Football Club before they moved to nearby Kenilworth Road. This was a smaller cinema than the Castle Street project, but it was the site ultimately chosen by Odeon. News of a planned Odeon in Dunstable Road no doubt soon reached the Union bosses' ears; indeed, they almost certainly heard about ABC's George Street project as well. John Maxwell's Associated British Cinema circuit plans submitted for a Regal in George Street were not approved straight away, but they got through in April, 1937. The cinema was also destined to undergo a change of name before it opened.

Cinema Craze Prompts Rumours

The cinema craze was under full steam in Luton during the mid-thirties. *The Luton News* reported:

> "Rumour has been very busy of late on the subject of new cinemas in Luton".

The writer of the "Around and About" column had observed a notice on land in Leagrave stating that it was "Reserved for Cinema" . William Southan Morris and Union parted company in what had been reported as not very friendly circumstances. He bought a cinema called the Luxor in Hemel Hempstead and then submitted plans for a new cinema to be built in Marsh Road in Leagrave. The plans were passed by Luton Council in February, 1937; the 1,000-seat cinema was also to be called the Luxor but was never built. *The Luton News* reported more planned cinemas. Passers-by noticed a prominent sign in Waller Street announcing that the site had been sold to Mr W. S. Scott of Wardour Street, London, for "The Waverley Cinema" but, once again, it never materialised. On the other side of town in Stopsley, a board described a piece of land as "... a site for a new cinema and temperance billiards' hall". *The Luton News* was unable to discover who was behind this prospective enterprise which also came to nothing.

This optimistic sign announces the forthcoming Waverly Cinema in Waller Street, but it was never built. (LN)

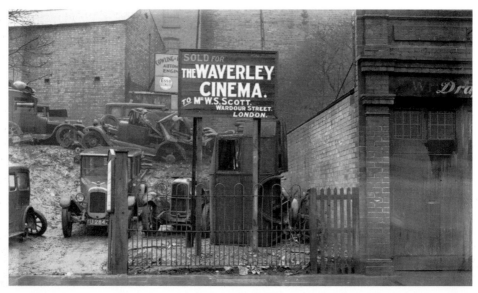

The Grand Keeps Pace

With so much cinema activity, the Grand resisted conversion (a fate which befell many live theatres up and down the land). In fact, in order to keep their audiences happy, the Grand produced plans in 1936 to re-arrange the balconies and closed for the whole of July for alterations. They also had to compete with the Alma's cine-variety and they did this by booking popular stars like Anona Winn, Bob and Alf Pearson and Albert Whelan. Although the Grand still operated a policy of presenting both variety and plays, the programme consisted almost entirely of variety when the theatre re-opened on August 3rd, 1936 with music hall star Ella Shields topping the bill. In September, Sunday variety concerts based on the "Brighter London" Sunday series at the Prince of Wales Theatre were introduced. Not that this was a new idea for Luton – both the Alma and the Palace offered leading dance-bands and variety stars in their Sunday concerts. Roy Fox, Charlie Kunz, Arthur Askey (4th billed!) and Wee Georgie Wood were just a few of the big names Luton audiences could see on Sundays in 1936. The invasion of variety stars and famous dance bands continued in 1937 – The Western Brothers, Joe Loss, Mantovani, Teddy Brown to name but a few.

The big stars didn't only visit Luton on Sundays. True, the Palace had virtually given up the concept of cine-variety by then, but it continued at the Alma where you could see Elsie and Doris Waters ("Gert and Daisy") topping variety as well as two films at the end of January, 1937. In March, the film double-bill was accompanied by Tommy Handley and his famous "The Disorderly Room" sketch, three other acts and the Compton organ!

The famous Music Hall star Ella Shields headed variety at Luton's Grand Theatre when it re-opened after a month long closure for alterations in the summer of 1936; she returned to play Dick Whittington in the Grand's second panto for the 1936/37 season. (LCL/LN)

The Grand introduced Luton audiences to "new" comedians Jewel and Warriss who were to find fame on the radio ten years later with their show "Up The Pole". The forty-year old theatre also brought back old favourites like Harry Tate, Leon Cortez and "The Ovaltineys", continental broadcasters on Radio Luxembourg, Britain's principal source of commercial radio at that time. However, the Grand did not ignore the playgoers. Tucked in amongst the variety performers, the famous actor and teller of Dickens, Bransby Williams, was booked. In 1937, interest in plays was being revived; for some years, there had been heated discussion on the area's theatrical taste, though it was admitted by the theatre that a mixed programme must continue. To promote interest in live theatre generally, the Grand instituted its "Monday Club" to:

i) popularize drama, variety and revue and
ii) to form a body of critical public opinion who will visit the theatre for the first performance each week and be able to recommend or condemn the show to their friends.

No doubt the Grand hoped that there would be more recommendations than condemnations! Even today, theatres recognise the value and importance of "word of mouth" which can often be more effective than newspaper advertisements.

In April, 1937, the Malvern Repertory Company offered a season of plays at the Grand, while Harold V. Nielson's Shakespearean Company performed no less than eight of the Bard's most popular dramas and comedies in May. The company featured "Luton favourite" Edward Dunstan who had successfully brought Shakespeare to Luton audiences throughout the twenties. In fact, Edward Dunstan had a very long association with the Grand Theatre. The theatre was also the home of the Luton Amateur Operatic and Dramatic Society whose 1937 productions were "The Desert Song", Ivor Novello's "Fresh Fields" and a now forgotten play called "On the Spot" which shared the week with the Novello play. As it happened, weekly rep was to gain ground in Luton, but that's a later story.

South Bedfordshire's Largest Cinema

Before Southan Morris left Union, he submitted plans for a large cinema to be called the Ritz in Gordon Street, Luton. The initial plans submitted in March, 1936 proposed a luxury cinema with 1,946 seats, one small and two large dressing rooms and a 21' deep stage in front of the screen. For some reason, these plans by architects Leslie H. Kemp and Tasker were not accepted and a further application was made in August. These too were rejected in September; more amendments

Above Luton's Union cinema in the early stages of construction in early 1937 during a period of great growth for the circuit. The same circuit's Alma can be seen in the background. (LN)

Below The brick cladding begins to be added to the steel skeleton of the Union cinema in Luton (destined to be the largest single-screen cinema in South Bedfordshire). (LN)

This thirties' shot of Luton's Union demonstrates how the Gordon Street slope was effectively used. (CTA)

The magnificent art deco pillars and ceiling in the foyer of the large Union in Luton were still in evidence when this photograph was taken during alterations to convert the building into a Liquid Night Club and Chicago Rock Cafe. (JC)

were made and a slightly larger cinema than that originally envisaged was finally approved on December 15th, 1936. In these revised plans, the stage remained intact, for it was assumed that this new "super" cinema would replace the Alma as Luton's principal cine-variety hall. With 1,412 seats in large blocks separated by three aisles in the stalls and a further 686 seats in the circle, the new cinema could now seat a total of 2,098. Two vomitory entrances gave access to the circle with the most expensive seats at the front. Inside the auditorium, lighting cornices in the ceiling gave a soft illumination during the intervals between the films which were projected onto the 28' X 21' screen.

The huge new cinema proved to be a big attraction. There was a "niche" under the double staircase on the right side of the large, airy foyer which contained an attractive goldfish pool and fountain surrounded by well-lit mirrors. The two sets of stairs either side of the niche led to a spacious circle foyer, offering plenty of space for audience circulation before and after performances. Looking back, it seemed absolutely right that these large cinemas should have such large foyer areas both upstairs and down. The upstairs foyer could easily have contained a modern-day "screen". Three sets of swing doors led into the cinema from the top end of Gordon Street with another set of swing doors before entering the foyer itself. As one entered, the pay-box was originally sited on the left hand side of the foyer, but was later moved to occupy a central position. The old pay-box area was then used to sell cigarettes and confectionery. Smoking was permitted in cinemas in those days.

The outside of the building was plain and functional, though it did have an attractive relief, windows and a false balcony above a shallow entrance canopy. It was all within the modern style which found favour with cinema architects of the period. The length of the cinema stretched part way down Gordon Street, with a large shutter opening on to the back-stage area at the Manchester Street end of the building. The shutter has now been bricked up and the inscription

Union Cinema 1937 – 1949
Ritz Cinema 1949 – 1971

has been etched in the space to remind Lutonians that the building was once a splendid cinema. Beyond the entrance area, the building was in brick. The bottom section was continuous, while the top section was divided with pilasters. The sloping site proved ideal for the cinema. Just like its smaller counterpart in Dunstable, it was to be called Union Cinemas Ritz, but opened with the name shortened to Union. Twelve years later, in 1949, the cinema changed its name to the Ritz!

A Grand Opening

Such a grand cinema had an appropriately grand opening on Monday, October 11th, 1937. A Wurlitzer organ had been installed and BBC organist H. Robinson Cleaver came along to play the magnificent instrument on that first night. There was also a full variety show featuring Terry's Juveniles (from whose ranks a young Jessie Matthews had graduated to stardom) and, like the Dunstable opening, a local "In Town Tonight" was presented on stage. Popular British film star Robert Douglas came to the official opening; he was the star of the Herbert Wilcox production "Our Fighting Navy", the first film to be shown in the new cinema. The film is largely forgotten today, but Robert Douglas did go to Hollywood where he was to play in more memorable fare. This first programme was a precursor to the cine-variety to come, though not for long. The concept of films plus a live show was dying fast. However, the beautiful organ was to be well used for many years. For the Union's second programme, H. Robinson Cleaver played the Wurlitzer between the two films on offer , "After the Thin Man" and "Parole Racket".

During the ensuing months, popular variety artistes such as Ronald Frankau, Tommy Fields (Gracie's brother making a name for himself) and music hall star

Billy Bennett appeared at Luton's Union Cinema. Meanwhile, the former leading cine-variety hall, the Alma, gave up live acts altogether, though they did schedule Sunday concerts with famous dance bands. In November, 1937, the ever popular Roy Fox and his Band put in a welcome appearance and there were many more to follow.

A Complaint Clocked in the Local Press

Cinemagoers soon got used to the comforts and luxury offered by the Unions in both Dunstable and Luton, though there was one complaint! A correspondent to *The Luton News* complained about the size and placing of the clocks in both cinemas, a key factor in the days of continuous performances. Members of the audience, who may well have come into the cinema while a film was running, would often sit and watch some of the show again before they had to leave. The writer could not understand why the clocks were so small and were placed at the back of the hall. "Super cinemas should have super clocks," he felt. Notwithstanding the size of the clocks, the cinema scene was changing rapidly. The Alma Cinema Cafe re-commenced lunches in mid-November and the "Chums Club" offered

The Wurlitzer organ was a popular feature of Luton's Union Cinema; Alex Taylor is at the keyboard in this early 1945 shot. (LN)

Saturday morning programmes for children, largely following the pattern set in Dunstable where the Chums Club gave an distinctive role to the older, largely superseded Palace.

Just three days after Luton's Union opened on October 11th, 1937, it was announced that the chain had been acquired by Associated British Cinemas, already well advanced with plans for their own cinema in the town. Initially, the Union circuit was operated as a subsidiary of ABC, with the phrase "managed by Associated British Cinemas" added to their newspaper ads, but the two chains were eventually integrated.

Dramatic Change to Cinema Scene in Luton

In Luton, the cinema scene was already set to change dramatically. In his report at the end of 1937, the Chief Constable for Luton reported that two cinemas had been closed by the County Council as "not being suitable for public performance". Initially, it had been assumed that the Picturedrome would remain open, but audiences soon defected to the new Union. When it did not pass a health inspection, there seemed little point in correcting the problems; "Hearts in Re-union" and "Thank You Jeeves" were scheduled to be screened from Monday, 25th October, 1937 but, when the few stalwarts still faithful to the Park Street cinema turned up, they found that the Picturedrome had closed its doors never to open again as a cinema. As it had been the Union circuit's policy to show the same film at both the Picturedrome and the Empire, the planned films were not lost to Luton audiences.

The High Town Plaza had closed earlier in the year due to a fire; it would be fifteen years before that little cinema would open its doors again. Even if the Union circuit had survived, they would never have controlled all the cinemas in Luton. Apart from the ABC plans, Oscar Deutsch saw Luton as an ideal town for one of his Odeons.

Acres of Seats

The pundits had great fun as they discussed the sudden increase in cinema seats in Luton. In March, 1938, *The Luton News* "Around and About" columnist had reported that the Odeon ("Luton's second 2,000 seater unless the ABC in George Street is opened first") will increase the number of cinema seats, "now numbering 6,070", by a third. The number of available seats in early 1938 totted up approximately as follows:

Union 2,000 plus
Alma nearly 1,700
Palace about 1,250
Empire nearly 800
Wellington 300 plus

Thus, "Around and About" pointed out, the older cinemas offered about 4,000 seats and the Union and Odeon would double that number. "With the opening of the ABC, which is to seat 1,948, seating capacity will have been increased by 150% in about a year." In the event, it wasn't quite so dramatic because the Empire closed as the "ABC" (as it was still referred to in the press in early 1938) opened.

Part of the stalls area of the Union in Luton can be seen while children enjoy their own show. (LN)

This magnificent view of the Odeon, Luton, taken in 1962, clearly demonstrates the circuit's famous style; as one of the few remaining examples, it was deservedly given Grade II listing. (EM)

Oscar Deutsch Plans to Entertain in Luton

The plans for a new cinema and car park in Dunstable Road were finally passed on September 21st, 1937. In August, it had been reported that the cinema had been approved "with modifications". It was necessary to hold an enquiry to build the cinema on the old Luton Town Football Club site, for a 1919 conveyance had restricted development to housing. Originally intended to occupy the corner of Dunstable Road and Hazelbury Crescent, the arbitrator called for the cinema to occupy a more central site with entrances from Dunstable Road only. Shops were also planned (and subsequently built) on the Hazelbury Crescent corner as part of the overall development. To preserve the residential nature of Avondale Road (which runs behind the site), that side of the cinema had to be built with red bricks and without windows. A car park with an entrance from Hazelbury Crescent was permitted. Despite these precautions, there were a number of objectors who received compensation because their view was blocked. There were those who suggested that the new cinema would present a more favourable outlook than the gas-works on the other side of the road!

Distinctive Odeon Destined for Preservation

The distinctive Odeon was designed by architect Keith P. Roberts whilst in the employ of Andrew Mather, one of the principal firms working on Odeons during the thirties. Like the Union, it has a steel frame clad in brick. The Dunstable Road entrance frontage, which is ranged to the right of the building as one faces it, is recessed above the canopy and made up of opaque cream glass panels. To the left, the outside wall of the auditorium is built in brick divided into nine bays by pilasters while the roof is hidden behind parapets. The building stretches some 178 feet with a typical Odeon tower (often known as a fin) between the recessed section and the auditorium wall. The fin-tower is marked out in horizontal sections; the top section originally held a neon illuminated 'O' which dominated that part of Dunstable Road on the south side and could be seen from quite a distance, especially as one approached it from the town centre. No one at the time could have guessed that the development would eventually become a listed building, an honour that certainly was not accorded the gas-works!

The ultra-modern style was pleasing to the eye, though similar in style to any number of Odeon cinemas being built in the country at that time. In drawing up the schedule for listing the building in 1999, the Department for Culture, Media and Sport clearly recognised that many Odeons had been razed to the ground and, having described the facade as "a remarkably sophisticated piece of purist geometry, entirely lacking historicist references or even Art Deco styling", it was all summed up thus: "Keith Roberts (1910 – 1994) was the outstanding designer of International Modern cinemas in Britain, and the former Odeon at Luton is the best remaining example".

The Odeon's Spacious Interior

Having entered the cinema by one of the five sets of double doors, one found six steps leading into a deep foyer. The attractive handrails were designed in the modern style with the typical liner effect so popular during the thirties. Once

The interior design of Luton's Odeon, like others in the chain, was inspired by Mrs Lily Deutsch. This view is taken from the circle. (CTA)

inside the foyer, two sets of doors on the left led into the stalls which contained 1,332 seats. An imperial stair at the far end of the foyer led to the upper foyer from which doors led into the 626 seat circle. Initially, the glass circular pay-box commanded a dominant central position. In later years, this was removed and the pay-box moved to the side opposite the stalls doors.

The interior design of the 1,958 seat auditorium was, in common with other Odeons, inspired by Mrs Lily Deutsch, wife of Odeon boss Oscar Deutsch. A general house style was imposed upon all Odeons built at that time, but the interior was different in Luton as the ceiling was not typical. The outer ring of lights in the ceiling was reminiscent of the style adopted by the new Gaumont Palaces being built in other parts of the country. The proscenium arch surrounding the screen was flanked by wide sections with openings for ventilation. These openings were disguised with narrow horizontal banding with a typical Odeon clock mounted on either side. Saucer domes with or without lights were also a feature of the decorative style inside the cinema. The discreet lighting was designed to be soft as it was raised or lowered before and after each performance. Curtains (or 'tabs') in front of the screen were decorated with a flying horse and were said to be the same design as Brighton's Odeon. In most respects, the interior was typical of the Odeon house design. It is interesting to recall that a smart salesman rapidly realised that Odeon could be an acronym for "Oscar Deutsch Entertains Our Nation". It quickly caught on and people believed that was why the cinemas were given that name, a view never discouraged or denied by Deutsch. Although the Odeon circuit had only come into existence in 1933, it had more than 250 theatres by 1938, with predictions that the number would shortly reach 300.

Stunning Opening for Odeon

The opening ceremony on Wednesday, October 12th, 1938, proved to be a stunning affair, marred only by the fact that the mayor Alderman Harrison was seriously ill and could not perform the official opening. His death shortly afterwards provided a sad footnote to a grand opening. Former mayor Alderman Wistow Walker took his place and, an hour before the opening, the Band of the

A grand "Imperial Stair" led up to the large circle area, making an ideal background for this decorative group in 1952. Note the circle seat prices. (LMS/LN)

1st Battalion of the King's Own Borderers marched up and down in front of the new cinema. The No 1 Ceremonial Fanfare was played as the guests arrived and then they were piped through the auditorium and up on to the stage. The party included Valerie Hobson, star of the opening film, and Mrs Deutsch, no doubt pleased to nod approval at the design of the interior. The proceeds from the opening went to the new Bute Hospital (later renamed "Luton and Dunstable"). Oscar Deutsch himself could not be present, but he made sure that he sent a telegram to be read out to the assembled throng.

The opening film was "The Drum" which, apart from Miss Hobson, starred Sabu (of "Elephant Boy" fame) and Raymond Massey. The film had been photographed in "gorgeous" Technicolor – a special treat as so few films were made in colour at that time. With a "Full Supporting Programme" consisting of Paramount News, a Mickey Mouse cartoon and a short entitled "North Sea", "The Drum" continued into the following week – "By Public Demand". Free aids were offered for the hard of hearing.

Even though it was drizzling with rain on that opening day, crowds lined the streets to catch a glimpse of the glamorous Valerie Hobson, reputed to be the best-dressed actress in British films. Dressed in a "sheath-like gown of black crepe, with yoke and long, tight sleeves of powder blue", she did not disappoint the fashion conscious who were very impressed with the foot-long train of her elegant skirt. The "waist-length cape of coffee-coloured fox fur" would undoubtedly cause frowns today but, in 1938, it was seen as a sign of the star's success and good taste. Valerie Hobson charmed everybody. She had never visited Luton before and was surprised how big the town was. She had imagined it to be no bigger than St. Albans – but she did know that Luton made hats!

ABC's Savoy Opens in Luton

Just days after the Odeon opened its doors, Lutonians had yet another new cinema offering up-to-date films in comfortable surroundings. For the opening of the Savoy in George Street, however, there was no grand ceremony. The original design called for a cinema with 1,948 seats, but this was finally increased to 1,990. The exterior had changed quite considerably from the original "Regal" design submitted in 1936, but it was the auditorium which took the breath away. It was extremely wide; the circle had to be held up by a single-span girder which was even wider than that required for the Alma. There's no doubt that the width of the cinema was to prove a very real asset when CinemaScope was installed in the fifties.

The Savoy's art-deco auditorium decorations in shades of pink and green

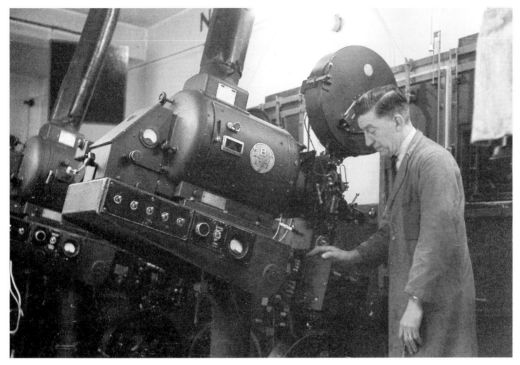

Above **Both projectors can be seen in this photograph of the Odeon operator's room. (LN)**

Below **In the days before "cakestand" projectors, which can hold a complete film and return it to the beginning after a screening, a re-wind room was necessary as each ten or twenty minute reel had to be made ready for the next showing. (LN)**

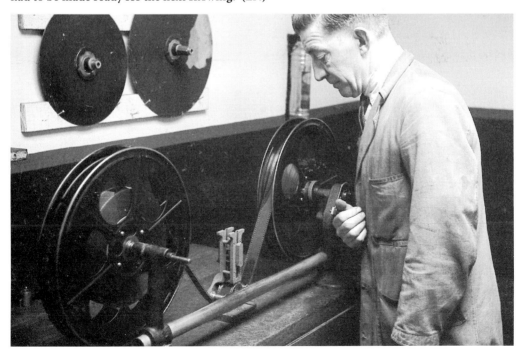

Above Only 5 days after the Odeon, the Savoy in Luton opened to the public without any ceremony. (CTA) *Opposite* Arguably most beautiful of all local cinema interiors, the Savoy's auditorium reveals its art deco splendour. (CTA)

stippled with gold made it the most beautiful cinema interior in Luton. The main entrance is on the corner of George Street and George Street West. When it first opened, there was another entrance for the front stalls further up George Street West, but it was not in use for very long. It has subsequently been bricked up, though it is still possible to see where it was. As we'll learn, the Savoy was to undergo a number of changes and ownership, but it was the only thirties cinema in the South Bedfordshire area to continue operating until 2000.

The Savoy actually opened its doors for the first time at 1.30 pm on Monday, October 17th, 1938. There was no band, no special personality – the first people to enter the Savoy were the customers themselves. Despite the fact that the Odeon had opened just five days earlier, the new town centre cinema had a full house on that first afternoon. Although one had been originally planned, no organ was installed in the Savoy. As the patrons filled the stalls and circle, recorded music came from behind the attractive curtain which hid the screen. The curtains were opened at 2.30 pm. A strong programme had been booked for that initial screening; that first audience saw Clark Gable, Spencer Tracy and Myrna Loy – all big names in 1938 – in MGM's "Test Pilot". It had been announced that programmes would be continuous, which was usual in those days. From Tuesday, October 18th, the cinema opened its doors at 1 pm with the programme starting at 1.30 pm.

Luton's Empire Closes but Luton has More Cinema Seats Than Ever Before

It was intended that the Savoy would be the only ABC cinema in town but, by the time it opened, Associated British Cinemas had acquired the Union chain. As a result, there were three other ABC controlled cinemas in Luton by the time the George Street cinema opened. Despite denying rumours that the popular Empire may close, ABC decided that it would not remain to compete with the Savoy. In fact, it did not remain open after the final screening of "Almost a Gentleman" starring British comic Billy Bennett on Saturday 15th October, 1938. The staff of twelve were transferred to other ABC cinemas in the town, including the Savoy. There was also some speculation over the future of the Alma, also now managed by ABC. One of the strong rumours at the time was that ABC would turn one of its Luton cinemas into a variety hall. Although it was hotly denied, the rumour proved to be prophetic, but more of that in the next chapter.

In less that two years, Luton lost three cinemas – the Plaza, the Picturedrome and the Empire. However, the town now had far more cinema seats than ever before, and most of these represented unparalleled comfort and luxury. All the front of house staff in the larger cinemas were uniformed – for example, commissionaires, cashiers and attendants at the Savoy all wore smart green uniforms. With more than nine thousand cinema seats, not to mention accommodation for nearly another thousand at the Grand Theatre, competition became very keen indeed. The two new cinemas which opened in 1938 both charged 1/6 and 2/- in the circle, while the Odeon charged 1/- at the back and 9d at the front of the stalls and the Savoy had a slightly better deal at 1/- and 6d in their downstairs area. For those who bought their ticket before 4 pm (3 pm on Saturdays and Holidays), the whole of the circle cost just 1/- and the stalls 6d in both houses. Not surprisingly, the day the Savoy opened, the Alma revised their prices – downwards!

Despite all this competition, not all the cinemas were behaving fairly according to correspondence in *The Luton News*. It was alleged that one cinema with a foyer notice offering lower seat prices for children except on Saturdays or Bank Holidays refused a half-price ticket to the mother of a four-and-a-half year old on a week-day afternoon. There were also several complaints about cinemas claiming that the cheaper seats were full. In order to avoid queuing, some cinemagoers reported that they had bought higher priced seats than they had expected, only to find that there were empty seats in the cheaper area. How times have changed! Multiplexes normally offer just one price for all their seats. Where superior seats are offered in older cinemas with booking facilities, it is these more expensive seats which sell first for the very popular films.

Luton's Palace Fights Back

The well-established Palace could no longer let the new cinemas get all the attention and – if they were not careful – all the customers too! So they closed their doors for two weeks from December 12th, 1938, for an auditorium re-fit. The circle was completely re-constructed, while the whole theatre had new seating and was redecorated throughout. Looking like a shiny new pin, the Palace re-opened on Boxing Day 1938 with Alfred Hitchcock's "The Lady Vanishes". Though the days of cine-variety had virtually passed, the Palace offered live shows on Sunday – the first following the re-fit came on January 1st, 1939, when "Big-Hearted" Arthur Askey came to town. The Palace retained its flair for showmanship, attracting large crowds when searchlights were installed to herald a major film. Even after the war, the Palace was very publicity-conscious – those who remember still talk about the live monkeys displayed in the large, glass fronted display cases which flanked either side of the entrance. The jungle film they were supposed to advertise has long been forgotten.

There were other live shows in town – it was the Panto season and Luton had three. A two-week run of "Jack and the Beanstalk" started at the Alma on Boxing Day, while "Aladdin" started a week-long run at the Grand on Christmas Eve. The following week, the Grand offered "Mother Goose".

Church Hall Cinema Shows Revived

The growth of cinemas in Luton and Dunstable was tremendous during the late thirties, but other opportunities for screening films were still being explored. A Mr Willis organised a film show for the old folk at Kensworth Methodist Church which proved to be a big hit. Even as late as 1938 there were many in the village who had never seen a moving picture. "This Saturday's entertainment is merely the beginning," commented Mr. Willis. It seemed that the well-tried concept of the travelling showman was still alive and well in South Bedfordshire, for it proved to be just the first in a series of film shows in Kensworth. Where Kensworth led, Luton could follow!

Waller Street Methodist Church introduced film shows on Sunday at 7.45 pm after the evening service. A flood of letters to *The Luton News* followed; most felt that the church was not the place to show films, though a few saw the advantages. When one recalls that some of Luton's earliest film shows were screened in chapels and church halls without opposition, it seemed strange that Luton's Methodists should now balk at the concept during the height of the cinema age. After all, one of their greatest benefactors was movie magnate J. Arthur Rank who had contributed to the cost of building Biscot Methodist Church. It is interesting to note that he insisted that the new church should have cinema-style tip-up seats – and these have lasted to this day! Eventually, Mr Rank was to control the company which operated two of Luton's major cinemas (the Odeon and the Palace).

A Final Thirties Closure

There was one more closure before the decade closed. The Palace in Dunstable retained a faithful audience for almost a year after the Union opened, but they gradually defected to the newer cinema next door. It finally closed its doors at the end of August, 1938. The theatre and cinema scene in South Bedfordshire was now set in place for the next decade, though the coming of war in September, 1939 brought about a number of changes.

CHAPTER EIGHT

The War Years

In America, the cinema enjoyed a vintage year in 1939 with films like "Gunga Din", "Stagecoach", "Wuthering Heights", "Goodbye Mr. Chips", "The Wizard of Oz", "Mr. Smith Goes to Washington", "Ninotchka", "Destry Rides Again" and "Gone With the Wind". For filmgoers in Britain, many of these films became war-time movies, for they did not reach local screens until 1940; in the case of "Gone With the Wind", it was not seen locally until 1942.

Cinemas and Theatres Close for a Brief Period
Before Meeting the Demands of Wartime

Upon the outbreak of war, all places of entertainment were closed, though not for long. It was soon realised that cinemas in particular could boost morale and provide a valuable channel for essential propaganda. Within days, they all opened again and cinemagoing became just as much a wartime activity for those left at home as it was before the war. There were changes, of course. Cinemas could no longer advertise their presence with neon lights and programmes often finished earlier to avoid having too many people on the streets late at night. "Message" films from the Government were included in programmes, with food hints becoming a staple of film fare to help eke out the rations, while warnings against "loose talk" were designed to thwart giving vital information to the enemy. There were also films about the black-out, so vital if German bombers were to be prevented from seeing intended or other targets.

A certain camaraderie began to build up between cinema staff and patrons. Not that the regulars remained unknown to the staff before the war, but now everyone was united in wanting to beat Nazi Germany. A noticeably friendlier attitude could be detected amongst people at home as together they faced deprivations, dangers and casualties of war. After a bombing raid, the cinema staff would look out for their regulars and, if someone didn't turn up on their usual night, the manager would make discreet enquiries to make sure they were all right. As a result, cinemas thrived as centres for meeting friends, old and new, during the dark days of the war.

Many more war films were shown to highlight the heroism of our servicemen; they often spelled out an important propaganda message as audiences were reassured that we were winning the war. Whilst Germans were depicted as dastardly villains, prompting a national antagonism to spur us on to victory, there were also the gaudily coloured musicals designed for pure escapism. The hero in these fast-paced tune-fests was invariably a serviceman who captured the heart of the beautiful heroine whilst on leave. These films suggested that the likes of Betty Grable or Rita Hayworth could only fall for a uniformed soldier on his way to fight the enemy.

CEMA, Distinguished Visitors and Non-Stop Revue

The government was fully aware of the part that entertainment and the arts could play during the war. They set up the Entertainments National Service Association (ENSA) and the Council for the Encouragement of Music and the Arts (CEMA). Under the umbrella of this wide-reaching organisation, a variety of events including opera, ballet and drama but mainly classical music and art exhibitions were toured, often finding their way into South Bedfordshire in general and Luton in particular. In November, 1944, the Ballet Rambert came to the Grand Theatre under the auspices of CEMA. The Luton factories were carrying out essential war work; entertaining the workers was seen as a vital contribution to stepping up production. After the war, CEMA developed into the Arts Council of Great Britain which has subsequently become individual Arts Councils for England, Scotland and Wales.

All the theatres and cinemas began to have distinguished visitors. In July, 1939, the Grand had followed a year of revue and variety with Frank H. Fortescue's Famous Players in a season of repertory. At the outbreak of war, the season came to an abrupt halt with the closure of places of entertainment. When the Grand re-opened, Frank H. Fortescue produced two more plays before turning to non-stop revue; he now presented his "Famous Funsters"! He gave Luton its very first non-stop wartime show, a comedy revue called "Spicy Bits" from 5.45 pm to 9.55pm every night – "Come when you like – Go when you like" coaxed the ads. More revue followed before "World Famous Stars of Radio Luxembourg" took the stage to open a twice-nightly variety season which included well-known bandleaders like Bertini and Billy Thorburn.

In April, 1940, Luton Operatic and Dramatic Society hired the Grand for their first war-time production, "The Arcadians", with the proceeds going to the Red Cross. The following week, Winston Churchill's actress daughter Sarah made a personal appearance in "Gaslight". Miss Churchill was supported by the London Coliseum Theatre Company. The Grand was determined not to get in a rut. By January, 1941, they announced a "Stupendous Attraction" with "Nature Parade", advertised as "The Greatest Road Show of 1941". Apart from "Luton Favourite" Jack Strand, the cast included La Moya from the Folies Bergere in Paris and "The Eight Nature Girls". Not to be outdone, both the Alma and Union cinemas ran competitions to support causes like "War Weapons Week".

Sunday Concerts and Other Live Shows

Although the age of cine-variety was virtually over, Sunday variety or band shows, which had proved so popular before the war, were presented at most cinemas as a vast army of top-ranking entertainers came to South Bedfordshire. Just about every cinema seemed keen to offer Sunday night entertainment of one sort or another. This did not include films, however; when the local population had been asked to vote on Sunday movie shows, this had been rejected in Luton and Dunstable.

The Palace was the first to introduce wartime Sunday concerts when Harry Fryer and his Broadcasting Band performed on 22nd October, 1939. Fryer and his band rapidly became wartime favourites for Luton audiences as he came back again and again to the Palace stage. On a couple of occasions, he introduced Luton audiences to "Britain's Shirley Temple", Petula Clark, one of the youngest performers to entertain during the war. In March, 1940, the Alma even tried to revive cine-variety by offering "The Great Nixon" twice-nightly in addition to a double-bill of comedy films. From September, 1940, the Palace began to present popular variety and broadcasting stars on Sunday evenings. Troise and his Mandoliers, Issy Bonn, Peter Brough, Derek Roy, Sid Phillips, Nat Gonella and Mantovani were all welcomed by Luton audiences before the year was out. Nat Gonella also appeared in events organised by the Royal Air Force at Leighton Buzzard's Corn Exchange Theatre. The Alma presented a pantomime instead of films from Boxing Day, while the Grand competed, as they had the year before, with two Pantos! The Palace now made their Sunday shows a regular weekly feature. In March, the Alma offered a week of variety headed by popular singer Hutch for War Weapons Week, followed on the Sunday by a special concert featuring Count John McCormack, the Albert Sandler Trio and the Luton Girls Choir.

ABC Cinemas, who operated the Alma, clearly realised that they, too, could offer Sunday stage shows, though they chose the Union as their main venue. In April, 1941, the Gordon Street cinema began a Sunday series called "Luton Meets the Radio Stars" and over the following months, a host of popular performers appeared, including among many others, Peter Brough, Norman Evans, Cyril Fletcher, Adelaide Hall, Harry Hemsley, Derek Roy, Albert Sandler, Stanelli, Suzette Tarri, Jack Train and Bransby Williams. Even the Savoy, never intended as a live theatre, provided Sunday concerts. Francis Cassel, the famous musician who lived at Putteridge Bury, organised "All Star Celebrity Concerts" in aid of the British Red Cross. Among the stars in just one such concert at the Savoy were Vic Oliver and Sarah Churchill. Francis Cassel played the piano with the Vauxhall Motors Orchestra making a welcome appearance. The Grand also offered radio stars and, by the end of 1941, Lutonians had been introduced to, among many others, Billy Reid and Dorothy Squires, British film comedian Leslie Fuller, Jack Payne, Felix Mendelssohn, Nellie Wallace, Jack Train (from ITMA), Naughton and Gold (of `Crazy Gang' fame), Ted Andrews, "The Canadian Troubadour", and his girl-friend Barbara (daughter Julie was destined to achieve the sort of fame they could only dream about). In addition to variety, the Alma offered the BBC Theatre Orchestra and others in 1942, while the Luton Girls Choir, the Luton Choral Society and the Luton Symphony Orchestra often supported distinguished visitors.

"Somewhere in Britain"

Luton's factories were making an important contribution to the war effort and this continual stream of star visits throughout the war undoubtedly contributed to morale. In addition to Sunday concerts, stars would also visit factory canteens for lunch-time shows. These were sometimes broadcast, though the location was never given over the air. The announcer merely announced that the show was coming from a factory "somewhere in Britain". There may still be those who remember the great Jack Buchanan dancing on the stage of the Electrolux canteen in Oakley Road. Electrolux also sponsored concerts under the general heading of "Lux Playtime" at the Odeon. Stars like Jack Warner were joined by the Electrolux Male Voice Choir for these Sunday concerts.

By 1942, the Union in Dunstable was offering the occasional Sunday concert as the stars continued to entertain South Bedfordshire. The year before, Dunstable Town Hall had played host to an army musical revue by the "Blue Pencils", a nationwide touring company designed to entertain both the troops and the public. On that occasion, the cast included Gunner Wally Spence, a former member of "Luton Operatic Society".

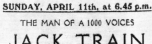

SUNDAY, APRIL 11th, at 6.45 p.m.

THE MAN OF A 1000 VOICES

JACK TRAIN

(Funf)

with

JACK SIMPSON

King of the Zylophone

AND HIS

BROADCASTING SWING BAND

with

BETTY KENT

JEAN SHAW

and

"DIANA"

The Latest Discovery

Your Compere

ALF GODDARD

Book your Seats at
ARTHUR DAY & SONS

SAVOY CINEMA
LUTON

SUNDAY, APRIL 4th
at 6.45 p.m

PROGRAMME.

TOMMY HANDLEY

with

HAL ("HAPPY DAYS") MOSS

AND HIS

MAYFAIR SWING BAND

PRICE THREEPENCE.

Above **Most cinemas and theatres offered Sunday concerts during WWII. This programme was for the Savoy, never intended for live performances. (CTA)**

ALMA CINEMA
LUTON

BBC THEATRE ORCHESTRA

Conductor:

Stanford Robinson

Sunday, 2 August 1942, at 7 p.m.

Programme Price Threepence

Right **One of the many concerts for Luton's cinemagoers during WWII was given by the BBC Theatre Orchestra at the Alma in 1942.**

Propaganda and Fund Raising

When Hitler invaded Russia, the Soviets became an ally. Lectures, film shows and talks were promoted as fund-raisers for the "gallant Soviets". It was not unusual for the cinemas to be used for such events; Harry Pollitt, leader of the British Communist Party, explained the "Communist Policy for Victory" at Luton's Savoy Cinema on Sunday, 21st December, 1941. All seats for that event were sixpence. The Ministry of Information offered a free film show at the Odeon the previous Sunday. Six films were included, one of which was called "Soviet Women". The propaganda and fund-raising machinery was at full throttle and the cinemas were playing their part.

Alma Becomes a Full-Time Theatre

Belatedly proving the truth of pre-war rumours, the Alma became a full-time live theatre in 1943. During that year, changes were made behind the scenes at Luton's fourth largest cinema. Since July, dressing rooms had been created from offices to add to those already in existence since the venue's "cine-variety" days during the thirties. The alterations and renovations included the construction of a bar under the stage, while the seats were re-upholstered. On Saturday, October 16th, 1943, the audience left at the end of the week's screening of "Money For Jam" starring the popular comedy duo Abbott and Costello. However, the lights did not dim, for workmen then removed the loud-speaker horns and the screen. By the time Monday, October 18th dawned, the Alma was a variety theatre. Work had lasted all week-end and Monday daytime to ensure that the transformation from cinema to theatre was completed without the need to close. A new booking office was installed in the foyer and, following seat re-numbering, advance bookings were proving popular even before the Alma ceased to be a cinema. In all, performers at the theatre could expect to find no less than eight dressing-rooms and, to use the words of the then manager R.C. Taylor, "The West End is coming to Luton and I think it has come to stay".

Harry Davidson and his Orchestra were employed, while the cinema staff were re-trained to operate the theatre. In addition to variety, musical comedies, road-shows and operettas were promised. The first show at the newly transformed Alma was Lew and Leslie Grade's "Tommy Get Your Fun!", a typical war-time variety show which starred Robb Wilton ("The Day War Broke Out") as well as the famous xylophonist and bandleader Teddy Brown. A further seven acts completed the bill. Luton now had two variety halls; the Grand offered "Vanities of 1943" to compete with the Alma Theatre's opening programme. Meanwhile, in addition to two live theatres, Luton still had a choice of five cinemas – the Palace, Union, Odeon, Savoy and the little Wellington. In the weeks following its opening as a full-time live theatre, the Alma offered Sandy Powell ("Can You Hear Me Mother?"), Naughton and Gold (of "Crazy Gang" fame), Vic Oliver, bandleader Maurice Winnick (famous for playing "the sweetest music this side of Heaven") and a production of the popular musical "The Chocolate Soldier".

The Grand Fights Back

Needless to say, the Grand fought back. Having had an extremely successful week in September with the "Master of Melodrama" Tod Slaughter in his production of the famous "Maria Marten or The Murder in the Red Barn", they brought Mr Slaughter and his company back in December. This time, the "King of Blood and Thunder" presented "Sweeney Todd The Demon Barber of Fleet Street" with Tod Slaughter's wife Jenny Lynn playing Mrs Lovatt. It was an astute move; Slaughter had already established his popularity with Luton audiences during the thirties, and his film and radio appearances kept his name fresh in the minds of theatregoers.

Though the war and all its deprivations had been dragging on for four long years, entertainment was not rationed in South Bedfordshire. As in former years, Christmas 1943 saw two pantos in Luton – "Jack and the Beanstalk" at the Grand and "Dick Whittington" at the Alma. Indeed, Luton audiences could look back on a very varied year of arts and entertainment throughout 1943. Before the Alma finally converted to full-time live shows, the Borough's Holiday Entertainment Committee had hired the theatre for a week-long presentation of Richard Tauber in "Old Chelsea" with music by Tauber himself. The Odeon found an enthusiastic audience for orchestral concerts on various

Right **Richard Tauber appeared in "Old Chelsea" at the Alma in 1943. (LMS/LN)**

The Luton Girls Choir performing in front of the Odeon's distinctive curtain (only two other Odeons in the country had the same design). In addition to several appearances at the Odeon, the Luton Girls Choir also gave Sunday night concerts during the war at the Alma and the Union. (LMS/LN)

Sundays. Luton Choral and Orchestral Society under the leadership of Arthur E. Davies (founder of the world-famous Luton Girls Choir) presented Sir Adrian Boult (courtesy of the BBC) and the National Philharmonic Orchestra in May, while the Entertainments Committee hired the Odeon for their August concert featuring the London Philharmonic Orchestra and pianist Eileen Joyce. These were just a few of the artistic events in town that year.

Alma Rapidly Reverts to Screening Films

After only a few months operating as a live theatre, the Alma opened a "Super Film Season" in January, 1944. Perhaps Luton couldn't support two full-time theatres after all; apart from Sunday concerts and the annual pantomimes, the Super Film Season ran for several years!

Orchestral and Choral Concerts Prove Popular in Wartime Luton

There were more exciting concerts at the Odeon. In February, 1944, the very active Luton Choral Society joined the world-famous operatic soprano Eva Turner and the London Theatre Orchestra for a Sunday concert called "Scenes from the Operas". January 1945 saw the return of Sir Adrian Boult and the BBC Symphony Orchestra who were joined by Luton Choral Society and the BBC Chorus for a concert which was broadcast from the Odeon. Members of Luton Choral Society were also frequent visitors to BBC's wartime studio in Bedford. Luton's taste for music had not ebbed away. Luton's own Symphony Orchestra performed with broadcasting pianist Irene Kohler at the Odeon and Frank H. Fortescue's No. 1 Company brought Bernard Shaw's "Pygmalion" to the Grand. Also at the Grand, CEMA presented a series of plays in November presented by, among others, Walter Hudd's Company (two Bernard Shaw plays) and The Travelling Repertory Company (Catherine Lacey in "Jane Clegg" which was produced by Lewis Casson).

The BBC Symphony Orchestra with the BBC Choir and Luton Choral Society conducted by Sir Adrian Boult in one of the last wartime Sunday concerts at Luton's Odeon in January, 1945. The concert was broadcast, though the venue would not have been revealed on air. The BBC microphone can be seen above the harp. Both the Luton Girls Choir and Luton Choral Society would give one more Sunday concert each before VE day. (LN)

Erratic Programming at the Grand

Notwithstanding these cultural excursions, programming at the Grand seemed to be as erratic as ever. Frank H. Fortescue's Famous Players continued to visit the theatre with West End hits, the ever-popular Tod Slaughter returned yet again with the sensational drama "Landru – the French Bluebeard", there was a revue called "Eve Goes Gay" and the Royal Allied Circus brought thirty "Wonderful Pigeons" and eight marvellous dogs to the theatre in December. The mixed bag of presentations continued into 1945. The pantomime "Little Red Riding Hood" was followed by "Swing Lady Swing" with Dorothy Squires and, much further down the bill, five classic nudes! In the midst of this very varied fare, the Grand did manage to present Schubert's "Lilac Time" among a plethora of shows with titles like "The Forties Naughty Naughties". Sadly, it was a harbinger of things to come. Though it had ceased to show films, even the Empire played its part during the war, for it was requisitioned for unspecified "Government purposes".

Left **The Palace celebrates Victory in Europe in 1945; by chance, an extremely popular wartime film, "Since You Went Away" was showing; it proved so popular, it was retained for a second week. (LN)**
Below **Children enjoying Saturday morning films at the Gaumont. (LN)**

At Last, the War Comes to an End

All those Sunday Orchestral concerts and CEMA productions made their impact, but Luton Choral Society, who had done so much to keep Bedfordshire's spirits up thoughout the war, felt compelled to cancel their May, 1945 performance of "The Dream of Gerontius" owing to the National Day of Thanksgiving. The war in Europe was over. Associated British Cinemas with three venues in Luton and one in Dunstable used a considerable part of their large advertising space in the press to make this announcement:

"We, the Directors and Staff of Associated British Cinemas, offer our sincere congratulations to General Eisenhower, Field Marshal Montgomery and all Allied Naval, Military and Air Force Commanders on their brilliant Victory and from our hearts we thank the Members of the Forces who did the job so gallantly.

Further, we extend our grateful thanks to the men and women of Great Britain who so courageously withstood the blitzes and who worked in the workshops, the factories, the mines and on the land, to make this Victory possible".

The Savoy was meant to have an organ, but it was never delivered. However, the intended space proved valuable when an orchestra played to celebrate a post-war birthday for the cinema. (LN)

The Odeon proved very successful in marketing its films as this 1947 display demonstrates. (LN)

The Sunday concerts continued for a time; the Odeon presented a programme with both Richard Tauber and Albert Sandler in June, the Grand announced a short season of Drama and Opera (which included "The Beggar's Opera" and Noel Coward's "This Happy Breed") and the Luton Choral Society went to Luton Parish Church for their Choral Thanksgiving.

Luton Music Club

Now that the war was over, there seemed to be a massive outpouring of artistic activity in South Bedfordshire. On April 24th,1946, Luton Music Club was formed at an open meeting. It was destined to reach national recognition and, to this day, remains one of the finest music clubs in Britain.

With the relaxation of wartime restrictions, the big cinemas now took every opportunity to promote their films with displays and other, more imaginative activities.

"The Three Musketeers" ride through Luton in August, 1949, to promote their film at the Savoy! (LMS/LN)

Cinemas Open on Sundays

1946 saw another innovation for Luton's film-goers; from May 5th, cinemas opened on Sunday for the first time. For the next ten years, only old films were screened on Sunday with the latest releases still starting on Monday. In February, 1956, the Odeon began seven-day programming with the new films starting on Sunday, but the practice of showing old films on Sunday persisted at some cinemas until 1965.

The Alma Becomes a Live Theatre Again

In 1948, ABC Cinemas had another go at full-time live theatre when they once again turned the Alma into a live theatre. On Easter Monday (29 March), the Alma Theatre opened its "1st Stage Production" – a touring production of the ever-popular "Me And My Girl" starring Lauri Lupino Lane, Barry Lupino and Wallace Lupino. Seats at 4/- in the stalls or 3/6 in the circle could be booked in

When Laurence Olivier's celebrated Oscar-winning film version of "Hamlet" was screened at the Odeon, the manager and his costumed team welcomed the audience. (LMS/LN)

advance. If you were prepared to risk that the performance of your choice had not sold out, you could make a considerable saving by popping along 45 minutes before curtain up to buy unreserved seats at 3/- in the stalls or 2/- in the circle.

During the next few weeks, audiences at the Alma saw the world's tallest man in Pete Collins' "Would You Believe It", the very popular comedian Max Wall, Carroll Levis' "BBC Discoveries" and International Ballet. Initially, films were still shown on Sundays, but this practice ceased after 29th August to allow longer prepararion for the coming week's show. This was probably because the Alma's very varied programme also included touring plays of note with the need to erect the set on the Sunday. By then, audiences had already seen, among other productions, Ronald Shiner's touring production of "Worm's Eye View" and Terence DeMarney as Heathcliff in a stage version of "Wuthering Heights". In December, old Grand favourite Tod Slaughter came to the Alma to give Luton audiences another chance to see him and his company in the Victorian melodrama, "Maria Marten or the Murder In The Red Barn".

"Rep" at the Grand

The Grand Theatre responded to this new threat with a strong season of repertory. The Theatre's own Falcon Players had had a successful season at the end of 1947. Following a short break for a visiting pantomime in January, 1948, they continued presenting popular plays like "The Winslow Boy", "The Shop At Sly Corner" and the old Aldwych farce, "Rookery Nook". To strengthen the whole operation, a new company, the Luton Repertory Company, was formed and worked jointly with the Falcon Players. At the end of December, Luton could choose between the Grand's 50th Anniversary Panto, "Little Red Riding Hood", scripted by Dan Leno Jnr., or the Alma's "Cinderella", both of which ran for two weeks. The Alma offered a strong programme of variety and tours in the new year, but it began to look as if the Grand would suffer at the hands of its new rival. At the end of January,1949, the Grand presented an exciting six week season of "Shakespeareana" from the Geoffrey Kendal Players, but the revues which followed ended in the first of a series of temporary closures at the beginning of May. One had to ask – could Luton support two full-time live theatres when the cinemas were still enjoying a post-war boom? In February, 1949, it had been announced that Mrs Rose Newton was going to put the Grand Theatre and the Royal County Theatre in Bedford up for auction. For many years, the theatres had been owned by Mrs Newton's family (her father, Edward Graham Falcon, had taken over the Grand a few years after its opening) and were now among very few British theatres left in private ownership.

Only months before in October, 1948, the old Empire was auctioned off for £8,500. It had been considered by the Luton Committee for Education for educational purposes, but they concluded that it was not suitable. The Council turned down a proposition to turn the building into a coach station and it was finally sold to the local Jewish community to become Luton's synagogue. Associated British Cinemas continued to run the Alma until they granted a twenty-one year lease to Alma Theatre (Luton) Ltd. in February, 1951, but live theatre continued for a few more years and the present staff were retained.

Luton Film Society

Meanwhile, film-going was still popular. Indeed, it was felt that Luton could support a Film Society and a meeting to determine the level of interest was called by Borough Librarian Frank Gardner in February, 1949. The Secretary of the London Film Club was invited to speak at the meeting and Luton Film Society was duly formed to screen classics, foreign language and other films not to be

The Geoffrey Kendal Players returned to the Grand Theatre, Luton, in 1949. Kendal himself played Romeo, while his wife, Laura Liddell played Juliet. It wasn't long after this engagement that the Kendals returned to India where, a few years later, they introduced their daughter Felicity to their Indian audience. (LMS)

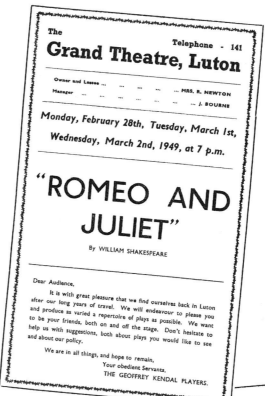

The
Telephone - 141
Grand Theatre, Luton

Owner and Lessee ... ... MRS. R. NEWTON
Manager ... ... J. BOURNE

Monday, February 28th, Tuesday, March 1st, Wednesday, March 2nd, 1949, at 7 p.m.

"ROMEO AND JULIET"

By WILLIAM SHAKESPEARE

Dear Audience,

It is with great pleasure that we find ourselves back in Luton after our long years of travel. We will endeavour to please you and produce as varied a repertoire of plays as possible. We want to be your friends, both on and off the stage. Don't hesitate to help us with suggestions, both about plays you would like to see and about our policy.

We are in all things, and hope to remain,
Your obedient Servants,
THE GEOFFREY KENDAL PLAYERS.

PROGRAMME

"ROMEO AND JULIET"
By
WILLIAM SHAKESPEARE

Cast

Escalus, Prince of Verona...	RONALD MEE
Paris, a young nobleman, kinsman to the Prince	REX DUTTON
Montague } heads of two houses at variance with each other	DAVID REYNOLDS
Capulet }	JOHN MAYES
Romeo, son of Montague...	GEOFFREY KENDAL
Mercutio, kinsman to the Prince and friend to Romeo...	MICHAEL TURNER
Benvolio, nephew to Montague and friend to Romeo...	JOHN DOWNING
Tybault, nephew to Lady Capulet	ROBERT ESSEX
Friar Laurence, a Franciscan	MALCOLM PHILLIPS
Friar John, of the same Order ...	ELWYN DANIEL
Balthasar, servant to Romeo	JENNIFER BRAGG

Peter, servant to Juliet's nurse ...	STANLEY RICHARDSON
An Apothecary ...	MICHAEL TURNER
Page to Paris	DAVID REYNOLDS
Lady Montague, wife to Montague	JOAN MILLS
Lady Capulet, wife to Capulet ...	ASTRID ANDERSEN
Juliet, daughter to Capulet	LAURA LIDDELL
Nurse to Juliet ...	BRYN BARTLETT

VERONA

SCENE ... Once, in the Fifth Act, at MANTUA

THE PLAY PRODUCED BY GEOFFREY KENDAL

Manager (for "Geoffrey Kendall Players") ... Gerald Saffery
Stage Managers ... ... David Reynolds and Stanley Richardson
Publicity ... ... Lawson Trout Ltd.

Costumes by Yorick   Scenery by Thomas Moule

found in the commercial cinemas. In its first year of operation, the 1939 French film "Fric Frac" with Fernandel and Arletty was screened and, in association with the British Film Institute, distinguished critic Dilys Powell commented on the British/Australian co-production "The Overlanders" (which was also screened). Luton's general cinemagoers had seen it in a double bill with a Barbara Stanwyck comedy called "The Bride Wore Boots" at the Odeon in November, 1946. The Society also formed a production group to make film records of various important local events, processions and celebrations which included the Luton

Coronation Pageant, "Merrie England", in 1953 and the Royal opening of Luton's new Central Library in 1962. Luton Film Society continued providing a programme of distinguished films until the Luton Film Theatre, supported by the British Film Institute, became a regular part of the Library Theatre's programme in 1969.

Left **Luton Girls Choir perform on the stage of the Gaumont, Luton prior to the World Premiere of "Old Mother Riley, Headmistress" in July, 1950. (LMS/LN)**

Above **The Luton Girls Choir sit in the circle of Luton's Gaumont cinema to watch themselves as the schoolgirls in "Old Mother Riley, Headmistress" . (LMS/LN)**

Cinemas in Luton Change Their Names

In 1949, two cinemas in Luton changed their names; in *The Luton News* of 30th June, the advertisement for the Union was now headed "Ritz – formerly Union". Back in 1937, the huge cinema was to have been called "Ritz", then "Union Cinemas Ritz", but when it opened, "Cinemas Ritz" had been dropped from the name. The Palace was brought into line with other cinemas in the Gaumont-British circuit when its name was changed to "Gaumont" from Monday, November 14th. However, the dark shadow of television would soon have a devastating effect on both theatres and cinemas in the area.

Above **Union, Dunstable foyer during promotion for "Father of the Bride" in 1950. (LMS/DG)**
Right **The Palace Theatre in Luton changed its name to Gaumont in 1949 to reflect circuit identity. (LMS/LN)**

Years after it closed, the Palace, Dunstable still stood next to the Union. (LN)

CHAPTER NINE

Decline and the Threat from Television

Following the post-war boom in attendances, theatres and cinemas were about to face their greatest threat. Television had actually started during the thirties, but made virtually no impact at all. Sets were very expensive and reception was confined to a small area – though it did reach South Bedfordshire and *The Luton News* printed television programme listings as early as 1936. When World War II broke out, the television service closed down for the duration.

The British Broadcasting Corporation (BBC) re-started their television service after the war, with more and more sets being installed in homes. With a tiny screen by today's standards and a very restricted programme schedule, the initial threat to the cinema was slight. Each street had its pioneer television set owner and, if the family included children, little friends were invited to huddle around the small patch of light to watch Annette Mills and Muffin the Mule. By today's standards, the pictures looked like something out of the ark but the television service gradually became much slicker. In America, a choice of stations stimulated competition and it was only a matter of time before the BBC had to face competition from Independent Television (ITV). Hollywood reacted with hostility towards the new medium as cinema audiences began to decline. The major film companies imposed strict controls on the showing of feature films and, even when they relented, only very old films could be beamed into homes. Feature films attacked television by ridiculing the little screen, but as television stars were born and television companies began to develop programmes which no longer looked like second-rate cinema, audiences became hooked on the newer medium.

Luton's Live Theatres Battle it Out

The full impact was not felt in South Bedfordshire until the early fifties when the first cinema closure occurred in Luton. By then the rot had set in, but there were those who still had faith in live theatre. The Grand Theatre announced its re-opening on Easter Monday, April 10th, 1950 – "Under Entirely NEW Management". The New Repertory Company – "NEW Cast; NEW Plays" – proudly presented "See How They Run" with "Popular Prices" ranging from 4/- to 1/6. Seriously threatened by competition from the Alma, which offered a strong programme of variety and high-profile touring shows, the Grand closed again in 1951. In January 1951, readers of *The Luton News* were horrified by this announcement:

"The New Repertory Company in announcing the termination of their Repertory Season this week at the Grand Theatre desire to express their appreciation of the support given them by the regular theatre patrons, and regret that it was not sufficient to enable them to continue to establish good repertory in Luton. They, however, hope that those who have given their support and friendship will take the oppoprtunity of visiting the theatre during the next three days and see their final performance in Sir James Barrie's "Mary Rose". Usual times and prices."

There was a ferocious outcry as a flood of letters showered the newspaper's offices. One correspondent hit the nail on the head when he commented on the great regret being expressed by people who only went to the Theatre "now and again". The letter was optimistic, however; houses during that last week had risen considerably as Luton theatregoers realised that this may be their last opportunity to see "rep" in their theatre. The correspondent felt that this support could be harnessed to keep the theatre open following "the widespread regret at this turn of events". Other letters expressed similar sentiments while chiding Lutonians for letting the theatre slip out of their hands. The warmth of those who did support the theatre was appreciated by the Misses Sonia Mackay and Jean Glen who ran the company. They even put an advertisement in *The Luton News* to express their appreciation and to say that their stay in Luton had been a happy one.

Grand's Premature Closure

The closure of the Grand early in 1951 proved to be a false alarm. The New Repertory Company may have left town, but once Lutonians realised they could lose their Theatre, the barrage of support caused the management to try again. The Grand re-opened on Easter Monday, March 26th, 1951, with a "carefully selected company of West End repertory artistes in well-known plays, farces and comedies". The theatre opened their new season with the well-known play,

GRAND THEATRE LUTON

THE GRAND THEATRE
COMPANY

present

"THE HAPPIEST DAYS
OF YOUR LIFE"

A Farce by JOHN DIGHTON

PROGRAMME 3d.

Monday, Wednesday, Thursday & Saturday, 6.20—8.30
Tuesday & Friday, 7.30

PRICES — 4/- : 3/- : 2/6 : 1/6
Saturdays & Holidays, 4/6 : 4/- : 3/6 : 3/- : 2/-

In 1947, Repertory under various names once again became a mainstay at the Grand Theatre in Luton, though the theatre suffered several closures from 1949. In 1951, the Grand Theatre Company counted Joan Sims and Arthur Howard among its numbers. (LMS)

PROGRAMME

"THE HAPPIEST DAYS OF YOUR LIFE"

A Farce by JOHN DIGHTON

Characters in order of appearance

Dick Tassel	ROBERT ESSEX
Rainbow	RAYMOND PIKE
Rupert Billing	ARTHUR HOWARD
Godfrey Pond	DEREK WATERLOW
Evelyn Whitchurch	PHYLLIS MONTEFIORE
Miss Gossage	HILARY MASON
Hopcroft Minor	BILL CROYDON
Barbara Cahoun	DOLORES LAYTON
Joyce Harper	JEAN BURGESS
The Rev. Edward Peck	ROBERT LONG
Mrs. Peck	JOAN SIMS
Edgar Sowter	CHARLES CALVERT
Mrs. Sowter	ANNE McGRATH

DIRECTED BY ROBERT LONG
Setting designed and painted by Colin Mackenzie

The action of the play takes place in the Masters' Common Room at Hilary Hall School for Boys, in Hampshire

ACT I	The first day of Summer Term
	INTERVAL
ACT II	Saturday afternoon—three weeks later
	INTERVAL
ACT III	Two hours later

Stage Director	John Wyckham
Resident Stage Manager	Bert Whyatt
Assistant Stage Manager	Joyce Gardner
Electrician	Harry Allen

Company Hairstyles by Caspar of Luton, Soft Furnishings by Old Times Furnishing Co., Furniture by John Edwards Stores of Luton and A. Cook and Sons of Dunstable, Other fittings and properties by Luton Co-operative Society, Messrs. Staddons, Boots, Wilds, Novelty Corner, Etherington, James Walker.
Telephone by the G.P.O.

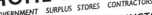

"Harvey", but the Grand's management was well aware of the cinema's dominance in Luton. They vied for audiences with this challenge:

"You may have seen the Film. Now see the Play – SEE THE DIFFERENCE".

The impressive cast included Arthur Howard and Joan Sims; capacity houses welcomed the re-opening of the Waller Street theatre and everyone breathed a sigh of relief. The Grand was as good as its word. "Harvey" was followed by a series of good, popular plays. As before, however, audiences began to dwindle as the occasional playgoers became complacent once again. The Grand tried a season of revue, musical comedy and "Novelty Festival Shows" from July.

The Grand Theatre Repertory Club had been formed by regular supporters. When the plays stopped, the Club used the money left in the kitty to purchase a cup in their name. It became a trophy to be won at the Luton Drama Festival, already establishing itself as an important annual event for groups from far and wide. The club also helped local amateurs by organising Sunday night productions at the Grand.

Bela Lugosi, Hollywood's most famous Dracula, making up for his performance in the play version at the Alma, Luton during his 1951 tour. Luckily, his image does appear in the mirror! (LMS/LN)

Having initially failed to keep a viable repertory audience, the Grand had resorted to shows like "Sensations of 1951" and "Skirts and Scanties". Repertory did return after another brief period of closure in September, 1952, with a company called "The Cry of Players". Their first production was Benn Levy's "Mrs Moonlight"; a season of strong plays followed, remembered to this day by the author and many others. When the company finally came to an end in June, 1953, two of the players left the profession and lent their considerable talents to local amateur companies – Geoffrey Deakin worked with a number of Luton companies while Bill Dellar was welcomed by the Dunstable Repertory Company.

The Alma Hits Back

It proved to be a great if short-lived period of live theatre in Luton; the Alma hit back with a very strong variety line-up which included Dick Emery, Derek Roy, Julie Andrews (not yet the huge star she became following "My Fair Lady"), Elsie and Doris Waters, Jimmy Wheeler and Harry Secombe – all big names in the early fifties. Sunday concerts were resumed.

Most people realised that it couldn't last forever. In many ways, it was surprising that Luton should have supported two full-time live theatres for so long, but few could have guessed that the Alma would be the first to go, especially as the Grand remained closed for most of 1954. However, after just six years as a full-time live theatre, the Alma closed its doors for the last time on Saturday, July 17th, 1954, with the final performance of "This Was the Army". The Grand re-opened with a three-week run of their panto "Little Red Riding Hood" on December 27th, but there was no return to weekly rep.

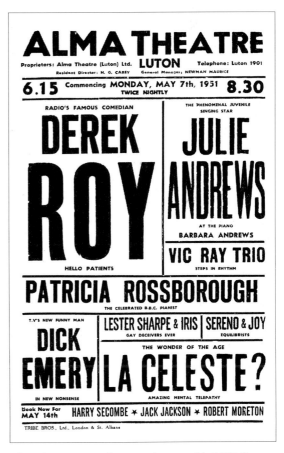

The Alma attracted top variety, as this 1951 flyer testifies. (LMS)

Ice being loaded into the Alma Theatre for "Round the World on Ice" in 1950. (LMS/LN)

Goodbye Wellington, Hello Coronet

The tiny Wellington cinema had escaped control by the major circuits and had remained in business since it opened in 1912. By 1950, few ventured beyond its small entrance to enjoy the re-runs on offer. The little cinema which had held its head up so proudly in the early years was now known locally as the "Flea-Pit" or the "Bug 'ole", dubious soubriquets confirmed in the minds of some as they observed the usherette spraying the audience with a 'flit-gun'. It also suffered from a scandal involving two part-timers who were sent to prison for offences against young girls. It seemed just a matter of time before cinemagoers would desert it forever, but someone had faith in the little cinema in the top half of Wellington Street.

Ex-Luton Police Inspector John Edward Perkins took control of the cinema in September, 1951. The former owner handed over his cinema to a small chain controlled by a three-person syndicate and the new owners redecorated their latest acquisition. Only the projectionist remained from the former staff and, after a couple of days closure, it re-opened as the Coronet on Saturday, September

Elephant entering the scenery dock at the Alma Theatre in 1952 when the "Hip Hip Zoo Ray Mammouth Circus" came to town. (LMS/LN)

22nd. "The Jolson Story" was chosen as the opening feature and "New Low Prices" were introduced – before 1pm, all seats were just 7d (very cheap, even in 1951); after 1pm, the ticket prices rose to 1/-. These special prices didn't last for long. By April 1952, seats cost 1/- and 1/6; 7d and 1/- for children. Until then, there was little perceptible change in the programming policy from the old Wellington, but changes were afoot.

Continental and Classic Films Come to Luton

The Coronet placed this ad in *The Luton News* for Thursday April 10th, 1952:

"SPECIAL ANNOUNCEMENT. – Commencing Monday, April 21st, for 6 days and each week thereafter, at 8 pm daily, we shall bring Luton the best Continental and Classic Films. Let us know what you would like to see. Watch for details of programmes."

The Coronet was responding to the increasing interest in foreign films which were beginning to be shown across Britain; hitherto, foreign language films were confined to major cities and film societies. *The Luton Pictorial* reported this unique development thus:

> "It is not often that Luton people have the opportunity of seeing a foreign film. This week there is an Italian film in town that has achieved an international reputation. The film is "Bicycle Thieves" with Italian dialogue and English sub-titles".

The Coronet continued to screen old favourites from 4.30 pm to 7.30 pm, though it wasn't long before the little cinema opened in the evenings only (with a matinee on Saturdays). In May, the cinema had such a success with the Italian version (with English dialogue) of "Les Miserables" with Valentina Cortese, it was retained for a second week. Hitherto, a two week run at the Wellington was unheard of. A couple of weeks later, Luton audiences had a chance to see Jacques Tati's "Jour de Fete" at the Coronet; that film is now regarded as a comedy classic.

Goodbye Coronet, Hello Plaza

Sadly, it didn't last. The Coronet finally closed its doors forever at the end of May, 1952, having served the town for forty years. The building was purchased by Gibbs and Dandy, the town's leading hardware and ironmonger's shop, in 1953 for £3,100 and converted for storage. The address reverted to 61, Wellington Street and, following a compulsory purchase order in 1965, was demolished to make way for the inner ring road.

Ironically, just before the old Wellington/Coronet closed, another cinema which had originally opened in 1912 was revived. Having been idle as a cinema for fifteen years, the Plaza in High Town (still owned by W. Southan Morris, Ltd.) opened its doors once again on April 28th. The cinema's management announced that the first film, "The Greatest Show On Earth", would run the whole week but that future films would be booked on a twice-weekly basis. There was quite a kerfuffle when, just before the cinema was about to open, it was discovered that there had been no application for the necessary music licence. A special court was held on the Monday morning it was due to open and the licence was granted. Good quality films like "A Streetcar Named Desire" and "Viva Zapata!" attracted Lutonians back to the small cinema which, in 1930, had been the last to install sound. What a delight it was for those of us who felt we were stepping back in history when we set foot inside the cinema for the first time.

Attracting a family audience, the Plaza enjoyed a revival when it re-opened in 1953. The portico has been bricked in. (LMS/LN)

Under the management of K.C. Johnson (Uncle Mick to the younger members of the High Town community), the re-opened Plaza acquired quite a family atmosphere. The "Mickey Pops Club" offered special shows for children on Saturday mornings. They even had their own club song composed by Master David Fox and members were encouraged to send their old magazines to children who had lost their belongings in the Lynmouth flood disaster. When the re-opened cinema celebrated its first anniversary in 1953, the birthday cake was cut by "Mickey Pops" member Janet Clarke whose grandmother had been born in one of the cottages which stood on the site before the cinema was built . In other respects, the programming policy was not that different from the old Wellington, with re-runs of mainly popular fare and a change of programme on Mondays and Thursdays. Like other cinemas in the district, a different programme of older films was offered on Sundays. Luton may have lost the Wellington, but its place had quickly been filled by the Plaza. It seemed as though the cinema and theatre scene would go on in the same old way forever. However, it proved to be a false sense of security for regular theatre and cinema patrons.

Coronation Boosts Cinema Audiences – and Television Sales!

In 1953, cinemas received an added boost to audience figures when they screened full-length Coronation films. At both the Odeon and Gaumont in Luton, "A Queen Is Crowned" in glorious Technicolor was shown, while the Savoy and Ritz simultaneously screened "Elizabeth Is Queen" in Warnercolor. Not a good week for anyone wishing to avoid the Royalist fervour which swept the country!. Not long afterwards, cinemagoers in Dunstable and Leighton Buzzard had their opportunity to see the Queen's Coronation on the big screen. As it was also the first coronation to be televised, the fact that both these films were in colour was very important; in 1953, colour television had not yet arrived, but this event still persuaded many to buy or rent their first television.

"Merrie England" at Luton Hoo

Week commencing Monday : December 14th : 1953

SAM WANAMAKER and RALPH BIRCH
present

THE BIG KNIFE
By Clifford Odets

•

Characters in order of appearance :

Russell	JOHN HARRISON
Buddy Bliss	PHILIP VICKERS
Charles Castle	SAM WANAMAKER
Patty Benedict	NATALIE LYNN
Marion Castle	RENEE ASHERSON
Nat Danziger	MEIER TZELNIKER
Marcus Hoff	FREDERICK VALK
Smiley Coy	GEORGE COULOURIS
Connie Bliss	JACQUELINE KOTT
" Hank " Teagle	STUART NICHOL
Dixie Evans	DIANE CILENTO
Dr. Frary	ARTHUR OWEN

•

Time : The present
Place : The " Playroom " of Charles Castle's house in Beverly Hills, California

•

ACT ONE
A summer afternoon
ACT TWO
Late one night, the following week
ACT THREE
Scene One .... Afternoon a few days late
Scene Two .... An hour later

The Play directed by Sam Wanamaker
Settings by Richard Lake

In addition to top variety, the Alma Theatre in Luton presented major tours. A truly distinguished cast performed "The Big Knife" in December, 1953.

In South Bedfordshire, the most exciting entertainment event of 1953 didn't take place in the cinemas, the Grand or the Alma, but in a natural amphitheatre in the grounds of Luton Hoo. As it was Coronation year, Arthur E. Davies, conductor of the world-famous Luton Girls Choir as well as the prestigious Luton Choral Society, came up with the idea of presenting a joint professional and amateur production of "Merrie England" to celebrate the Crowning of Queen Elizabeth II. The idea grew into a magnificent venture with nearly one thousand performers presenting Edward German's operetta on an outdoor stage, separated from the audience seated on a gentle slope on the other side of the lake. The water became an integral part of the action as Good Queen Bess was brought by boat to the huge stage. The magnificent setting re-created the outer walls of Windsor Castle and thousands of

Hollywood star Douglas Fairbanks Junior was among the guests invited to see "Merrie England" at Luton Hoo. (LN)

people enjoyed a memorable evening of music, theatre and spectacle. Popular singers Anne Ziegler and Webster Booth were among the professionals who were joined by Luton's leading amateur performers.

Meanwhile, the Alma introduced a policy of presenting pre and post West End plays and musical comedies from September, 1953. Emile Littler's "Blue For A Boy" was followed by a series of plays which brought such stars as Vivienne Merchant, Kathleen Harrison, Jack Hulbert, Sam Wanamaker and Diane Cilento among many others to Luton. The Grand had closed again when the Cry of Players came to an end, but it re-opened at the end of August with twelve weeks repertory from Fitzgerald Productions. With so much enthusiasm, who would have thought that Luton's professional theatre scene would completely collapse within a few short years? Ultimately, it couldn't compete with all the new developments, including those being made by the cinemas to persuade people to leave their television sets.

In 1953, a magnificent Coronation Pageant offered an outdoor production of "Merrie England" in the grounds of Luton Hoo. As this scene demonstrates, full advantage was taken of the site. (LN)

183

The Cinemas Fight Hard to Regain Their Audiences

Alive to the competition from television, the film industry went all out to make sure that the cinema experience was beyond the realm of small screen entertainment in the home. A considerable investment was made in "3-dimensional" (3-D) films; the first to arrive in South Bedfordshire came to Luton's Savoy on Easter Monday (April 6th), 1953 when the Kirk Douglas/Lana Turner drama "The Bad and the Beautiful" was accompanied by "Metroscopix". At least these shorts were shown locally as the second feature; in some places, "Metroscopix" was advertised as the main feature, pushing the likes of Clark Gable into supporting place!

At the end of September, 1953, the music and dancing licence for the Plaza was transferred to Peter Edward Philpotts. The little High Town cinema now had a "New Management Policy" which involved new prices and not opening until 4pm Mondays to Wednesdays. Clearly, audience figures were not as good as had been hoped. It was a brave attempt to keep going, but the little Plaza was destined to close within eighteen months. However, it did outlast the Alma.

Audience reaction to "Metroscopix" at the Savoy, the first 3-D films shown in the area. (LN)

Following its closure as a theatre, the Alma became the Alma Ballroom in April, 1955. After a brief closure for redecoration, the venue re-opened as the Cresta Ballroom in November, 1955. These musician demonstrate the hall's flair for publicity. (LMS/LN)

Alma Converted into Ballroom

Following the closure of the Luton theatre in 1954, the seats were removed, the stalls area was given a level floor and the "New Super Alma Ballroom" opened with a Grand Gala Dance on Friday, April 1st, 1955; the April Fools were the theatre-lovers who hadn't supported the venue when it was open as a live theatre. The new Ballroom went all out to woo local dancers; during the following months, Sid Phillips and his Band, Johnny Dankworth with Cleo Laine, The Modernaires, Vic Lewis and his Orchestra as well as Ken Mackintosh and his Orchestra were among the famous bands who came to Luton before it was announced that the hall would close for re-decoration at the beginning of November.

Had this venture also failed? Quite the reverse, in fact. The Alma changed its name and re-opened just two weeks later. Friday, November 18th saw the "Grand Opening Night Gala" of the Cresta Ballroom with Sabrina and Paul Carpenter in attendance. An exciting line up of the best bands in the land were booked, while a series of Jazz Nights with the likes of Ken Colyer, Alex Welch, Chris Barber and Cy Laurie was arranged. These "Trad Bands" were hugely popular at the time, but the other bands were not forgotten. Among other big names to visit the Cresta in 1956 were top British bands Joe Loss and Ted Heath as well as American superstars Stan Kenton and Lionel Hampton.

Above **The Luton Music Club organised Symphony Concerts at the Alma Theatre and these continued following its conversion to the Cresta. It will be noted that, as the former stalls had been removed to create a dance floor, seating had to be set out on the flat floor. The size of the audience indicates how popular these concerts proved to be. (LMS/LN)**

Below **Chris Barber at the Cresta. (LN)**

3-D and Those Special Glasses

If live theatre found it difficult to compete with television, the cinema was determined to fight off the challenge. Two rival developments vied for cinema audiences – 3-dimensional (3-D) films and CinemaScope. Following that first tentative screening at the Savoy, the Ritz installed 3-D equipment and scared the living daylights out of Luton audiences when they presented "House of Wax" for two weeks in August, 1953. As wax models burned in a conflagration at the heart of the plot, it seemed as though burning eyeballs fell into our laps!

In order to experience the three-dimensional effect, it was necessary to wear special glasses which translated the green and red fuzz on the screen into a picture that jumped out at the audience. Two copies of the early 3-D films were required; one suited to the left eye, the other to the right. In order to show the film, both projectors had to be used to screen each reel simultaneously and this presented problems. First, with both projectors in operation, it would not be possible to show the film without breaks. Each standard reel ran for about twenty minutes

Arguably the most successful of all the 3-D films to be produced during the early fifties, "House of Wax" was heavily promoted the week before it came to Luton's Ritz (formerly Union) Cinema in August, 1953. It ran for two weeks. (LMS/LN)

so, unless a solution was found, no less than three "intervals" would be required to show the 83 minute film. This was considered unacceptable, so the projectors were fitted with double-size reels which ran for some forty or so minutes. Thus, the film could be screened with just one interval. In order that the two copies were kept in exact synchronisation, a special bar was fitted to govern the speed of the projectors and ensure that they ran in exact parallel. "House of Wax" was a spectacular success, but the inconvenience of wearing special glasses meant that the novelty soon wore off.

CinemaScope and the Wall-to-Wall Pictures

The alternative was to make the screen so wide that television could not possibly copy the panoramic effect created by CinemaScope. The first cinema in South Bedfordshire to install this revolutionary system was Luton's Savoy. It was a good choice, for the width of the cinema made it ideal for the new wide screen process. In fact, the auditorium was so wide, virtually no structural changes were necessary to the proscenium. The first film to be advertised for the "New Giant Screen" was "Androcles and the Lion" in April, 1954 (the same week as "Kiss Me Kate" in 3-D at the Ritz). However, "Androcles and the Lion" was not made in the new wide-screen process; the first true CinemaScope film to be screened in Luton, "The Command", came to the Savoy on May 10th, 1954, more than a month after the new screen had been fitted. It would be August before Luton saw its next CinemaScope film – "Knights of the Round Table"; in the meantime, films in ordinary ratio were advertised for the big screen. The ever-popular

When "House Of Wax" was shown in 3-D, both projectors were required simultaneously. (LMS/LN)

The screen area had to be widened to fit a CinemaScope screen in the Oriel, Leighton Buzzard, but little of the attractive interior was lost. (BY)

"Genevieve" was advertised as "Funnier than ever on the Giant Screen".

The week before its second CinemaScope presentation, the Savoy showed Alfred Hitchcock's celebrated 3-D film "Dial M For Murder" – but it was screened flat! Luton audiences at last had the opportunity to see the first film made in CinemaScope, "The Robe", at the Savoy in October, the very week the Gaumont had its first CinemaScope film, a pre-release screening of "The Black Shield of Falworth". The Ritz installed CinemaScope and in January, 1955 they screend their first film in the wide system, "The Student Prince". Bringing up the rear, Luton's Odeon showed their first CinemaScope film, "Sign of the Pagan", from January 31st, 1955. The Savoy now had wide-screen competition from all the other major cinemas in the town, so they went one better by introducing Luton audiences to Perspecta Stereo Sound when they screened "Seven Brides for Seven Brothers" in February.

The little Plaza could no longer compete; its brief revival came to an end when it closed on April 2nd, 1955, having never embraced the new technologies. The building remained derelict for ten years until, in June, 1965, Luton Corporation bought the old Plaza for £9,000 and gained planning permission to use the premises for "slipper baths", surely one of the more bizarre uses for an old cinema. They were meant to replace those in Waller Street, destined to be demolished for town centre redevelopment. The Waller street baths did come down, but the old Plaza was never converted to its intended new use and was leased to Grosvenor Car Sales in 1967 on a three-year lease for £350 per year. In the meantime back in the fifties, there was a brighter note, for the cinemas in Dunstable and Leighton Buzzard were soon to offer wide-screen entertainment.

Grand's Desperate Bid to Stay Open Fails

The Grand had closed again at the beginning of 1954, but re-opened with a pantomime in December. Luton Amateur Operatic and Dramatic Society, who had moved to the larger and more central Alma, returned to their old home at the Grand which once again had become Luton's only live theatre. For the Grand, however, it now proved to be a continuing battle against financial losses. Desperate attempts were made to attract audiences with nude shows and the like, but to no avail. Towards the end, passers-by could hear the efforts of a non-stop pianist engaged to play for the whole week. A loudspeaker had been fitted outside the theatre as the marathon pianist strove to break some record or other. It left most Lutonians cold and few were tempted inside to actually see the ordeal. Following a seemingly interminable stream of shabby shows, the Grand presented a play, "My Wife's Uncle", and after its final performance on May 4th, 1957, the theatre finally closed for the last time. Since 1950, each brief closure had been met by a storm of protest and the theatre was tempted to start again. Now the few letters to *The Luton News* were written more in sadness than anger.

What with television, CinemaScope and the other innovations designed to tempt audiences into the cinemas, the Grand could no longer compete. Eight months after the Grand closed, it still stood intact, though plans were already in hand to turn the building into offices and shops. Such development meant changing the frontage as the Council had pushed back the building line in order to widen Waller Street. It was with this understanding that Luton Corporation had granted planning permission for the conversion. The building had a structural wall running parallel with the frontage which was almost exactly on the proposed new building line, so it would not be necessary to pull down the whole building.

Amateurs Try to Save the Grand

Estate agents Ronald Mayne and Company were actively looking for a tenant to convert the building into shops "and so on" but, as no progress had yet been made, arts enthusiasts in the town tried to save the Grand. The Ustinov Players, who had performed "The Love Of Four Colonels" to enthusiastic audiences just a couple of months before the theatre closed, asked the Council to save the Grand for the town provided they found an initial £5,000. Councillors refused to "take any action in the manner indicated", stating that they could not grant any financial assistance. The Arts League of Luton seemed reluctant to offer the scheme any support, with their then chairman Arthur Mandy declaring that he thought it would be "a white elephant". His argument was that had there been enough people to fill the theatre, it would never have closed; in any event, he thought it unlikely that the town's amateurs could afford to run the place. Meanwhile, the Arts League was trying to raise £100 by their next annual meeting to establish an arts centre. After more than a year, only £85 had been raised. With such limited fund-raising success, Mr Mandy said "I cannot see anyone ever raising £5,000 to save the Grand".

In retrospect, we can only mourn the loss of the Grand Theatre. To have pulled it down may seem like authoritarian vandalism, but it is important to see the situation in context. Had the theatre carried on for another decade, the possibility of saving it would have been far greater. It would have been most unusual for a Council to have such vision at the end of the fifties – if they had, they would almost certainly have been heavily criticised.

Luton Loses Professional Live Theatre

Luton now had no professional live shows and, although the towns-folk didn't know it, the cinemas would soon come under threat as well. In 1959, former theatregoers watched aghast as the front of the Grand was demolished. The back part of the theatre remained intact with the words "Grand Theatre" painted on the back wall plainly on view to tease new-comers who arrived in the town by train. Though live performances had long since ceased, Luton still had the old Palace Theatre. It had changed its name to Gaumont in 1949, but it was destined to be the next to go. By 1961, cinema audiences had declined to the point where only two major release circuits remained. Gaumont had been absorbed into the Rank circuit some years before, but had continued to offer a separate programme of equal quality for many years. As the production of new films began to decline, so only Odeon (operated by Rank) and ABC remained as major releasing circuits, with a third "independent" circuit showing the less commercial films.

Cinema Audiences Continue to Decline

More and more people were staying in to watch television. The screens were getting bigger – in fact, in January, 1958, *The Luton News* carried the headline "Those 14" TV tubes arrive at last". Viewers were so keen to improve their sets that a shortage of tubes and valves made the news. Another factor contributed to the growing stay-at-home culture. "Teddy Boys" had gained a reputation, often unfairly let it be said, for rowdyism and hooliganism. When *The Luton News* readers read this page one headline – "Hooliganism In Luton Cinemas To Be Stamped Out" – their worst fears were no doubt confirmed. As it happens, the

In October, 1962, the former Palace/Gaumont was converted into the Majestic Ballroom. Sadly, the attractive pre-WWI building was obscured by the new, very plain frontage. (LMS/LN)

Teddy Boys were not necessarily the culprits. Ritz manager Charles Smith was quoted as saying "The most annoying thing to customers is when, during a quiet episode in a picture, some loud-mouth will come out with an offensive word that can be heard all over the house." Cinema staff often knew who the culprits were and they were often girls! "Girls – who use the most atrocious language imaginable," said Mr Smith.

Realising the adverse effect this behaviour could have upon ticket sales, the managers of all four Luton cinemas decided to revive the Luton Cinema Managers' Association to tackle and eradicate the problem in a concerted campaign to stop this "movie madness". Well known Savoy manager John Lake stated that "this hooliganism will be No 1 priority on our agenda." Cinemas reserved the right (as they still do) to refuse entry to troublemakers and this became the policy in all local cinemas. None-the-less, cinema audiences continued to decline across the country with more and more empty seats evident during performances.

The Former Palace in Luton Finally Succumbs to Dancing and Bingo

Rank therefore decided to convert the Gaumont into a ballroom at a cost of £80,000. The Alma had been converted into a ballroom in 1955 but it closed in May, 1960, a couple of months after the California Ballroom had its Grand Opening in Dunstable on March 12th. Notwithstanding the popularity of the new Dunstable venue, Rank clearly thought Luton still needed its own dance venue. When news of Rank's decision to close the Gaumont and convert it into the Majestic Ballroom leaked out, there was an immediate protest. Originally, the cinema was to have closed on September 2nd, 1961, but when a spokesman for Top Rank Dancing admitted "we have not got our costing and budgeting plans ready yet", the Gaumont was given a temporary reprieve. The 49 year old cinema finally closed on Saturday, October 14th, 1961, having devoted its last week to a highly nostalgic double-bill of popular British films, "The League of Gentlemen" and "Whisky Galore". In the meantime, in line with other cinemas in the ABC chain, the Savoy changed its name to "ABC" from 2nd October, 1961.

Interior of Alma/Cresta during demolition. The decoration surrounding the organ chamber is clearly in view. (LMS/LN)

Above The interior of the Majestic Ballroom. The original circle has been replaced by a gallery on three sides with steps leading down to the stage area. (LMS/LN)
Left above The old Palace Theatre ended its days as The Top Rank Bingo Club. Following the building's destruction by fire at the end of 1982, Luton's Odeon closed and was converted into a Bingo hall. (LN)
Left below The Majestic Ballroom also operated as a Bingo Hall which, as this queue indicates, proved popular. (LN)

A year later on Saturday, October 20th, 1962, the Majestic Ballroom opened to the general public, having played host to the Mayor's Charity Ball the previous evening. The stalls area of the former Palace Theatre had been flattened and converted for five hundred dancers, while the circle had been replaced by a gallery on three sides of the dance floor below. It was also designed for Bingo; the Top Rank Bingo and Social Club opened on Tuesday, October 23rd. During the thirties, Lutonians could find live performances at three theatres; now it had none. In fact, there were just five cinemas left in the whole of South Bedfordshire – three in Luton and one each in Dunstable and Leighton Buzzard. Television was increasing its audience more and more at the expense of theatre and cinema. Despite the glories of CinemaScope and the sort of screen spectacle not possible in the average living room, the cinema industry was at a low ebb. It decided to fight back in the sixties – with live shows! 1963 saw the return of star performers at the Odeon and Ritz but, by then, a new live theatre had been built in Luton.

A New Theatre for Luton

The attractive Carnegie Library on the corner of Williamson Street opposite the Town Hall had been bursting at the seams for many years. It could no longer satisfactorily serve Luton's growing population, so a new state-of-the-art library was built in Bridge Street at the back of the area which eventually became St. George's Square. The plans for Luton's new library included a lecture theatre on the third floor, but the Borough Librarian Frank Gardner had a broader vision. By various means, he was able to make sure that the lecture theatre had enough facilities to allow it to be used for more conventional theatrical events. In the early days, these facilities were undoubtedly limited but, without Mr Gardner's foresight together with the enthusiastic and active interest of the Arts League of Luton, it is unlikely that the magnificent small-scale theatre Luton still enjoys would exist in a form which was destined to host a wide variety of activities.

The new library itself was officially opened by H.M. The Queen on Friday, November 2nd. With an audience of civic dignitaries, Her Majesty and the Duke of Edinburgh heard the Luton Girls Choir conducted by their leader Arthur Davies sing from the stage of the new Library Theatre. It fell to Luton Arts Council, which grew out of the old Arts League, to mount an inaugural programme and, indeed, to make sure that the theatre was fruitfully employed for almost a decade. So it was that the Library Theatre opened to the public that same evening with a Musical Comedy Cavalcade presented jointly by Luton Operatic and Dramatic Society and Luton Band. On the following evening, Lutonians realised they had acquired a superb recital hall. Pianist Clive Lythgoe presented a "Pianoforte Recital" and he was so overwhelmed by the intimacy of the new theatre, he could not help himself voicing his enthusiasm to the very receptive audience. It was only a small hall, but its huge potential was already being realised.

A celebrity lecture followed on the Sunday (after all, it had been initiated as a lecture theatre!) and another well-established local group took the stage on Guy Fawkes night when Luton Choral Society presented a concert version of "Merrie England". Luton Music Club, who had brought famous conductors and symphony orchestra to perform at the Alma and Union cinemas, still use the Library Theatre as their home and have used the theatre more than any other group. Their debut came on Tuesday, November 6th when they presented the Intimate Opera Company under the direction of Antony Hopkins (who, as President of Luton Music Club, became a regular visitor to the theatre). Luton Music Club made the Library Theatre their home and they continue to this day to showcase the small theatre as a perfect recital hall by presenting professional music of the highest order to their Monday evening audiences. Luton Arts

Following a five-year period when Luton had no live theatre, the compact Library Theatre opened in 1962. This view shows the attractive stage area. (LMS/LN)

Council sometimes supplemented the excellent Music Club programme with other professional musical events, an early example being the Western Theatre Ballet. The organisers had their work cut out to make sure the stage was suitable for dancers.

Luton Film Society Moves to Library Theatre

Luton Film Society, which formerly used the lecture hall in the Carnegie Library, also decided to make the Library Theatre their home. The Society had been sorely tempted when it was offered the old Wellington Cinema, not least because they would have been able to screen their choice of films in 35mm instead of 16mm. That didn't happen, but now they had the perfect venue for their screenings. Their first film at the Library Theatre, included as part of the inaugural programme, was the classic "The Red Shoes". Sadly, a film break occurred in the 16mm film, but those of us in the audience (from memory, a full house) still realised that the Library

This view from the stage of the Library Theatre, Luton shows the small auditorium, which proved ideal for local productions, Luton Music Club, small-scale touring companies and visiting personalities from the worlds of music, jazz and theatre. It also proved to be the perfect size for art-house and other cinema presentations. (LMS/LN)

Theatre could also serve as an excellent cinema. With Experimental Theatre on the Thursday and the Community Theatre Movement's amateur production of "The Miracle Worker" on the Friday and Saturday, the highly successful inaugural programme not only came to an end, but had demonstrated the flexibility of a small theatre which could be used as a recital hall, a theatre for both professionals and amateurs and a cinema – oh, and also as a lecture theatre!

Initially, the theatre had just 240 seats, though it wasn't too long before sixteen rows were extended by one seat each to give seating for 256. The auditorium had a very shallow rake with almost an eighteen inch rise from the stage end to the back of the hall. The proscenium opening was approximately 25 feet wide, with a depth of about 21 feet. Both the opening and the depth have since been increased. There is virtually no wing space on "stage right" (the left side of the stage as seen by the audience), though enough room exists for entrances and exits to be made. The stage area is backed by a fine cyclorama, behind which lies a corridor and two dressing rooms. When it first opened, wing space "stage left" was also limited, but adequate for scenery to be moved on and off stage. A steel shutter opened onto a roof garden, though this was subsequently reduced to almost nothing when the wing space was extended, room was made for scenery storage and two further dressing rooms and a shower were added. During those early years, the voluntary Luton Arts Council provided a continual stream of plays, films and music. Many of the local amateur dramatic societies found the venue to be the ideal size for their productions, though it was clearly too small for the operatic societies. Some of the musical societies tried to shoe-horn middle and large scale shows on to the stage of the little theatre, but soon realised it didn't work.

Luton Film Theatre

After a gap of eight years, professional theatre returned to Luton with various touring companies. In 1969, the Library Theatre also became home to the Luton Film Theatre, one of a loose chain of regional film theatres supported by the British Film Institute. By then, 35mm projectors had been installed, though the 16mm projector was also retained. Luton Film Society decided to support this new venture rather than compete, so having given Lutonians an appetite for quality cinema, it ceased to exist. It must be said, however, the Library Theatre met only a part of Luton's artistic and entertainment needs, as various proposals for a concert hall had come to naught. It had been proposed that Luton buy the Alma Theatre when it closed, but the Council thought a twenty-one year lease was too long as they still hoped to build a new hall. With its choral society and choirs, its orchestras and musical societies, Luton had been a very musical town for well over one hundred years. When the Library Theatre opened, the singers, the musicians and their audiences still hoped that a suitable venue would be built. To date, it hasn't materialised.

The Library Players

Nevertheless, the new Library Theatre was very welcome and certainly helped to perpetuate and strengthen drama in the town. Shortly after it opened, Luton Arts Council set up an ambitious company called the Library Players, intended to give all local actors, directors, designers and back-stage enthusiasts an opportunity to work in productions normally beyond the reach of individual amateur companies. This large group, which had no permanent membership, operated alongside the existing companies and groups for many years, sometimes giving local amateurs the opportunity to work with professional directors and writers. With the dawning of the seventies, Luton Arts Council bowed out of running the Library Theatre and a full-time professional theatre manager, Chris Potter, was appointed. He rapidly achieved a keen rapport with the local drama fraternity while increasing the amount of professional theatre coming into the town. The theatre has been professionally managed ever since, though its special relationship with Luton Arts Council (until its demise in 2006) and the local amateur companies has been maintained.

The Stars Return to Luton

The opening of the Library Theatre was an undoubted bright spot – apart from giving a home to most of Luton's amateur companies, outstanding touring companies such as Cheek By Jowl, Middle Ground, Compass and Snap were regular visitors for many years. For such a small venue, the list of star names is impressive – Cyril Fletcher, Joyce Grenfell, Warren Mitchell, Stephane Grappelli, Alan Price, Ken Dodd, Alec McCowan and Prunella Scales, to name but a few. The theatre also proved to be an ideal venue for jazz musicians, with Chris Barber, Humphrey Lyttelton, George Melly and Kenny Ball among the regulars. Luton Music Club ensured that most of the country's top musicians and singers put in an appearance, while opera and ballet companies also graced the small stage.

Though far too small for large, or even middle scale, performances, the Library Theatre has kept live theatre afloat. It has also given Luton audiences a far wider range of cinema than that provided by the commercial cinemas which were in decline during the sixties. Though it did not fufill all of the town's theatrical requirements, the little theatre on the third floor of Luton's Central Library was a very welcome addition to the area's somewhat limited facilities and, after its opening, encouraging developments were also taking place in the rest of South Bedfordshire.

CHAPTER TEN

Signs of Revival

Luton was not alone in wanting and getting its own theatre. With great enthusiasm, Dunstable decided to build its own Civic Hall. Work began in 1962 and the brand new building opened on the 17th April, 1964. Unfortunately, the building replaced the old Town Hall, the scene of so many touring theatre companies in former years and, since their first production, "The Sacred Flame", in April, 1945, the home of the Dunstable Repertory Company. The "Rep" performed their 63rd and final production in the Town Hall in March, 1964. It was a farce called "Brush With A Body", but the company was about to have more than just a brush with change and challenge. With nowhere else to go, the Rep had to move into the new Civic Hall. By comparison with their old home it was vast – it could seat 810. What should they perform in this large hall? The Council was approached for a grant of £50 with a view to mounting a grand Shakespearean production ("The Merry Wives of Windsor") as their inaugural presentation in the Civic Hall. One alderman was less than impressed by this idea – he said: "The only time there would be a rush to see Shakespeare at the Civic Hall would be if he appeared in person"!

Dunstable's Queensway Hall, which had opened as the Civic Hall in 1964, was also a popular venue for pop and rock concerts as well as other events. (DG)

CECA – Council for the Encouragement of Cultural Activities in Dunstable

Luckily, such a philistine attitude did not stop Dunstable forming their "Council for the Encouragement of Cultural Activities" (CECA) in 1965. The Council believed that the Civic Hall could put them at the centre of cultural activity in South Bedfordshire. After all, they reasoned, no town (including the much larger Luton) could offer such a substantial venue. Dunstable Council voted a farthing rate, which generated £2,000, for CECA to promote bigs arts events. £1,000 was spent on a concert and a ballet, though the Chairman of the Council admitted that it would take at least five years before the people of Dunstable "can be brought to accept and support ballet and regular concerts".

In addition to this initiative from the Council, the Dunstable Amateur Operatic Society was launched in 1964. It certainly looked as if things were looking up for the arts and entertainment in Dunstable, but the euphoria was relatively short-lived. By October, 1964, changes were being called for in the Civic Hall; a year or so later, poor visibility prompted a suggested scheme to stagger the seats in the hall. This was initially opposed by the Chief Fire Prevention Officer on the

Pink Floyd at the Queensway Hall, Dunstable circa 1969. (LMS/DG)

The Rolling Stones at the California Ballroom which was one of the area's major venues for performing artists throughout the sixties and seventies. (LMS/DG)

grounds that staggered seating could cause an obstruction in the event of an emergency. A modified plan staggered the seats in the central block with a loss of only eleven seats. It soon became obvious that the hall was inflexible and the acoustics were not really good enough for a wide range of performances. However, it was an attractive building both outside and in and proved popular for pop and rock concerts. That did not stop the carpers who were very critical of the town's new hall; quite a contrast to the town's very real desire to keep the hall when it came under threat during the late nineties. Dunstable may have been hostile to its new asset, but it came to love its hall with a passion.

Rock, Pop and Dancing in Dunstable

In fact, Dunstable now had two venues for regular pop and rock concerts – the California Pool Ballroom had opened in a blaze of publicity on Saturday, March 12, 1960. A newspaper ad in *The Dunstable Borough Gazette* said it all:

"THE SPECTACULAR OPENING
by the
MAYOR OF DUNSTABLE OF ENGLAND'S MOST
MODERN AND LUXURIOUS BALLROOM
built high above the town, overlooking thousands of illuminations
SATURDAY, MARCH 12 * 8 p.m. – midnight
STUPENDOUS ALL-STAR CHARITY DANCE
Proceeds In Aid of the Old People's Welfare Association
Personal Appearance of
TV Personality * Recording Star
RONNIE CARROLL
Stage and Film Star
NON-STOP DANCING TO TWO STAR BANDS".

Admission on that opening night was 7/6, while additional benefits included fully-licensed bars, spacious lounges and late coaches to Luton, Bletchley, Leighton Buzzard, etc. The California meant business; popular groups and bands were booked on a regular basis and proved to very successful. The Rolling Stones came in January 1964 and the Beatles were expected in July 1965. In January, however, there were rumours that the California Ballroom was to be sold and the Beatles didn't come after all.

The Dunstable Repertory Company

The Dunstable Repertory Company presented "The Wizard of Oz" at the Civic Hall in January, 1966. The production was deemed a great success, but with only a few hundred in the audience, it was clear that the Hall was far too large for the Rep. Dunstable was going to get a brand new library almost opposite the Civic Hall which meant that the old library in High Street South would fall vacant. The Rep were quick to seize their opportunity – the Chew's Trust governors leased them the vacated building and they formed themselves into the Dunstable 'Rep' Theatre Club, turning the old library into a delightful Little Theatre. In the meantime, the Rep presented their plays at Brewer's Hill School and Luton's Library Theatre. They also toured their productions around the Bedfordshire villages. After months of alterations, decoration and sheer hard work, Dunstable's Little Theatre was opened by Bernard Bresslaw on 5th October, 1968.

At first, the theatre had just eighty-seven seats on a flat floor. These were later replaced with the seats and the raked floor from Whitbread's Lecture Theatre. When these seats came to the end of their life, the rake remained, but

When the Dunstable Town Hall was demolished, the Dunstable Repertory Company lost their home. Various venues were used but, in 1968, they opened their own Little Theatre which has proved to be a huge success. (DG)

with major changes to the auditorium, the Little Theatre now had the ninety-nine seats plus space for a wheelchair it can offer to this day. The stage, with a proscenium opening of twenty-one feet and a depth of sixteen feet, is small but totally adequate. There's also room for set-building and storage with dressing-room facilities to suit the Rep's needs. With workshop facilities and extensive wardrobes, the company is self-contained and well able to present five full-length productions during its season from September to May. There's no doubt that the Dunstable 'Rep' Theatre Club has become a resounding success, fully justifying their affiliation to the prestigious Little Theatre Guild. Their membership is so large, nine performances of each production are required to satisfy demand. Such a long run for an amateur company demands a considerable commitment from its members. The Theatre Club encourages young people and offers "open" auditions to local actors in Dunstable, Luton and the surrounding district. Both Luton and Dunstable now had facilities for stage performances. Exactly eleven years later, Leighton Buzzard would join their ranks. However, there were other developments before the western side of the county got its own venue.

A Civic Hall for Luton at Last?

There was still talk of a civic hall for Luton. When it came to regular live shows, little Dunstable beat their larger neighbour hollow. The huge Ritz and Odeon cinemas did bring the big pop and rock stars to the town several times a year, but Luton desperately needed a hall of its own. The Odeon and Ritz concerts proved to be hugely popular. When the Odeon presented "The Beatles Show" in September 1963, a suitable stage had to be installed. It proved to be a good investment; the two shows on September 6 were a sell out and other stars including Freddie and the Dreamers, Billy J. Kramer and Duane Eddy had all appeared before the year was out. As it happens, an earlier appearance by the Beatles at the Majestic Ballroom went almost unnoticed.

ABC's "Top Stage Shows" at the Ritz followed quickly on the heels of the Odeon. Their first show featured Billy Fury in October who was followed by Gerry and the Pacemakers, The Bachelors and Helen Shapiro later in the year. The next two years saw a seemingly continual stream of pop and rock stars at the Odeon and the Ritz, with Cliff Richard and The Rolling Stones making repeat visits. The Beatles also returned to Luton in 1964, this time at the Ritz. The Rolling Stones

Left **In order to accommodate the Beatles, the Odeon fitted a special stage. (LMS/LN)**
Below **This queue shows how popular The Beatles were when they performed at the Odeon, Luton in September, 1963. (LMS/LN)**

and other leading groups who had visited Luton also appeared at Dunstable's California Ballroom which offered star names on a more regular basis. In fact, for a glorious if brief period, both Luton and Dunstable had a regular diet of the biggest names around. Even more stars arrived when Cesar's Palace opened on the very edge of Luton. Even with this seemingly unbounded interest in live performances, Luton still had no large dedicated live venue.

In March, 1966, *The Luton News* reported that a special committee was to be formed to press for the building of a civic centre. Town centre redevelopment plans were under study by Luton Town Council and, as these were to be put before the full council within the next month or so, the Luton branch of the Musicians' Union called a meeting attended by the Arts Council, Luton Band and the Trades Council. Support was sought from businessmen, trade unions and various groups interested in the arts and entertainment. The question of a civic hall for Luton had been the subject of reports and discussion since the twenties; this initiative was no more successful than its predecessors.

The Beatles performing on the specially prepared stage at the Odeon, Luton in 1963. The "Fab Four" had appeared at the Majestic in April, 1963, but were virtually ignored by the press. They came to Luton for a third time in November, 1964, when they appeared at the Ritz. (LMS/LN)

Like many cinemas in the circuit, Dunstable's Union changed its name to ABC. (DG)

More Cinema Closures

Dunstable's Union Cinema, now called ABC, responded to falling audiences by introducing Bingo three days a week in January, 1969, but it was only putting off the inevitable. By 1973, audiences for the big-screen in Dunstable had diminished to the point where the cinema decided to operate as a full-time Bingo Hall. The last film to be screened was "Fear is the Key" on February 14th. An attempt to revive cinema was made when films were shown in the Civic Hall (now called the Queensway Hall), but with no lasting success.

1969 also saw changes in Luton. With falling audiences, cinemas tried various alternatives to get them back. The Odeon's solution was to have a face-lift and remodel the interior of what seemed a vast space when audiences were small. Stricter fire regulations after the war had forced cinemas to remove seats which impeded the exits. At that time, the Odeon's seating had been reduced to about 1,800; they now decided to reduce the number quite drastically in order to offer "more leg-room for fewer patrons" as *The Luton News* put it. The cinema was given new carpets and just 1,300 seats. To complete the make-over, the kiosk in the foyer was re-designed, new lighting was installed and attention was given to the exterior.

Luton, and indeed South Bedfordshire, lost its largest cinema in September, 1971. Some six months before, the ABC Cinema (formerly the Savoy) had closed for major structural alterations. It re-opened as the triple ABC 1-2-3 on Thursday, 23rd September, 1971 and, as a result, the Ritz showed its last film on Friday, 24th September and closed its doors following wrestling "live on the stage" on Saturday, 25th September. The last film programme to be screened at the Ritz included a revival of the ten-year-old "Eyes Of Hell" (with sequences in 3-D) and "The Haunted Palace", a horror film starring Vincent Price. Both films carried an 'X' certificate.

Multi-Screen Cinema Comes to Luton

One way in which the cinema industry fought back as television took more and more of its audience was to provide more but smaller cinemas with particular attention to audience comfort. All over the country, large cinemas were being doubled, tripled and, in some cases, quadrupled. The interiors were gutted and two, three or four new, smaller cinemas replaced the large auditoria which, with only small audiences scattered across acres of seats, had given a cavernous, unfriendly feel to cinemagoing. Multi-screening offered a far more flexible programming policy; the week's main release no longer moved on after the normal seven-day screening, but would stay as long as it attracted an audience. If audience figures decreased, but a film still had "legs" (i.e. audience potential), it would move down to a smaller screen to continue its run. If a film proved really popular, it could be shown in more than one screen, though this option was rarely exercised.

The ABC, Luton's first triple, turned out to be a very good conversion. The former circle was extended forward and became the 628-seat ABC 1. Decorated with attractive red curtains which swept back from the screen to cover the side walls, there was no longer an ornate ceiling, but plain, dark "amethyst violet" tiles to maximise lighting on the screen. Before the auditorium was darkened for the screening, it was lit by concealed lighting which enhanced the flame effect of the red curtains. The first film in "Screen One" was "Love Story" with Ali McGraw and Ryan O'Neal. Clearly, the major releases would be screened first in this ample and attractive auditorium.

Screen Two was fitted with 70mm projection equipment and stereophonic sound. The colour scheme, brown and orange, was completely different to the larger hall upstairs. The only curtain was for the screen and that was in oyster, with illumination from the stage. The 458 seats could be booked for separate performances of the block-buster "Ryan's Daughter". Incidentally, this was not Luton's first taste of 70mm presentation, for the huge wide-screen system had been introduced at the Ritz in April, 1969, with "2001: A Space Odyssey". Ironically, ABC 2's screen was smaller than that in ABC 1 which seemed to negate the screening of films in 70mm in that auditorium. This had not been the intention of the planners, however. ABC 1 was intended for 70mm presentations, but the switch was made when the local authority would not allow the bar to be sited on the upper floor above the foyer. The cinema's operator felt that the bar would be patronised more by those who had booked in advance and should therefore be associated with the auditorium showing films in the bigger format. As a result of this change of plan, the space above the foyer remained unused for the rest of the cinema's life. Enclosed within a glazed screen, the bar was built on the ground floor with discreet lighting to create a friendly, relaxed atmosphere. The bar closed in 1998.

With only 272 seats, Screen Three was described as intimate. Crystal glass brackets, imported from Austria, were fitted to the walls for lighting before and after the film. The screen curtains, lit from the stage, were gold. The first presentation in Screen Three was Kirk Douglas in "A Gunfight". Screens Two and Three occupied the former stalls area. While Screen Two was well proportioned, Screen Three (though "intimate" as described) had something of a narrow feel which accentuated the very slight dip which used to lead to the centre of the former stalls. Screens One and Three maintained continuous performances with all unreserved seats. The seats and carpets in each auditorium were given their own, distinctive colour scheme. There was no doubt that the conversion was "state of the art" for 1971 and offered the comforts and services which would encourage audiences away from their television sets. Initially, a single projection suite served all three auditoria, but as this necessitated a "mirror periscope" for Screens One and Two, a very minor picture distortion occurred during panning shots. To rectify this, a separate projection box was later erected in the largest auditorium. It meant the loss of some seats, but projection was improved to give excellent presentation. It also meant that Screen Two could, like Screen Three, have direct projection. The new fitted cinema now had Philips DP 70 projectors with transistorised amplifiers for the optical sound. For Screen Two, projection for 70mm films was installed with six-track stereophonic sound.

The Savoy's Beautiful Art-Deco Interior Disappears

The downside to the conversion was that the magnificent art-deco interior, where it survived, was hidden from view in the auditoria and the foyer area. The modernisation of the foyer was totally insensitive to the original design, especially as the ceiling was lowered to hide the art-deco lighting which was originally suspended from the roof. However, with two pay-boxes as well as a sales kiosk, the design in natural tones with splashes of turquoise, purple and "flame" was undoubtedly inviting, with good entrance lighting and an up-to-date canopy to advertise the films. The vital poster display panels were also well placed to make sure that passers-by knew what was showing. ABC appointed one of their most experienced managers, Bob Parsons, who maintained a high standard.

Luton now had just two cinemas, but with four screens and a fifth part-time screen at the Library Theatre, cinemagoers were offered a wider choice. Incidentally, the Odeon was not keen to allow the ABC to gain all the attention, so manager Jeff Way invited a local reporter to spend a day working in the various departments of his theatre. What resulted was an entertaining article printed a week before the ABC re-opened. Such up-staging would ensure that film-goers did not forget that the Dunstable Road cinema was still open for business! In Dunstable, the Queensway Hall offered a live alternative when they presented the Syd Lawrence Orchestra playing – Glenn Miller style!

Leighton's Last Cinema Closes

Over in Leighton Buzzard, after fifty years service, the popular Oriel Cinema was struggling to find adequate audiences for films. Following their last film programme, Frankie Howerd in "Up The Chastity Belt" and Dave Allen in "Squeeze A Flower", the venue finally succumbed to full-time Bingo on 15th January, 1972 .

Odeon 1,2,3

In 1974, Luton's Odeon tripled, though the conversion was not as good as the ABC. The circle was retained, as was the original screen. Together with the very front stalls, this became Odeon One. The dramatically reduced stalls were only used for very popular films (like "Close Encounters of the Third Kind") and had to be approached through a corridor at the side of Screen Three. For most films, only the old circle seats were offered. A wall was dropped from the front of the circle to make room for two much smaller cinemas below. The area under the circle was then halved to make two small auditoria, each with just over one hundred seats.

All Night Elvis

Every so often, a special event would be mounted to attract audiences. The

ABC decided to offer a "through the night" tribute to Elvis Presley following his death in 1977. Five films were shown in all three screens, involving very strict planning. This proved no problem to chief Vic Harvey who scheduled the films from 10.45pm on the Friday to 8. 51am the next morning – just nine minutes before the ABC Minors Club were about to enter the cinema! It is a tribute to Vic Harvey that Philip Turner should choose to relate this event in his 1998 book about MGM Cinemas, and a credit to the Luton cinema that it was one of only seven major refurbishments he described in detail . Apart from the specialist film programme at Luton's Library Theatre, the six screens in the tripled ABC and Odeon now served the whole of South Bedfordshire, but that situation was not allowed to last for long.

The Luton Community Arts Trust and Refleks

During the early seventies, a loose collective of performance artists (mainly musicians) regularly played at Luton's Royal Hotel on the corner of Mill Street and Old Bedford Road. On Thursday evenings, they also took over a room upstairs, installed their 16mm projector and showed films to audiences of between 30 and 40. Refleks joined Luton Arts Council and, in 1977, moved to their premises at 33, Guildford Street. At the same time, the Luton Community Arts Trust was set up as a charitable trust with Refleks and with the support of the Gulbenkian Foundation; they shared the building with Luton Arts Council for some time before taking over the building as a whole. When they moved in, the top back room was converted into a "black box" performance space and cinema. Eastern Arts installed two interlinked 16mm projectors. 40 old cinema seats were raked on removable rostra to give stadium seating for a small cinema audience. The seats were sometimes reoriented to make the space more flexible for live performances.

It proved to be a popular venue for specialist audiences and 33 Guildford Street played host to a cult film festival, a series of 'B' movies and one-off screenings of early classics such as "Things To Come". The cinema operated on a regular basis until the mid-eighties, but the availability of suitable films on 16mm was becoming more limited and expensive as video began to take over. Luton Community Arts Trust set up a professional video unit which became an important training ground for such future Hollywood talents as David Arnold, Danny Cannon and Mike Figgis. The unit made "Death Valley Days", notable as the first "scratch" video to be shown on Channel 4. Films utilising professional and amateur talent were made on video, setting a pattern which was also reflected in live stage performances. The "People Show", David Rappaport and the Random

Band, John Hegley's one-man show and semi-professional productions (which included a stunning production of Strindberg's "Miss Julie") were among the regular performances at 33.

Leighton Buzzard and "A Gentleman in an Old Jacket"

The various developments in Luton and Dunstable were welcomed by audiences in the area and, with the opening of a new Library and Arts Centre in Leighton Buzzard, the news continued to be encouraging. Lord Miles of Blackfriars opend the new multi-purpose centre on 5th October, 1979 – eleven years to the day after Dunstable's Little Theatre had opened. *The Leighton Buzzard Observer* reported that "A gentleman in an old jacket that his wife bought for a pound from an Oxfam shop unveiled a plaque and opened Leighton's new library". The occasion was given a delightfully informal air as Lord Miles told the assembly that he owed the area a lot. As Bernard Miles, he had based his Music Hall act on the days when he lived in Ivinghoe Aston. Those of us who remember listening to his familiar tones on the radio were proud that he put Ivinghoe so firmly on the map and in the affections of the nation. He recalled that he used to cycle from Ivinghoe to Denham Studios and then described the new library as "lovely". "You are lucky you got in before somebody said 'no you can't have one,'" he added.

Leighton Buzzard's "Studio Theatre and Cinema"

The theatre, described as a "studio theatre and cinema", has raked seating for 170 which faces a wide stage with a traditional proscenium arch. The theatre on the second floor of the modern library has full facilities for film shows, professional touring stage performances and amateur productions. Like Luton's Library Theatre, it was initially equipped with 16mm projection equipment, but Leighton Buzzard audiences were given a full, wide-ranging film programme. Whereas Luton Library Theatre was typical of BFI-run Film Theatres in showing art and repertory films to complement the main-stream films at the ABC and Odeon, Leighton Buzzard Library Theatre had no competition from a commercial cinema. Consequently, both specialist and main-stream films were screened. Leighton Buzzard's Theatre finally installed a modern 35mm projector with Dolby "surround" sound in 1992. With the opening of the Leighton Buzzard Theatre, all three towns in South Bedfordshire had thriving, well-supported live theatres. As now, the amateur dramatic societies were vital to the success of these theatres.

Both Luton and Dunstable had good venues for small-scale performances; in 1979 it was Leighton Buzzard's turn when the Library Theatre (later called the Leighton Buzzard Theatre) opened. This grand view shows both the auditorium and the stage area. (BLARS)

Tragedy in Luton and a Swift Change in Plans

There was one sad foot-note however. Cinema audiences were still going down and it became clear that Luton was over-screened with two three-screen cinemas. In 1982, ABC's owner EMI applied for planning permission to convert the old Savoy into a Bingo Hall. The Council had always declared that the George Street site should be used as a cinema, but even they could not deny the commercial reality. As a result of this decision, Rank decided to upgrade the Odeon in Dunstable Road. Among other improvements, it was decided to increase the size of Screen Three.

However, before anything happened, tragedy struck. As the new year was about to dawn, the old Palace Theatre suffered a very bad fire. At the time of the fire, the old theatre was operating as the Top Rank Bingo Club. It wasn't long before Rank decided to move the Bingo operation to the Odeon. All plans came to a halt as the promise of cinema improvements gave way to a call for "legs eleven". It looked as if Luton would be left with just the part-time Luton Film Theatre based at the Library Theatre. However, when they heard that the Odeon was closing as a cinema, EMI had a change of heart and decided to keep the ABC open. The Palace was a tragic loss and the cessation of films at the Odeon was a blow, but if Luton was to be left with only one cinema, the town was probably better off with the town-centre site. After all, the ABC conversion to three screens was far more successful than that at the Odeon. It really did look as if the days of commercial cinema were drawing to a close, but the cinema industry was as tenacious as ever.

A cinema revolution was about to burst upon the scene.

CHAPTER ELEVEN

Cinema Revolution

I n 1985, the latest cinema revolution occurred in Milton Keynes, which was within easy reach of South Bedfordshire. Right in the centre of the new city, a ten-screen multiplex cinema was incorporated into a leisure complex called The Point. There were those who thought the concept of putting so many screens in one site was lunacy – but then, back in 1909, local businessmen in Luton thought that the opening of the tiny Anglo American Electric Picture Palace was equally mad. In both cases, the pessimists were proved wrong. As much as anything else, the timing was just right. Although television had decimated the cinema industry even more than the cinemas had damaged the live theatres fifty or more years before, the little screen was beginning to be passe. Young people in particular no longer wanted to sit at home watching "the box". As far as they were concerned, that's what their parents did!

Moviegoing – Eighties Style

Good old variety had brought out audiences to the Cesar's Palace Night Club on the edge of Luton; the new type of cinema now attracted young people with enough cash to enjoy a night out. The trouble was, people didn't want to go to old-fashioned cinemas, even if they had been doubled and tripled. Modern audiences demanded more and that's precisely what the multiplex gave them. As part of an entertainment centre, members of the audience could make a night of it. They could eat and drink in the Point and drop into a night-club if they still wanted to be entertained after the movie! The ten-screen cinema was well equipped with sales points. There was plenty of leg room, and the architect had even had the foresight to include cup-holders in the arms of the seats! The auditoria were very plain by the standards of the thirties, but the comforts of a new generation of cinemagoers had been taken into account. The building may have lacked the architectural and design panache of earlier cinemas, but audiences were made very welcome. Just as important, the design of each auditorium had the largest possible screen to fill the end wall. Even if the space was quite small, an impression of size was created by giving the eye no diversion from the projected picture and everyone got a good view. Dolby stereo also added to the enjoyment; at last, the cinema had brought itself up to date and was very acceptable to young audiences – and older people came to like it too!

Marketing Movies in Multiplexes

There was advance booking, but if you just turned up, there was always another film if your first choice was "sold out". In fact, this turned out to be a master stroke in terms of marketing. Most people drove to the multiplex and didn't really want to go home without seeing something. If a film was really popular, movie fans soon learned to book in advance if that was the only film they wanted to see. Many people were prepared to be offered an alternative however, for a night out was a night out! This way, films which may have only lasted one week in a triple-screen cinema, could run three or four weeks simply on the back of a popular film which was perpetually sold out. When a film proved really popular, it would be shown in two, or even three, screens. Once again, flexibility became all important. Overall, the Point had well over two thousand seats, but even the largest auditorium had no more than a few hundred.

In the thirties, it was not unusual to find two or even three thousand seats in a single auditorium. As a result, films seldom lasted more than a week and the cinema had to sell as many seats as possible for just one film programme whether it was a "blockbuster" or not. In the multiplex, the operator put the blockbusters in the auditoria with the most seats, while films with less appeal would be put into a much smaller "screen". There was even the promise of regular "art house" movies, but in most cases, this has turned out to be no more than a one-night-a-week event.

Multiplex Success

The immediate success of the Point in Milton Keynes ensured that multiplexes would be built elsewhere. However, unlike Milton Keynes with its spacious and generous parking in the central area, town and city centres were thought unsuitable for such developments. As a result, they were built on the edge of urban areas. During the next decade, multiplexes opened on the outskirts of Bedford, Hatfield, Hemel Hempstead and Stevenage. Milton Keynes became the first town in the area to have two multiplexes when a sixteen-screen Cineworld opened within sight of the Point in 2000. The Luton-Dunstable conurbation began to stand out as the biggest population area in the region without its own multiplex, so it wasn't surprising that various proposals began to emerge.

Bringing Luton up to Date

There was talk of a multiplex near Vauxhall Motors on the Brache Sports Ground between Park Street and Gypsy Lane. Vauxhall, who owned the land, were keen, but Luton Council wanted to build a leisure complex in the centre of town. Discussions ensued, but when it was realised that the Brache was directly under the flight path into Luton Airport, fears were raised. It would be bad enough for an aircraft to crash as it approached the runway, but if it crashed into two-thousand or more cinemagoers, it would be a disaster of monumental proportions.

Luton Council had set its sights on the derelict Co-op site in the very centre of the town. It was an eyesore and gave that part of the centre a very run-down feel. Not surprisingly, the Council was looking for a way to regenerate the town centre and a leisure park seemed to be the ideal solution. The big problem was, would anyone want to operate a cinema in an area without adequate parking? It was a conundrum which kept the Co-op building still standing years after its sell-by date and then, when the rotting building was finally pulled down, the site made money for the Council as a temporary car-park for several more years.

Goodbye Library Theatre – Hullo St. George's Theatre

The Central Library was run by Bedfordshire County Council and had been since Luton lost its County Borough status with local government re-organisation in 1974. The theatre on the third floor was still operated by Luton Borough Council, however, and it was decided that it should no longer be called the Library Theatre. Several ideas for a new name were suggested, but the councillors decided to let Luton have its say. As a result, a competition to find a new name was organised, though cynics suggested that, as the building was in St. George's Square, whoever came up with the name St. George's Theatre would win! Many new names were suggested – Theatre in the Square, the New Grand, but the Library Theatre became the St. George's Theatre in 1985.

In 1986, the Theatre's lovely old Gaumont Kalee projectors were ditched in favour of a modern, "cake-stand" machine . This undoubtedly had advantages, not least because Dolby Sound could be, and indeed was, installed. The complete film was made up on to a horizontal platter, thus eliminating the need to switch from one projector to another every twenty minutes. The film ran from one platter to another and rewinding each reel before it could be shown again became redundant. The film wound itself in the correct order and could be shown again within a few minutes. Initially, the projector only had two platters, but it was quickly realised that a third was needed for efficient operation. Apart from anything else, the platters were smaller than those to be found in most commercial cinemas. They could only hold about two hours and twenty minutes of standard film stock, thus making it impossible to run longer movies without an interval. As there were operating advantages in holding two shorter films made up on the platters, the third platter was soon installed. Incidentally, when a new, thinner but much stronger film stock was introduced during the nineties, the small platters could accommodate longer films.

Complete Refit for St. George's

In 1989, St. George's Theatre had a complete facelift. The whole auditorium was gutted and a new, raked floor installed. Although the original seating was not on a flat floor, the rake was very shallow. It was now raised so that the back row was about six feet higher than the front, creating stadium style seating for the theatre. Instead of two aisles against the walls of the auditorium, a single, central aisle was created. The back of the space was now enclosed, with members of the audience entering the auditorium through a new, vomitory entrance with several steps to reach the seats. At the front, seats were designed to be readily removed, thus making it much easier for people in wheel-chairs to visit the theatre. All these changes meant that the seating was reduced from 257 to 240. As two of these had to be used by stewards, only 238 seats were available for sale. The theatre re-opened with the Trestle Theatre Company, and everyone had a wonderful view. The new rake improved viewing immensely for both live performances and films, though the size of the theatre meant that seats could not be staggered.

The stage was also extended forward by about four feet with a flexible system which could be altered, or even removed, if required. Over the years, lighting and sound have been improved dramatically and this has continued. Since the theatre opened, programming has changed considerably. Many professional touring companies visited the town, but funding constraints meant that these visits began to decline. The amateurs still offered a wide variety of productions; apart from the societies producing big musical productions unsuitable for the small space, most of Luton's amateur societies regarded St. George's Theatre as their home. It was also the home of the very successful Luton Music Club whose programme of "Music on Mondays" passed its fifteen hundredth concert with no sign of diminishing interest!

Luton's Library Theatre was given a much steeper rake and a vomitory entrance to the auditorium during the extensive 1989 refit. (JC)

The Dragon Club

While professional theatre for adults declined, professional theatre for children increased. For many years, the theatre had successfully offered shows for children on Saturday mornings. Doc Watson, the theatre's manager since 1988 and a recognised authority on children's theatre, introduced Luton's younger audiences to a wider range of professional productions on Saturday mornings through the now well-established Dragon Club. Through the years, St. George's Theatre always seemed to manage to keep up with changing demands, but tough battles still lay ahead. The nineties saw less money for the theatre and an increase in the film programme; could it succeed with this policy when Luton eventually got its own multiplex cinema? As things turned out, that would not become a problem until the end of the century.

The Developing Nineties

After years of cinema closures and stagnation, the nineties saw an upsurge in activity. Talk of building a multiplex cinema on the old Co-op site in Luton had taken root during the latter half of the eighties when the Council had decided to create a leisure park in the town centre. There were many problems to solve – could a cinema chain be found for such a site? Would the road system be able to cope with the extra traffic and that all-important question – would parking be adequate for such a development?

It had been hoped that the site would include the live theatre Luton's residents had been led to believe may be developed. Such a venue was not included in the plans, but the council deflected criticism by setting up the "Bute Street Arts and Media Trust Limited" which would develop and operate a major arts centre in a former hat factory at the top of Bute Street. It transpired that revenue grants fell short of the sum required to carry out the initial plans and a plea for extra cash from the Arts Council of England was refused.

The trust was set up, but only one councillor sat on the board; it was suggested that the Council adopted something of a "hands off" policy in case it didn't work out. In view of the sorry catalogue of events which were to follow, it was felt by some they didn't really have their heart in the project, though there were councillors who were committed to the arts.

Who Would Operate Luton's Multiplex Cinema?

When the road system and parking facilities were deemed satisfactory, Luton waited with interest to see which chain would run the multiplex cinema to be built on the old Co-op site. It was thought that Odeon would be the right operator. In addition to running the cinema, they would be able to incorporate their bingo operation from the old Odeon in Dunstable Road. There was also the suggestion that, once bingo moved out, the Council could purchase the cinema for local use but, as it happened, Odeon did not take up the option and the Bury Park building was destined for a different use. Then there was talk of Warner Brothers operating the cinema, but that option also faltered. By 1995, building the leisure park on Luton's Co-op site seemed as far away as ever.

Changing Ownership for the ABC

Meanwhile, the George Street cinema, now called Cannon, was looking decidedly run down. Associated British Cinemas had been absorbed into the EMI empire in 1969, though the cinemas were still called ABC. In 1979, EMI merged with Thorn Electrical Industries to become Thorn EMI Screen Entertainment, but the cinemas continued to close; by 1984, the chain had just 107 sites with a total of 287 screens. In order to reverse its fortunes, the cinema industry launched British Film Year in 1985. It proved to be a worth-while initiative which was enthusiastically embraced by Thorn EMI, for the cinema closures began to slow down. Overall, cinema audiences rose by over 20%; it was also the year in which the multiplex (in the shape of the Point in Milton Keynes) came to Britain. Then EMI decided to build an eight-screen multiplex cinema at Salford Quays (Manchester) in December, 1986. The cinema mergers continued and ABC became a part of Cannon, by now the largest chain in Britain. In October, 1986, the ABC cinemas began to change their names to Cannon (a process finally completed by March 1987). Thus, EMI's Salford Quays multiplex opened as a Cannon.

In the early nineties, the Cannon chain was taken over by Pathe Communications shortly before it acquired Metro Goldwyn Mayer cinemas. In March, 1992, Pathe changed the names of its West End Cinemas to MGM and followed this by renaming their multiplexes (including Bedford) and certain city-centre cinemas. Although it was an important cinema in the chain, the Luton cinema retained the name Cannon. Nevertheless, one could understand why little investment had been put into the Luton triple. With the continuing threat of competition from the proposed town-centre multiplex, it must have seemed to MGM Cinemas that any real investment in an old cinema more than fifty years old would be a waste of money.

Luton's Cannon Refurbished

As a shift in the pattern of cinema-going became apparent, MGM changed their minds. By the mid-nineties, town centre cinemas were found to succeed alongside multiplexes. Bearing that in mind and with the new multiplex development still on hold, MGM decided to invest a quarter of a million pounds and upgrade their Luton triple. Over a period of several months, the whole building was redecorated and refitted but, although the town's dignitaries were invited to a splendid "re-opening" do in April 1995, the cinema never actually closed while the work was going on. It proved to be a very sound investment. New seating in all three auditoria, the introduction of superior seating, front-of-house improvements, improved sales facilities, modern signage, computerised booking and Dolby stereo in all screens brought the cinema up to multiplex standards within the restrictions of the smaller space available. The seating was actually reduced slightly in screens One and Two, making them appear more spacious.

The refurbishment was widely promoted and an immediate increase in audience figures was the happy result.

The gamble had paid off. The management diligently maintained a high standard of neatness and cleanliness to the very end. In 1996, ownership passed to Virgin, but they were only interested in multiplexes and certain key city sites. That left quite a large part of the old ABC circuit intact. It was eventually bought out by the old circuit management and the name was changed back to ABC. An updated version of the former logo was created and an old friend returned to the national cinema scene. The Luton Cannon changed its name back to "ABC" on 14th June that year.

Cinema 100

As it happened, 1996 saw the centenary of cinema in the United Kingdom. Although the first projected film programme had occurred in Paris at the very end of 1895, the rest of the world considered this year to be the centenary. The British Film Institute (BFI) were determined to celebrate in style and encouraged cinemas across the country to join in. They also decided to make plaques to commemorate important cinema sites around the country. They were particularly interested in very early screenings and three plaques were awarded in South Bedfordshire. One was mounted on the site of Leighton Buzzard's Oriel Cinema which had served the town for fifty years. Leighton Buzzard also celebrated Cinema 100 by mounting an excellent exhibition supported by theatre manager Stuart Antrobus and an enthusiastic group of former cinema musicians, projectionists and other interested persons.

The other two BFI plaques were in Luton. One plaque, unveiled in Gordon Street in May, was placed on the site of the very first permanent cinema in Bedfordshire which had opened in 1909. The second marked a public cinema presentation in the town in 1896, the very first year of projected film exhibition in the country. The BFI identified less than one hundred such screenings outside London and listed them in their prestige publication "Cinema 100 Projections" in Summer 1995. The final such provincial presentation listed was the Boxing Day screening in Luton.

Luton also celebrated the centenary with two major events. The first was a season of films at St George's Theatre during May and June called "Reel Wheels". The season, sponsored by Vauxhall, also recognised the centenary of the motor car. The season included car-related films and an illustrated talk by the distinguished film historian John Huntley. The second event was an open-air concert, "Hooray For Hollywood", given by the Symphonia of Luton in Stockwood Park in August.

Cesar's Palace Relaunched With a New Name

The Skimpot Lane night spot was acquired by the Mean Fidler Organization and relaunched as "The Palace". As before, the club offered a starry array of performers who, in an earlier period, would have played the variety halls. Among the stars slated for the early part of the year, Sister Sledge, Clannad and Showaddywaddy satisfied the music fans, while comedy was well catered for by stars such as Freddie Starr, Mike Reid, Lenny Henry and Joe Pasquale.

Would the Multiplex Ever be Built?

Around this time, it seemed as if developments on the Co-op site had come to a halt. A large, brave sign announced the coming leisure complex to be opened in Summer 1996, but as that date came and went, it was clear that things were not going as smoothly as planned. When challenged, the planners claimed that they had to get the plans right for such a major development, but one cannot help but feel that more than a few sighs of relief were heard in the Town Hall when the relatively new Cine-UK cinema chain signed up to operate the multiplex. Initially, it was announced that the multiplex would contain eight screens (an even earlier estimate suggested only five). Now a far more realistic and exciting eleven screens were planned. Cine-UK had opened their first multiplex, the twelve-screen site in Stevenage, on 12th July, 1996. This nearby cinema complex was called Cineworld and offered a more imaginative programming policy than other multiplexes in the area.

CHAPTER TWELVE

Renewal and Optimism in Luton and Dunstable

Cineworld, Luton's eleven screen multiplex, finally opened to the general public in the Galaxy leisure complex in the heart of Luton on Friday, October 23rd, 1998. Apart from Cineworld, the centre included a Riva bingo hall (changed to Gala a year or two later), a Namco "Bar N Bowl", a J.D. Weatherspoons pub (The White House), a Fatty Arbuckle's restaurant (which subsequently closed and was replaced with other restaurants) and room for further facilities, some of which have subsequently been taken up. A Brannigans bar and night spot ("Eating, Dancing & Cavorting") also opened, but the eating, dancing and cavorting came to an end in March, 2004, seen by some as an indication that there was a possible decline in Luton's flourishing night-life. Before the official opening day, a glitzy preview was arranged for town dignitaries and the press; three special preview nights were also arranged for those who applied for sneak previews on October 19th, 20th and 21st. It was the eighth complex to open in the Cineworld chain.

A total of 2,148 seats within the new cinema complex are distributed across the eleven auditoria ("screens"); the exact number in each screen can be found in appendix 1. Dolby Surround Sound is standard, with digital sound in screens 4,5,6,8 and 11. The new Dolby E-X system was installed in the three largest auditoria for the eagerly anticipated "Star Wars Episode One: The Phantom

Left above **Cineworld, Luton under construction. Girders for the "stadium" auditoria are clearly identifiable. (EG)** Left below **The nearly completed Luton Galaxy Centre, which includes the Cineworld multiplex cinema, can be seen in the foreground. The Library Theatre at the top of the Central Library is on the other side of St. George's Square. (EG)**

Menace", screened in four screens with fourteen performances per day from Thursday, 15th July, 1999. Three of the screens – 4,5 and 11 – have stadium (or stepped) seating which gives these auditoria a very roomy feeling with excellent sight lines for the screen. With 421 seats, screen 5 is one of the largest multiplex auditoria in the country. The attractive carpeting throughout the complex is mauve with a distinctive film and star motif typical throughout the Cineworld chain. The walls in each auditorium are two-tone grey – a broad dark grey band passes through a light grey background. Oblong wall lights are mounted on the dark grey band. In 2006, digital projection was installed in screen 6. The first film to be screened in this process was "Adrift" from 1st September.

Left above With more than 400 seats, "Screen 5" is the largest auditorium in Luton's Cineworld. (CG)   *Left below* A view of the screen in the largest Cineworld auditorium. (CG)   *Above* The smallest auditorium in Luton's Cineworld. (CG)   *Below* Screen 11 in Luton's Cineworld has a traditional vomitory entrance with a central aisle. (CG)

Luton Gets All the Current Releases

The opening films in 1998 offered the wide range available at Multiplexes – Walt Disney's "Mulan", "Small Soldiers", "Ever After" and "Dr Dolittle" together with Saturday morning shows ("Space Jam" and "A Little Princess") showed that Cineworld wanted to attract family audiences. Films for adults included "Halloween H20", "Velvet Goldmine", "A Perfect Murder", "Elizabeth", "The Truman Show", "Saving Private Ryan", "There's Something About Mary" and "Lethal Weapon 4". In addition, two major Indian "Bollywood" films – "Kuch Kuch Hota Hai" and "Bade Miyan Chota Miyan" – were also on offer. After a long break, Luton audiences could expect to see the full range of current releases without having to leave town. The normal adult ticket price at the Cineworld's opening was £5, but the following deals were also on offer: Bargain Tuesday (all seats £3), Bargain Matinees before 6pm (£3.50), a £3.50 price tag for Senior Citizens, registered unemployed, children 14 and under and NUS members from Monday to Thursday together with Saturday morning "Movies for Juniors" for just £1.

Luton's ABC Remains Open

The ABC decided to stay open; in order to compete, they charged just £3 (£2.50 for matinees and concessions) for their standard seats. When the cinema was refurbished in 1995, superior seats were installed; these cost an extra 50p. The ABC had maintained a high standard since the re-fit and was able to find an audience which preferred the older style of cinema-going (the lower prices didn't hurt either!). The main releases continued to be shown, but the gradual introduction of a more adventurous programming policy didn't last. Although the ABC experienced a drop in audience figures, it remained open until the end of 2000.

There had been some suggestion that the sixty-year-old cinema should be listed, but English Heritage decided that the changes to the interior when the cinema was tripled were too great for it to be of interest. They did like the corner entrance and the parade of shop frontages attached to the building and suggested that these be retained should the building itself be demolished. The leaseholder applied for planning permission to replace the cinema with shops. Luton Borough Council acceded to the application on condition that the corner and frontages were retained in accordance with English Heritage's view that these were in keeping with the George Street conservation area. However, work could not commence as ABC held a firm sub-lease until 2011 and manager John Mellor confirmed that the cinema would remain open – which it did until 23rd

The last of the big thirties cinemas finally closed in 2000. (EG)

November, 2000. For two more years, Luton cinema audiences could choose between the new multiplex style of Cineworld or the more traditional ABC. At the time of writing, the future of the building remains uncertain.

Artezium Brings Imaginative Cinema and Other Riches to Luton

Before the full launch of artezium in September, 1998, a first phase opened at the end of 1997. This included a basement performance area and bar, a restaurant in the old factory tunnels and a large coffee shop, box-office and meeting area on the ground floor. Luton could afford to be optimistic about the future of the arts and entertainment in the town. The trust running artezium in close co-operation with Luton Council won a multi-million pound National Lottery grant from The Arts Council of England (one of the first awarded) and turned the old hat factory at the top of Bute Street into an award-winning art centre deserving of regional status. It was a condition of lottery funded capital projects that part of the grant should be spent on public art. To meet this condition, artezium commissioned distinguished artist Tim Head who designed the impressive "Light Rain" which adorns the side of the building.

For months after opening the first phase, the building was hidden with scaffolding, giving the centre a far from welcoming front. However, once the work was completed, the new building behind the Bute Street frontage emerged to provide a valuable addition to the arts and entertainment scene in South Bedfordshire. The new building included video and recording studios and a flexible dance studio with fold-away seating for 96 which converted the space into a comfortable, small-scale "black-box" type of theatre. Sadly, rumours that a larger theatre would be built at the back of the courtyard area proved unfounded; many felt that an opportunity had been missed. The inclusion of modern projection equipment meant that the studio could and did also operate as a part time art-house cinema. From June 1999, artezium fulfilled its promise to show minority films with a splendidly imaginative programme which included a week of American independent films. Designed to be used by the centre's own film makers, it also served as an "arts cinema".

St. George's Theatre Becomes The Library Theatre . . .

St. George's Theatre changed its name to The Library Theatre in 1997 after Luton became a unitary authority and regained control of its libraries. The theatre often included films of restricted appeal in its programme; absolutely the right policy, of course, as it meant complete cinema programming for the area. The trouble was, a small audience was sometimes lost in the 238 seats and it wasn't economic. The 96-seat cinema at nearby artezium was ideal for such programming. In the light of these developments, the Library Theatre initially reduced its screenings to concentrate on live performances, but found there was still an audience for quality movies in Luton's traditional part-time film theatre. In South Bedfordshire at the end of the twentieth-century, Luton led the field in terms of cinema, just as it had led in the field of live theatre at the end of the previous century.

Professional Theatre at Luton's Library Theatre Hangs On – Just

Unfortunately, the situation as far as live theatre was concerned was not so good. For some years, live venues have been struggling against rising costs and diminishing grants. This had been the situation in all venues offering professional live product in South Bedfordshire and is in line with national trends. At Luton's Library Theatre, reduced funding meant a decline in touring professional theatre, but

The impressive "Light Rain" decoration on the side of artezium (now The Hat Factory). (HF)

professional theatre was not lost altogether. A number of very good small-scale touring companies were prepared to perform at the theatre on a "split box-office" basis, thus keeping professional theatre alive in the town. Another imaginative initiative from manager Doc Watson could have seen the growth of professional theatre in the town. He set up a company called the Acting Mechanicals which offered work to local professional actors, writers and directors on a "profit-share" basis.

In the first instance the theatre presented a couple of "rehearsed readings" of new work. Support for these was encouraging and, when The Library Theatre was forced yet again to close for a period while the Central Library was refurbished and stripped of its lingering asbestos, a further two rehearsed readings were staged at artezium. Both were well attended by an enthusiastic audience prepared to offer encouragement and constructive criticism. As a consequence, rehearsed readings by professional actors of new plays in the theatre's cosy bar area became a regular feature. The Acting Mechanicals performed their first true production in the now asbestos-free Library Theatre in April, 1998. With such a name, the fledgling company could only perform one play, "A Midsummer Night's Dream", but the directorial style definitely looked forwards rather than backwards. Sadly, lack of funding brought even this inexpensive initiative to a halt.

Venue Under Threat

The situation in Dunstable was more fraught. The Queensway Hall in Dunstable was proving to be a money-pit and South Bedfordshire District Council felt they had to do something. Because of the way in which it was built, the Queensway was very inflexible. It also had serious problems for performers, not the least of which were the acoustics. Dunstable was facing another major problem – with an increasing number of shops closing down, the Council was anxious to regenerate business in the town centre. They concluded that a major supermarket would do the trick and that the best site would be that occupied by the Queensway. For the councillors, it seemed to kill two birds with one stone. In reality, this decision unleashed a rush of hostility. A "Save the Queensway" group was born and The Dunstable Gazette conducted the "Queensway Debate".

It was clear that Dunstable was not prepared to lose its only large performance space, however inadequate or expensive it may be. South Bedfordshire District Council made a cast-iron promise that the money gained from selling the valuable site would be used to build a brand new theatre. A feasibility study was commisioned and various possibilities were reduced to two possible solutions – a middle-scale theatre with 600–700 seats, or a small-scale theatre with less than three hundred seats. The latter option was quickly dismissed. Dunstable wanted a space which could include the sort of product they had been used to in the Queensway. If the smaller option had been accepted, the popular Dunstable Amateur Operatic Society would have been forced to follow the lead of Luton operatic societies and stage their major productions in Hertfordshire. Luton had been criticised because their leading amateur societies had to stage their productions outside their home town; Dunstable wasn't about to follow suit.

Following its closure as a cinema, the Ritz operated as a night club under various names. Before a major conversion to a Liquid Night Club and Chicago Rock Cafe, it was known as The Zone. (EG)

Despite Promises and Studies, No Large Venue in Sight for Luton

While all this was going on, Luton was pursuing its own feasibility study. The final plans for the Co-op site did not include a live theatre, but a number of possibilities were considered in the study. In March, 1998, the chairman of Luton Arts Council believed the Council was interested in developing one of three sites – the ABC Cinema (which many felt would close when the multiplex opened), the Zone Night-club or land in Guildford Street which it owned. However, it was reported that the ABC was ear-marked for possible retail develoment, while the Zone was converted into a Chicago Rock Cafe and a Liquid Night Club; the possibilities for a middle or large scale venue in Luton were diminishing.

Leighton's Theatre Also Under Threat

While Dunstable was fuming over the fate of the Queensway Hall, theatre-goers in Leighton Buzzard woke up one morning early at the end of 1997 to find that their own theatre was under threat. The operator, Bedfordshire County Council, no longer had the cash to support the imaginatively-programmed venue. The Council were soon left in no doubt that Leighton Buzzard, like Dunstable, had no intention of allowing its theatre to close. Over the years, it had become very popular and audiences quickly realised that they would be left with no stage or film entertainment if the theatre was to close. A compromise was reached when manager Stuart Antrobus, who was responsible for the theatre's continuing success, took early retirement, thereby reducing the running costs. To date, this strategy has enabled the theatre to remain open.

The Fate of the Odeon and the ABC

The cinemas in Luton were in the news again when the ABC circuit came under Odeon management. The fact that these two chains, which had been leading competitors in Britain for so many years, could merge with virtually no adverse comment indicated how very much the operation of cinemas had changed during the final years of the twentieth century. The next decade would see multiplex mergers, with the fledgling Cineworld chain growing as a result.

There had been local objection when the name of the Top Rank Bingo Club (formerly the Odeon Cinema) was changed to Mecca Bingo and it wasn't long before it closed. The building was purchased in June, 2000 by the Church of God in Christ (Calvary) Ltd (COGIC) with plans to convert the large building into a church and the UK headquarters of an international pentecostal organization based in Memphis, Tennessee. Before modifications took place, COGIC held its first service in August, with regular services from December. The official opening took place in February, 2001. As the former cinema is Grade II listed, this has proved to be a most satisfactory outcome for a building which continues to be used as an auditorium, albeit for church services rather than films. It certainly seems more appropriate than bingo!

A Multiplex for Dunstable?

The success of multiplexes in the area had prompted one developer, Burford Property Investments, to plan a multi-screen cinema for Dunstable within a leisure park on the old AWD site behind the new Sainsbury's in Luton Road. Certainly, when these plans were first revealed in 1999, it looked as if cinema audiences in Britain as a whole were increasing at a remarkable rate. However, this assessment was almost certainly made after a year of strong "blockbuster" releases.

The huge audiences were not maintained when the following year failed to produce as many popular films and the development company was forced to admit in March, 2000 that they had not yet found an operator for the cinema. A spokesman said that, as a result, the envisaged leisure park could not proceed as the cinema was the "anchor for the project". One Dunstable councillor expressed surprise that the situation could change so dramatically within a year, but he was told that the ever-changing film exhibition business meant that "the multi-screen market, for eight to ten screens, is dead". This situation was revealed after a council discussion on the requirements for the arts venue planned to replace the now doomed Queensway Hall. When a local councillor asked if the cinema provision in the proposed building would be compatible with the "Burford scheme", it was hinted that the "scheme had run off the rails". Needless to say, this made the front page of *The Dunstable Gazette* and, once again, doubt was cast on the future of entertainment in the town, especially as it had been reported that the cost of a reasonable arts venue would be double the £7.3 million which had been set aside for that purpose.

The Queensway Hall is Finally Destroyed

In August, 2000, *The Dunstable Gazette* carried a picture of the destruction of the Queensway Hall, thus confirming the end of an era. By then, 2000AD (Action Dunstable) had been set up to ensure that the Queensway Hall would be replaced with the right venue demanded by the town. In July, *The Dunstable Gazette* reported that Hetherington Seelig Theatres had presented a feasibility study suggesting that Dunstable's new theatre could be part of a "revamped leisure centre" which would include, among other facilities, a 4-screen cinema. It was clear that the £7.3 million which Dunstable would receive from ASDA would not be enough to build a theatre with between 500 and 700 seats and that a commercial partner would be needed. Despite the difficulties, Dunstable was destined to get its theatre. There had been considerable controversy over the closure of the Queensway Hall, but it became clear that the residents of Dunstable had a very clear idea of what they wanted. Though there were many hurdles to clear, success proved sweet indeed when it finally came.

Milton Keynes Scores Again

A new development across the border in Buckinghamshire gave theatregoers in South Bedfordshire an opportunity to see West End shows and tours for the first time in years. To add to its smaller venues, October 1999 saw the opening of the Milton Keynes Theatre with a very promising first season. Needless to say, the new theatre identified potential theatregoers and targeted Luton and Dunstable for audiences. Together with a new sixteen-screen Cineworld within the recently opened Xscape leisure complex, the city now had a fine "theatre district".

Artezium Falters

With heartbreaking irony, following the award of a "Best Regeneration Scheme", Luton's artezium went into administration in mid 2000, causing shock waves

throughout the artistic community. Applications for a National Arts Council grant failed and an Administration Order was granted. The Bute Street venue closed its doors and the windows were pasted over. Clearly, the financial situation (whatever that may have been) had to be resolved; as we will learn, optimistic suggestions that it would re-open as a centre for all the town's arts activists proved correct, though not without a struggle.

A New Millennium, New Hopes

If the arts and entertainment scene had seemed a little uncertain at the end of the twentieth century, the twenty-first was to prove considerably brighter. In February, 2001, a new Chicago Rock Cafe opened in the former Union Cinema in Luton, followed in March by the opening of a Liquid Nightclub in the same building. The former cinema had been used for various nightclubs since the seventies; these developments ensured that an important entertainment venue would remain in use. In 2002, it was the Dunstable Union's turn to make the news. Having been given consent by South Bedfordshire District Council for

Left **Taken during the extensive alterations made when the former Union/Ritz cinema was remodelled as a Liquid Night Club, part of the old foyer could still be seen, but the huge circle has been removed. (JC)** *Above* **Having served as a Bingo Hall for many years, Dunstable's former Union Cinema now operates as the Cubes Night Club. (DG)**

such a conversion the previous November, the distinctive former cinema opened on 13th June as Cubes night-spot, operating as a cafe-bar during the day.

In March, 2005, the Dunstable Rep celebrated their Diamond Jubilee at the Little Theatre when friends and members old and new could enjoy recent extensions made possible through a bequest from the late Eileen Dymond, a long-time stalwart of the Club.

Filmstock

When aspiring film-makers Neil Fox and Justin Doherty realised their dream of bringing an international film festival to Luton, they sparked a real appetite for non-mainstream cinema in the town. Their vision was both broad and daring. They set up a company, Zero Balance Ltd., (so named, it was rumoured, because it reflected the state of their bank account!) to front the business side of their

Below **Cubes Night Club entrance. (DG)** *Right* **The interior of the Cubes Night Club captures some of the splendour of the old cinema, no doubt keeping faith with the building's Grade II listing. (DG)**

festival and, after an eighteen month gestation period, Filmstock Luton Film Festival brought fifteen days of films and events at the beginning of June, 2000 to an eager audience. They had attracted support from important film personalities and presented an illustrated talk by Ray Harryhausen, a legendary film-maker who specialised in stop-motion animation. Much to their credit, Cineworld embraced the concept by offering screen space for some of the screenings and events. The Ray Harryhausen talk, other events (including the International Short Film Competition) and screenings were held at artezium before its closure, while the University of Luton hosted workshops. Filmstock has continued as an annual event ever since.

Artezium Row Finally Resolved

The wrangle over the future of artezium continued as Luton Borough Council, who own the building, and the administrators failed to agree. It was finally resolved in November, 2001 when the keys were handed back to the council. An immediate announcement promised a programme of "quality arts and media projects" in 2002. In April, 2002, Luton's council placed an advertisement in the Guardian for a new boss for what the press called the "failed arts centre artezium". Meanwhile, the building was opened for limited, small-scale events, including the screening for the cast and crew of a short film called "They Came For A Day" produced by Zero Balance.

The Hat Factory

artezium re-opened as The Hat Factory (HF)

Luckily, though artezium had ceased to operate, the big building at the top end of Bute Street was given new life when it was refurbished and opened as The Hat Factory. An experienced theatre and cinema manager, Andrew Grays, was appointed in 2003 to develop the renewed arts and media centre. Grays had been responsible for the development of arts centres, the development of a major multiplex cinema in Lancashire and had managed theatres in the West End. In September, under Andrew Grays' guidance, The Hat

Factory started an "unofficial" limited programme of events before the official opening in April, 2004. The programming policies were given a complete face-lift as a multitude of artistic and other activities began to blossom, but the first year of operation provided valuable experience for guiding the centre's activities. The audience target of 30 to 40 per cent was achieved, but audiences for the various activities varied widely. Comedian Ricky Glover attracted a near-capacity audience, while music events and films were disappointing. Important lessons were being learnt. Although publicity had been given to the centre, there were still too many people who didn't even know the centre existed. A free weekend of activities was organised from 16th to 18th April, 2004, when more than a thousand visitors enjoyed exhibitions, music and performance artists.

Now officially open, The Hat Factory offers an arts floor, a ninety-seat cinema/theatre space which could also be converted for dance. There's an exhibition gallery, an arts innovation centre, rehearsal and workshop spaces and a music and comedy basement for about a hundred. Equally important, the occupants of 33 Guildford Street, including 33 Records, moved into the re-opened venue, as did Zero Balance, the company which handles the eagerly awaited annual Filmstock festivals. Filmstock05 utilised the Hat Factory facilities when it took

The basement of The Hat Factory makes use of an original architectural feature as an attractive lounge. (HF)

place from 1st to 15th June, 2004, less than two months after the centre's official opening. As a curtain-raiser to the international festival, Filmstock presented a "Day of Rock" on Market Hill from 5.30 pm with an open-air screening of "School of Rock" as darkness fell.

The studio theatre and the basement area are also used by several companies resident in the Hat Factory for both the rehearsals and production of works being created at the centre itself. Through hosting classes as well as these creative activities, The Hat Factory is fulfilling the community based arts role which artezium seemingly had not focused upon sufficiently to maintain box office support. The Arts Council England East has recognised the innovative programming and activities of the Hat Factory and awarded them a grant of £90,000. Among the projects to benefit was a Jazz Development Programme. In an effort to extend the appeal of the centre, the Hat Factory organised a tea dance aimed at senior citizens; it proved to be a great success. The Library Theatre's management was combined with the new centre and, with film exhibition apart from charity screenings concentrated at the Hat Factory, it became mainly a live theatre.

Grove Theatre, Dunstable

Perhaps the most exciting development of all was the building of Dunstable's Grove Theatre. After all the discussions and problems, the land was cleared and construction started on the theatre, described as the centre piece of a twenty million pound development off Court Drive. A partnership of companies and organisations has delivered an entertainemnt and recreation complex to replace the Queensway Hall in accordance with South Bedfordshire Districot Council's commitment. The building has a terrace of six restaurants and licensed premises. The theatre's developers, Complex Development Projects (CDP), worked with South Bedfordshire District Council, Dunstable Town Council, the East of England Development Agency (EEDA), the Office of the Deputy Prime Minister (ODPM), the building contractor SDC Construction Group and the contracted theatre operators, Leisure Connection, to create a facility which will undoubtedly have regional significance. The Grove Theatre cost £16 million made up of the £8 million reserved from the sale of the former Queensway Hall (slightly more than originally anticipated), £10.5 million from the sale of residential land and commercial units to be developed by Bellway Homes and £1.5 million from ODPM and EEDA. The area gets the brand new theatre it craved and needed, but it can only survive with support from surrounding towns.

Clearly, this development puts paid to a similar project in Luton. However, the

The Grove Theatre in Dunstable begins to take shape (DG)

larger Luton musical societies, who for too long have had to travel to theatres in Hertfordshire to perform, will welcome this development and, like Dunstable's own societies, will want to perform there. Dunstable can be proud that they have had the initiative and courage to proceed; theatregoers in Dunstable, Luton and the surrounding district will be delighted and wish the venture every success.

The Grove Theatre has been designed as a multi-purpose venue with a total of 780 seats on two levels (492 in the stalls and 288 in the circle). 320 seats in the stalls are retractable in order to provide flat floor space suitable for large concerts, giving a potential total capacity of about 1,000. Following a consultative study, a gap in the market for this type of development in the area was identified, the economic benefits of which will not have escaped the council or the developers who anticipate that the facility will attract some 300,000 visitors a year to Dunstable (an important consideration for certain businesses in the town who will expect to benefit).

The brochure outlining the opening season gives a clear indication of what audiences can expect. Following an Opening Gala presided over by the distinguished actor Brian Blessed on Saturday, 21 April, 2007, the opening show from the following Monday is Bill Kenwright's production of Tim Rice and Andrew Lloyd Webber's "Joseph and the Amazing Technicolor Dreamcoat". Just like Luton's Grand Theatre more than a hundred years before, The Grove sets the ball rolling with an established favourite. Being a musical, it also reflects the most popular stage fare currently on offer in London's West End.

Indeed, the Grove captures the current affection for musical theatre by offering the West End hit, "The Rat Pack Live From Las Vegas" in June. The programming allows for various one and two night stands which include dance, opera, jazz and pop, demonstrating that all tastes are to be catered for. On Saturday 2 June, Ken Dodd's "Happiness Show" proves that the popular comedian is determined to get in early in his bid to play every theatre in the land (he had great success some years ago with two hilarious performances in Luton's Library Theatre, which were fully booked weeks in advance).

Although musical events appear to dominate, drama is certainly not excluded. The first play, J.B. Priestley's "Dangerous Corner", is another established favourite, but the inclusion of Theatreworks' dramatisations of "The Railway Children" and "Little Women" shows the sort of imagination that should spell success for the future. The programme also allows for the inclusion of films.

State of the Art Technology

Modern stage, lighting and sound equipment as well as projection equipment have been installed, while visiting companies will find that every care has been taken to ensure that "get-ins" (the delivery of scenery, etc) are as easy as possible. Like all modern public buildings, easy and convenient parking and access for disabled theatregoers has been provided. Following its opening in April, 2007, The Grove Theatre is clearly an integral and important feature of a land-scaped "leisure quarter" for Dunstable which will include the existing leisure centre, the Bowling centre and Grove House Gardens, to be known as Grove Park. It must be considered the most important theatre development in South Bedfordshire since Luton's Grand Theatre was build over a century ago.

What Next for South Bedfordshire?

Now that Dunstable has built its theatre, is there still an opportunity for further development? Taken as a whole, the area has a beautiful new theatre to complement the smaller venues in Luton, Dunstable, Leighton Buzzard and Toddington. The Hat Factory in Luton is already fulfilling its huge potential for the region and the area is blessed with the eleven-screen Cineworld in Luton (which, incidentally, reflects the multicultural nature of the area in its programming). However, the area still does not have the concert hall it really needs. Such a hall could offer tremendous opportunities for large musical events and conferences. It could also

act as an important focus for bringing the various strands of a diverse community together and would undoubtedly bring economic advantages (a point not lost on Dunstable in its decision to proceed with the Grove Theatre complex). Where should such a concert/conference hall be situated? Perhaps Luton Council could at last fulfil the many promises made since 1924. After all, despite everything, we should always be optimistic.

Above **Artist's impression of the approach to Dunstable's Grove Theatre. (SBDC)**
Below **Artist's impression of the Grove Theatre auditorium with its sweeping balcony. (SBDC)**

The Venues

This chart contains details for all performance venues opened in South Bedfordshire. Alternative names are given, but full data is normally included under the opening name. Dance Halls and Night Clubs are only included where these have been created from existing theatres or cinemas, or they became significant public performance venues. Unrealised projects are not included; for these, please refer to the index.

Dunstable

ABC Cinema
– see Union

California Ballroom
Whipsnade Road, Dunstable
opened 12 March, 1960 as "California Pool Ballroom" with personal appearance by TV and recording star Ronnie Carroll; before it closed 31 December, 1979, became a significant performance venue.

The Cinema Theatre
High Street North (opposite Town Hall)
original proprietor: Charles Abrahams
architect: A. Wilkinson (Luton)
opened: unknown
first advertisements gave notice of programmes from 12 July, 1915 (serial: "The Million Dollar Mystery" episode 1 – "The Airship in the Night")
seating: 256 on one floor
closed: unknown

Civic Hall
opened 17 April, 1964
seating (not permanent) 810, reduced shortly after opening to 799.
Changed name to **Queensway Hall**

With important rock and other concerts, became a significant performance venue before closing in 2000.

Cubes Night Club
– see Union

Grove Theatre
Grove House Gardens
Opening Gala: 21 April, 2007;
opening production: "Joseph and the Amazing Technicolor Dreamcoat" (23 – 28 April, 2007)
seating: stalls – 492*, circle – 288
*in the stalls, 320 seats are retractable, allowing a total capacity of up to 1,000 for certain events

Little Theatre
High Street South
opened 5 October, 1968
seating: originally 87, now 99 with wheelchair space.
owned and operated by Dunstable "Rep" Theatre Club

Palace
High Street North
opened 1912
proprietor Fred Marchant

seating (on a single floor): 375
remained open until Fred Marchant's new
Palace opened next door

Palace
High Street North
opened 1919/20 (exact date unknown)
original proprietor: Fred Marchant
architects: Franklin and Deacon
seating: stalls – 400
gallery – 112
a stage was added in 1923 in order that the
Dunstable Amateur Operatic and Dramatic
Society could use it for their first production,
"The Geisha Girl".
closed end August, 1938

Queensway Hall
– see Civic Hall

Town Hall
High Street North
regularly used as a performance space for
visiting theatre companies; after World War
II, principal theatre user was Dunstable
Repertory Company
closed 1964; demolished

Union Cinema
High Street North
opened 27 September, 1937
original owner: Union Cinemas (acquired
by Associated British Cinemas 14 October,
1937)
architect: Leslie H. Kemp
seating*: stalls: 803, circle: 278
* these figures are based on the penultimate
plan which was substantially the same as
the final plan, though one or two seats may
have been added; two previous plans had
envisaged a larger hall; see chapter 7 (some
local histories give greater seating, probably
based on one of these earlier plans).

films ceased 2 Feb, 1973
Name changes: **ABC, Star Bingo, Union**;
currently operates as **Cubes Night Club**
Grade II listed 1999

Leighton Buzzard

Empire
Bridge Street (Leighton Road, Linslade)
built by Frederick Yirrell (Leighton Buzzard)
opened 1922
closed June, 1922
reopened as **Grand Cinema** 3 August, 1922
seating: approx 500
Renamed **Hippodrome** after a brief closure
for alterations and opened as a live theatre,
3 September, 1923 with "Jingles and Smiles".
Under the ownership of London and County
Cinemas, reverted to showing films a few
years later; name also reverted to the **Grand
Cinema**.
closed 3 September, 1932 having been
bought out by Shipman and King (owners of
the **Oriel**)
closing film: "Frankenstein".
In recent years, until it was destroyed by fire
during the first half of 1999, the building
was used by Dunham and Haines as a car
showroom.

Exchange Theatre
Lake Street
name given to Corn Exchange when taken
over by Captain Webb in 1922. The ground
floor was used as a cinema for a few years
during the "silent" period, though the
venue also continued to be used as a live
theatre (as it had been when it was the Corn
Exchange).
Building now replaced with shops, though
the distinctive arch-tower has been re-
created to reflect the significance of the site.

Grand
– see Empire

Hippodrome
– see Empire

Leighton Buzzard Theatre
as part of Leighton Buzzard Library & Arts
centre
opened 5 October 1979; films from 6
November 1979
Bedfordshire County Council Leisure
Services venue which came to be known
as the Library Theatre before changing to
Leighton Buzzard Theatre in September
1992.
Proscenium arch stage – 170 raked seats

Library Theatre
– see Leighton Buzzard Theatre

Oriel Picture Theatre
Lake Street
original proprietors: a local consortium of
businessmen which included Steve Young
and Ben Brown
Built on the site of Oriel House (the original
frontage remained intact until it was
replaced by a modern frontage during the
thirties) by A. E. Dawson
opened 26 December, 1922
opening film: "Smiling Through"
seating*: stalls – 550
balcony – 326 (initially, the balcony had no
seats; these were added later)
*the 1919 plan gives seating capacity as
"Ground Floor – 518
Balcony – 260".
final film screening: 15 January, 1972
used as a bingo hall until it was replaced by
a supermarket; a BFI "Cinema 100" plaque
marks the site and records fifty years as a
cinema.

Victoria Electric Picture Palace
Hartwell Grove
original proprietors: Captain F. Webb & Mr
Trigg
opened 12 June, 1911(initially part time
only)
capacity (seating & standing) approx 300
re-opened as **Ye Olde Vic** 31 March, 1928
after a period of closure.
re-opening film: "Painting the Town"
closed 1930 (exact date not known)

Ye Olde Vic
– see Victoria Electric Picture Palace

Luton

ABC
– see Savoy

Alexandra Theatre
*– see People's New Temperance Music Hall &
Palace of Varieties*

Alexandra Palace Circus
Waller Street (corner of Melson Street)
opened 27 March, 1880
Temporary building constructed without
planning permission, it remained open for a
very short period.

Alma Ballroom
– see Alma Kinema

Alma Kinema
Alma Street/Manchester Street
original proprietor: Sydney Dillingham; part
of Union Circuit from mid-thirties – *see
note ** below*; officially opened as a cine-
variety hall 21 December, 1929; opened to
public 23 December, 1929
architect: George Coles

first cinema to open in the "talkie" area; silent films never shown. Fitted with wide-screen system Magnascope and a Compton organ. Building also included small ballroom and tea lounge.

total seating in stalls and circle: 1,664 (approx 600 in circle)

stage: 36 feet wide; 25 feet 6 inches deep

converted to live theatre use as a full-time variety hall from 18 October, 1943

changed name to **Alma Theatre**

seating reduced slightly to 1,648

reverted to films January 1944

finally became full-time live theatre in 1948

closed 17 July, 1954

converted into **Alma Ballroom** which opened 1 April, 1955; changed name to **Cresta Ballroom** 18 November, 1955

closed May 1960; building demolished and replaced by an office block.

**Before being absorbed into the Union Circuit, the Alma was part of the Reed circuit, but the ownership of the Alma was fairly complicated. Before it had even opened, Leicester Square Estates had acquired an interest in the theatre, but sole ownership reverted to Sydney Dillingham in June, 1931. Early in 1934, L & S Investments bought the Alma and, as a result, a new operating company called Luton Theatres Property Company was formed, but it quickly became part of Reed's Circuit (A.H. Reed was a director of L & S). Reed's circuit also included Regals in Kingston, Beckenham, Sidcup, Yarmouth and Gravesend as well as the Plaza in Catford and the Majestic in Gravesend. When the Reed circuit was absorbed by Union through the newly formed Alliance Cinemas Ltd., it was announced that it had become part of a chain of over two hundred cinemas. This figure included some forty-seven picture palaces currently being built by the fast-growing chain.

Alma Theatre
– see *Alma Kinema*

American Rink and Picture Hall
Dunstable Road
opened as cinema March 1911
(formerly Luton American Roller Skating Rink)
film shows alternated with skating sessions for a short period only

Anglo American Electric Picture Palace
Gordon Street
operated by Luton Electric Theatre Ltd.;
converted from a building originally leased from T & E Neville (until it was sold)
built by A. Attwood (Luton)
opened 16 October, 1909
capacity (seating & standing) up to 400
changed name to **Gordon Street County Electric Pavilion/Gordon Street Electric Pavilion**
first cinema in South Bedfordshire to install sound (first talkies 1 July 1929)
closed (through fire) 15 October,1929
A furniture store was built on the site; it is now used as a photographic studio. A BFI "Cinema 100" plaque marks the site of Bedfordshire's first permanent cinema.

artezium
Bute Street
opened in two phases in 1997 and 1998
various performance areas:
– the dance studio with 96 retractible bench-type seats easily converted into small "black-box" style performance space or cinema (projection box included 35 mm "cake-stand" projector, 16 mm projector and video projection); although the space remains the same, only ninety seats are now offered for sale.
– basement bar with wide performance

platform (ideal for "comedy-store" style performances, but also used for plays on occasion)
– exhibition space could also be used for certain types of performance
also includes many other arts facilities, a coffee bar and restaurant
went into administartion mid-2000; reopened as **The Hat Factor**y for a limited programme of events in September, 2003 before the official opening in April, 2004.

Cannon
– *see Savoy*

Caesar's Palace
– *see Cesar's Palace*

Cesar's Palace
Skimpot Lane
members only night club opened in 1966 offering a 58 ft bar and a casino; played host to big-name entertainers who, in an earlier era, would have appeared in variety theatres like the Alma.
name changes: **The Palace, Caesar's Palace**
acquired by Mean Fidler Organization mid nineties
premises now used for bingo

Chicago Rock Cafe
– *see Union*
(please note: an earlier Chicago Rock Cafe opened in Park Street)

Cineworld
Galaxy, Bridge Street
operated by Cine UK
opened 23 October, 1998
eleven "screens" (auditoria) multiplex cinema
a total of 2,148 seats are distributed as follows:
screen 1: 114
screen 2: 75
screen 3: 112
screen 4: 284
screen 5: 421
screen 6: 212
screen 7: 123
screen 8: 217
screen 9: 137
screen 10: 213
screen 11: 240
Wheelchair bays are provided in each screen proportionate to the size of the auditorium, the most (6) being in screen 5

Colisseum Night Club
– *see Union*

Corn Exchange
Market Hill
Victorian building (1869) with a gallery (able to seat almost 150) often used for public meetings, concerts and early cinema shows

Coronet
– *see Wellington*

Cresta Ballroom
– *see Alma Kinema*

Empire
Bury Park Road
original owners: Luton Cinemas Ltd
architects: Brown and Parrott, Castle Street, Luton
opened 29 November, 1921
opening programme: "Three Men in a Boat"
seating: stalls – 320; balcony – 120
original plans called for a total of 494 seats; during the late twenties, the size of the Empire almost doubled to provide stalls – 553; balcony – 228

The chief constable's report of seating in local cinemas for 1937 gives a total of 769
closed 15 October 1938
final film: "Almost a Gentleman"
Building was converted to a synagogue in the fifties; now used as an Islamic centre.

Gaumont
– see Palace Theatre

Gordon Street Electric Pavilion
– see Anglo American Electric Picture Palace

Grand Theatre
Waller Street
proprietor at opening: Reginald Turner
opened 10 December, 1898 (preview);
12 December, 1898 (general public)
opening production: "Sign of the Cross"
architect: Charles J. Shoppee
seating*: stalls – 321 (+ 90 standing)
dress circle & balcony – approx 170
gallery – approx 400 with standing
6 private boxes
* based on sale prospectus for 1903 (the plans in January 1898 envisaged seating for 806)
stage: width 50 feet (proscenium opening 24 feet) depth: 33 feet
dressing rooms: 10
Like most theatres, the seating changed over the years.
The chief constable's reports of seating in local theatres for 1937 & 1939 give a total of 761.
When the Grand came up for sale in 1949, the prospectus gave the seating capacity as 781 made up as follows:
stalls – 349
dress circle – 78
balcony – 84
gallery – 250
4 boxes with 3 seats each & 2 boxes with 4

seats each
closed 4 May, 1957
closing production: "My Wife's Uncle" (play)
replaced with a supermarket; site now part of Luton's Arndale Centre

The Hat Factory
– see artezium

High Town Electric Picture Palace
High Town Road
opened 24 August, 1912
architect: W.H. Guest Hubbard (Luton)
built by T. Day of Smart Street, Luton
seating: stalls – 331 (incl 24 triple seats)
balcony– 84
opening programme included "The Picture Idol" starring Maurice Costello, two dramas, three comedies, a western and Pathe's Animated Gazette (which became a regular feature at the cinema)
The High Town Electric was enlarged when it was taken over by Palace Theatre (Luton) Ltd in 1927; after a brief closure, the cinema re-opened Boxing Day 1927 with the following seating:
stalls – 418 (including 16 triple seats)
balcony – 75 (37 double seats plus one single seat)
Change name to **Plaza** May 1931
closed mid 1937
re-opened (as Plaza) 1952 under the ownership of the small Allwood Circuit (5 cinemas)
closed 2 April 1955
Ten years after its closure, the former cinema was purchased by Luton Corporation for use as "slipper baths" but this plan was never realised; in 1967, the building was leased for three years to Grosvenor Car Sales. Now demolished, the site is part of a redevelopment which includes a car park and industrial premises.

Library Theatre
St George's Square
2 November, 1962; The Luton Girls Choir
"christened" the Library Theatre stage when
they sang for Her Majesty Queen Elizabeth
II and civic dignitaries on the occasion
of the official opening of the new Central
Library. That same evening saw the first
public performance: "Musical Comedy
Cavalcade", presented jointly by Luton
Amateur Operatic and Dramatic Society and
The Luton Band
seating: 240 on single floor (very rapidly
increased to 256)
stage: proscenium opening – approx 25 feet
depth – approx 21 feet
Changed name to **St. George's Theatre** in
1985.
A number of alterations have been made
since the little theatre opened, the most
important being a complete refit of the
auditorium in 1989. This included a sharp
increase in the rake and a centre aisle. The
seating was reduced to 240 including 2
stewards seats, leaving 238 for sale.
Name reverted to **Library Theatre** in 1996.

Liquid Nightclub
– see Union

Majestic Ballroom
– see Palace Theatre

Mecca Bingo Hall
– see Odeon

Odeon
Dunstable Road
proprietor Odeon Cinemas (Oscar Deutsch)
architect: Keith P. Roberts (firm: Andrew
Mather)
opened 12 October 1938
opening film: "The Drum"

seating: stalls – 1,332
circle – 626
The chief constable's report of seating in
local cinemas for 1939 gives a total of 1,980.
Like many large cinemas, the seating was
reduced after WWII to comply with more
rigid fire regulations which required fewer
seats near fire exits; by 1963, the seating
had been reduced to less than 1,900. Stalls
and circle accommodation severely reduced
to 1,300 in 1969. Tripled 1974 – the circle
remained intact as Odeon 1 with two 100+
seat auditoria built as Odeons 2 & 3 under
the balcony. The front stalls also remained
intact and were occasionally used when
Odeon 1 had a particularly popular film.
Closed 1983 and converted into a **Top Rank
Bingo Club/Mecca Bingo Hall** which
closed 1999
Grade II listed –1999
Converted into a church whilst retaining the
essential aspects of the building – 2000

Palace Theatre
Mill Street
proprietor at opening: Mrs Millie Williams
opened 26 December, 1912
the opening programme was not advertised;
the earliest notable film screened at the
Palace was "Les Miserables" for one week
from 10 February, 1913.
seating: stalls – 702
circle – 416
boxes: 4 (each containing two seats)
stage: depth – 17 feet
the stage included an illuminated board to
indicate the number of the act on stage (a
common feature in variety theatres).
The Palace opened as a cine-variety theatre
which included films and variety acts in
the same programme. The orchestra was a
feature of the theatre's performances.
The chief constable's report of seating in

local cinemas and theatres for 1937 gives a total of 1,150.

closed for auditorium re-fit 12 December 1938; reopened 26 December 1938 with "The Lady Vanishes".

The chief constable's report of seating in local cinemas and theatres for 1939 gives a total of 1,076.

changed name to **Gaumont** 1949

closed 14 October 1961

final films (double bill) "League of Gentlemen" & "Whisky Galore"

converted to ballroom

re-opened as **Majestic Ballroom** 20 October 1962 (incorporating Top Rank Bingo and Social Club which opened 23 October 1962)

Building destroyed by fire December 1982; site now occupied by office buildings.

The Palace
Skimpot Lane
– see Cesar's Palace

Paragon Picture Palace
Castle Street
opened 25 September, 1909
Frank Blythe presented a short season of variety and cinematograph entertainment; operated as a full-time cinema for a short period, but could not compete with the Anglo American Electric Picture Palace in Gordon Street.

People's New Temperance Music Hall & Palace of Varieties
Manchester Street
opened December, 1880; formerly the Alexandra Skating Rink
initially used as a music hall, but a theatrical licence was sought and acquired shortly after opening; name changed to **Alexandra Theatre**

Picturedrome
Park Street
lessees: Luton Picturedrome Ltd (part of the Lion Circuit)
built by A. Attwood (Luton)
opened 8 April, 1911
opening programme comprised ten shorts
seating in stalls and balcony (approximate total – 600)
cinema closed for extensive alterations and enlargement in 1928; re-opened 29 September 1928 with a total of 985 seats (including 176 in the balcony) and a new orchestra pit.
closed October 1937 and lay empty for many years; converted to shop use during the fifties; now redeveloped as a snooker hall which incorporates a recognisable part of the cinema.

Plait Hall
Waller Street
seating for approximately 1,000 when used as a music or concert hall; plans to convert the hall into a permanent Concert Hall in 1924 envisaged 700 in the stalls with a further 300 in the gallery. The conversion never took place as the hall was used as part of Luton's new covered market.
Site now part of Luton's Arndale Centre; a BFI "Cinema 100" plaque marks the Plait Hall and records it as the site of Luton's first public cinema show in December 1896.

Plaza
– see High Town Electric Theatre

Ritz
– see Union

St George's Theatre
– see Library Theatre

Sand's Night Club
– *see Union*

Savoy
George Street
initial proprietor: Associated British
Cinemas
opened 17 October, 1938
total seating: 1,990
organ planned but not installed
opening film: "Test Pilot"
first cinema in area to show a 3-D film (a
short) (April 1953)
first cinema in South Bedfordshire to install
CinemaScope and stereophonic sound (first
CinemaScope film: "The Command" 10 May
1954)
changed name to **ABC** in 1961
tripled 1971 –
ABC 1 – 628 seats
ABC 2 – 458 seats
ABC 3 – 272 seats
re-opened as **ABC 1-2-3** 23
September,1971(following 6 months closure
for major structural alterations)
changed name to **Cannon** in 1987
changed name back to **ABC,** June 1996
Operated as a triple cinema until 23rd
November, 2000; planning permission has
been sought and granted for alternative use.
The planning consent calls for the corner
site and present shop frontages to remain as
they are considered by English Heritage to
fit in with the George Street conservation
area.

"33"
33, Guildford Street
In November, 1977, the newly formed
Luton Community Trust occupied part of
33, Guildford Street which was a base for
Luton Arts Council. The top floor included
a "black-box" performance space with

variable seating. The space was also used
as a part-time cinema; when used in this
capacity, removable stadium seating for 40
was available. Cinema shows lasted until the
mid-eighties when availability of film on 16
mm became too limited.
Operations at "33" were compromised when
artezium opened and operated as a rival;
activities moved to the newer premises
when re-opened as The Hat Factory.

Top Rank Bingo Hall
– *see Palace Theatre and Odeon*

Town Hall
– used as both theatre and cinema before
purpose-built venues established.
Burned down 1919

Tropicana Beach Night Club
– *see Union*

Union
Gordon Street
original proprietor: Union Cinemas
(acquired by Associated British Cinemas 14
October, 1937)
architect: Leslie H. Kemp and Tasker
opened 11 October, 1937
seating: stalls – 1,412
circle – 686
Wurlitzer Organ fitted; planned as cine-
variety hall, but rarely used as such after an
initial period
The chief constable's reports of seating in
local cinemas and theatres for 1937 & 1939
give a total of 2,094
changed name to **Ritz** 1949
first cinema in area to show a 3-D feature
("House of Wax" – August, 1953)
closed 1971 when the ABC in George street
was tripled.
converted into a night club and, under a

variety of names (**Sands, Tropicana Beach, Colisseum, The Zone,** etc) continues in that capacity; following extensive refurbishment 2000/2001, has re-opened as a major **Chicago Rock Cafe** and **Liquid Nightclub**.

Wellington (New Wellington Street Picture Palace)
Wellington Street
proprietors: Goodwin and Smith
opened 2 May, 1912
seating: 393 (cinema opened with non-fixed seating); 377 following re-fit in 1944
opening week, programme of shorts included two coloured films and a film about the sinking of the Titanic (which proved very popular).
closed briefly after change of ownership September 1951;
re-opened as the **Coronet** 22 September 1951 under the ownership of Clewer and Blake; closed mid-1952 and used by Gibbs and Dandy as a warehouse before being demolished to make way for the new ring road.

Zone Night Club
– see Union

Toddington

Cozy
– see Picturedrome

Picturedrome
Gas Street (later Conger Lane)
converted from old Guides Hall
opened September, 1925
seating for approximately 140 in stalls and a small balcony;
soon changed its name to **Cozy**; after World

War II, it was known as the **Toddington Cinema** before becoming known as the **Rex** under the ownership of the small Midland and General Circuit (4 cinemas) which had its head office in Dunstable before moving to Little Brickhill.
closed October, 1958
Converted for use as a 150-seat hall for St George's Parish Church (from 23 April 1960).
Building now used by TADS (Toddington Amateur Dramatic Society) as **TADS Theatre**.

Rex
–see Picturedrome

TADS Theatre
– see Picturedrome

Toddington Cinema
– see Picturedrome

APPENDIX 2

Chronology of Initial Venue Openings and Closures

Excludes those opened as night clubs

Date	Opening/closure
1862	Corn Exchange (later Exchange Theatre), Leighton Buzzard opens
27/3/1880	Alexandra Palace Circus, Luton opens (for brief period only)
12/1880	People's New Temperance Music Hall and Palace of Varieties (later Alexandra Theatre), Luton opens
10/12/1898	Grand Theatre, Luton, opened by Lillie Langtry (open to public from 12/12/1898)
1908	Alpha Cinema, St. Albans opens
25/9/1909	Paragon Picture Palace, Luton opens (for brief period only)
16/10/1909	Anglo-American Electric Picture Palace (later Gordon Street Electric Pavilion), Luton opens
3/1911	Luton American Roller Skating Rink, Dunstable Road, Luton becomes "American Rink and Picture Hall" (for brief period only)
8/4/1911	Picturedrome, Luton opens
12/6/1911	Victoria Electric Picture Palace (later Ye Olde Vic), Leighton Buzzard opens
1912	Palace ("Marchant's Picturedrome"), Dunstable, opens
2/5/1912	Wellington, Luton opens
24/8/1912	High Town Electric Picture Theatre (later Plaza), Luton opens
26/12/1912	Palace Theatre (later Gaumont), Luton opens
c 1914/5	The Cinema Theatre (Electric Kinema), Dunstable opens
1919/20	(New) Palace, Dunstable opens
29/11/1921	Empire, Luton opens
early 1922	Empire Cinema (later Grand and Hippodrome), Leighton Buzzard/Linslade opens
26/12/1922	Oriel Picture Theatre, Leighton Buzzard opens
9/1925	Picturedrome (later Cozy, Rex, Toddington), Toddington opens
15/10/1929	Gordon Street Electric Pavilion, Luton destroyed by fire
21/12/1929	Alma Kinema (later Alma Theatre), Luton opening ceremony (open to the public from 23/12/1929)
1930	Ye Olde Vic, Leighton Buzzard closes

3/9/1932	Grand, Leighton Buzzard/Linslade, closes following acquisition by Shipman and King
mid 1937	Plaza, Luton closes
27/9/1937	Union (later ABC), Dunstable opens
11/10/1937	Union (later Ritz), Luton opens
25/10/1937	Picturedrome, Luton failed to open and was never again used as a cinema
12/10/1938	Odeon, Luton opens
15/10/1938	Empire, Luton closes
17/10/1938	Savoy, Luton opens
end 8/1938	Palace, Dunstable closes
29/3/1948	Alma, Luton becomes Alma Theatre as it finally converts to full-time live entertainment
28/4/1952	Plaza, Luton re-opens
28/5/1952	Coronet (formerly Wellington), Luton closes
17/7/1954	Alma Theatre, Luton closes
1/4/1955	Alma Ballroom, Luton (soon renamed Cresta Ballroom) opens
4/5/1957	Grand Theatre, Luton closes
12/3/1960	California Ballroom, Dunstable opens
5/1960	Cresta Ballroom closes
14/10/1961	Gaumont, Luton closes
20/10/1962	Majestic Ballroom, Luton opens (formerly Gaumont)
2/11/1962	Inaugral programme, Library Theatre, Luton
17/4/1964	Civic (later Queensway) Hall, Dunstable opens
5/10/1968	Little Theatre, Dunstable opens
23/9/1971	Following a short period of closure for conversion, ABC (formerly Savoy), Luton re-opens as a triple cinema
25/9/1971	Ritz, Luton closes
1972	Oriel, Leighton Buzzard closes as cinema and offers bingo
14/2/1973	Union, Dunstable closes as cinema; continues with full-time bingo
1974	Odeon, Luton tripled
5/1/1979	Library and Arts Centre, Leighton Buzzard opens
12/1982	Top Rank Bingo Club (formerly Palace/Gaumont), Luton destroyed by fire
1983/4	Odeon, Luton closes as cinema and offers bingo
1985	The Point, Milton Keynes opens
1997	artezium, Luton (first stage) opens
23/10/1998	11-screen Cineworld, Luton opens
mid 2000	artezium goes into administration
23/11/2000	ABC Cinema Luton closes
4/2004	The Hat Factory (formerly artezium), Luton, official opening (an "unofficial" limited opening had occurred in September, 2003)
21/4/2007	Grove Theatre, Dunstable, opens

BIBLIOGRAPHY

ABC The First Name In Entertainment Allen Eyles, Cinema Theatre Association & BFI Publishing, 1993

"About It and About" Nicolas, Bedfordshire Magazine Vol VI, Staddon's, The Crescent Press, 1959

"About It and About" Nicolas, Bedfordshire Magazine Vol VIII, White Crescent Press, 1962

"Alma Cinema, Luton" John T. Squires, Bedfordshire Magazine Vol XXVII, White Crescent Press, 1979

Bedfordshire Cinemas G.C. Peck, Bedfordshire County Council, 1981

Bourne and Bred Colin Bourne, The Book Castle, 1990

Building the Name – Neville Nigel Watson, St. Matthew's Press, 2000

The 'Cali' Album Diane Ilka, The Book Castle, 2005

Cathedrals of the Movies David Atwell, The Architectural Press, 1980

The Changing Face of Luton Stephen Bunker, Robin Holgate & Marian Nichols, The Book Castle, 1993

"Dunstable and the Drama" R.P. Mander, Bedfordshire Magazine Vol IV, Leagrave Press, 1953

Dunstable, Its History & Surroundings Worthington G. Smith, Homeland Association, 1904, reprinted 1980 © Bedfordshire County Library

Gaumont British Cinemas Allen Eyles, Cinema Theatre Association & BFI Publishing, 1996

Girls in Blue Christine Turner, The Book Castle, 2001

A Hatful of Music Stuart Goodyear, The Book Castle, 2003

History of Bedfordshire 1066–1888 Joyce Godber, Bedfordshire County Council, 1969

The History of Luton and its Hamlets William Austin, County Press, 1928

The History of British Film 1918–1929 Rachel Low, George Allen & Unwin, 1971

The History of British Film 1929–1939: Film Making in 1930s Britain Rachel Low, George Allen & Unwin, 1985

The History of the Hathern Station Brick & Terra Cotta Company Kevin Wheelan, The Mercia Cinema Society, 1982

"The Itinerants" part IV Thomas W. Bagshawe, Bedfordshire Magazine Vol VIII, White Crescent Press, 1962

Jessie Matthews Michael Thornton, Hart-Davis, MacGibbon Ltd, 1974

"Leighton Buzzard Cinemas" Stuart Antrobus, Bedfordshire Magazine Vol XXV, White Crescent Press, 1996

Luton (Archive Photograph Series) Mark Stubbs, Chalford & Luton Borough Council, 1997

Luton From The Wings Greta Kent, Borough of Luton in conjunction with Luton District Libraries, 1975

"The Luton Palace (later Gaumont)" John Squires, Picture House No 4, Cinema Theatre Association, 1983

Memories Are Made of This P.C. Vigor, Borough of Luton Museum & Art Gallery, 1983

MGM Cinemas Philip Turner, 1998

Odeon Cinemas 1: Oscar Deutsch Entertains Our Nation Allen Eyles, Cinema Theatre

Association & BFI Publishing, 2002

Odeon Cinemas 2: From J. Arthur Rank to the Multiplex Allen Eyles, Cinema Theatre
    Association & BFI Publishing, 2005

Old Dunstable – A Collection of 110 Pictures White Crescent Press, 1975

Old Luton – A Collection of 145 Pictures White Crescent Press, 1974

The Oxford Companion to the Theatre edited by Phyllis Hartnoll, 4th Edition, Oxford
    University Press, 1983 (1st edition, 1951)

Red Roses Every Night Guy Morgan, Quality Press, 1948

The Story of Luton James Dyer, Frank Stygall & John Dony, White Crescent Press, 1964

Theatre Un-Royal Lou Warwick, Lou Warwick, 1974

"Union Cinemas" Allen Eyles, Focus on Film No 37, The Tantivy Press, 1981

A View From the Alley Aubrey S. Darby, Borough of Luton Museum and Art Gallery, 1974

White Cargo Felicity Kendal, Joseph, 1998

PHOTOGRAPH AND ILLUSTRATION SOURCES

BLARS – Bedfordshire & Luton Archives & Records Service

BY – Brian Yates

CG – Chris Grabham

CTA – CTA Archive (Cinema Theatre Association) www.cinema-theatre.org.uk

DG – Dunstable Gazette

EG – Eddie Grabham

EM – Eric G. Meadows

H – T.G. Hobbs

HF – The Hat Factory

JC – Jo Cross

LCL – Luton Central Library

LMS – Luton Museums Service

LN – Luton News

SBDC – Artists impressions courtesy of South Bedfordshire District Council

TL – Tom Lawson/Tom Lawson Collection

Other items from the author's collection

INDEX

Totternhoe 125

Train, Jack 152

Travelling Repertory Company
157

Trigg, Mr 53–54, 250

Troise and his Mandoliers 151

Tropicana Beach Night Club
256–257

Turner, Eva 157

Turner, Philip 213

Turner, Reginald Frank 15–16,
18–22, 25–34, 253

Turvey, Mrs Violet 125

U

Union Cinema, Dunstable iii,
122–126, 135, 148, 152, 168,
170, 209, 239, 248–249, 259

Union Cinema, Luton 18,
130–137, 139, 151–152,
155–156, 168, 187, 196, 239,
252, 254–257, 259

Union Cinemas Ritz,
Dunstable 123

Union Cinemas Ritz, Luton
134, 168

Union Cinemas 48, 72, 77, 115,
119–123, 127–128, 130, 136,
146, 249–251, 256

Ustinov Players 190

V

Vauxhall Motors 219, 224

Vauxhall Motors Orchestra
152

Victoria Electric Picture Palace,
Leighton Buzzard 53–54,

68, 70, 84, 88, 250, 258

Vincent, Mrs D.A. 66

Virgin Cinemas 224

W

Walker, Alderman G. Wistow
141

Wallace, Nellie 152

Wall, Max 163

Waller Street Wesleyan Chapel,
Luton 36, 147

Wanamaker, Sam 181

Wardown Park, Luton 32, 37,
57

Warner Brothers Cinemas 222

Warner, Grace 47

Warner, Jack 152

Warren, Councillor 28

War Weapons Week 151

Warwick, Lou 5

Waters, Elsie and Doris 116–
117, 129, 175

Watson, Doc 221, 233

Waverley Cinema, Luton (not
built) 128

Way, Jeff 212

Weatherspoon, J.D. 227

Webb, Captain Fred 53–54, 68,
84, 88, 249–250

Webb, Frederica 53

Webb, Larry 53

Webb, Mrs Sybil 53

Welch, Alex 185

Wellington Cinema, Luton 57–
60, 70, 91, 114, 120, 137, 155,
176–179, 197, 252, 257–259

Westerman, Edwin 127

Western Brothers 129

Westminster Bank 102

Wheeler, D.A. 63

Wheeler, Jimmy 175

Whelan, Albert 129

White House, The 227

Why Axe Ye Cottage 16

Wildman, E 6

Wilkinson, A 67, 248

Williams, Bransby 130, 152

Williams, Mrs Millie 63–64,
254

Willis, Mr 147

Wilton, Robb 154

Winn, Anona 129

Winnick, Maurice 155

Winter Assembly Hall, Luton
73, 90

Woburn 5

Women's Temperance
Federation 28

Wood, George S. 55

Wood, Wee Georgie 129

Wurlitzer Organ 134–135, 256

Y

Ye Olde Vic, Leighton Buzzard
68,94,250,259

Yirrell, Thomas 82,249

Young, Steve 250

Z

Zero Balance 240, 242–243

Ziegler, Anne 181

Zimmerman, Max 54

Zone Night Club 235–236, 257

THE CALI ALBUM
Life and Times at the California Ballroom, Dunstable

Diane Ilka

Hundreds of the now iconic pop stars of the sixties and seventies performed live at the unique California Ballroom in Dunstable. Thousands of their fans, local and nationwide, flocked to revel in the unforgettable atmosphere thus created.

Diane Ilka – granddaughter of the 'Cali's' founder – lived and worked there. A generation on, she has compiled a tribute to this very special phenomenon in pop music's history, including many pictures and contract details from her private collection of memorabilia. All those who were part of the 'Cali' era can now reminisce over the stars and dates that formed a highlight of their most impressionable years.

The 'Cali' lives on in the reunions and websites it still inspires. Now it also has a fitting pictorial souvenir and record of those idols and dreams of yester-year.

A HATFUL OF MUSIC
The Dance Band Days in Luton, Dunstable & District

Stuart Goodyear

In 1939 Lutonian Stuart Goodyear was born into a musical household, whose father, also Stuart, encouraged him to embrace his love of music.

As a millennium project, Stuart was asked by the Luton Historical Society to write a page or two about the local "dance band days" of the last century, and drawing on his own involvement as novice pianist through to bandleader, was happy to undertake the challenge.

Starting in a modest way in the 1950s with fellow airport apprentices, his first band The Rainbow Melody Makers, rapidly became a larger and more polished dance band, and was subsequently renamed The Ray Miller Band. Remaining as leader of the band through to the 1980s, he became well connected with the local musical establishment, and has comprehensively collated his experiences during that time, although it soon became apparent that the finished article would be a book, rather than a dossier.

In a most fascinating personal and wider-ranging survey of musical days gone by in Luton, Dunstable and the surrounding area, Stuart has compiled a detailed impression of how he remembered the busy dance scene, and the many brilliant musicians who contributed to a period of live musical entertainment that will never return.

Deliberating over a title, he shortlisted "Batons and Bows" and "You've gotta lot to learn my boy", but thinks that a "Hatful of Music" just about strikes the right chord. The book contains over 300 photos of events covered over the years. People born and bred in Luton will be pouring over the nostalgia for weeks to come.

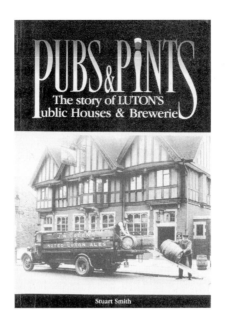

PUBS AND PINTS
The story of Luton's Public Houses and Breweries

Stuart Smith

Whilst the town of Luton is well documented in other ways, this book is the first comprehensive history of its important brewing industry and retail beer outlets – linked, staple trades in the area for over five hundred years.

The development of the modern public house from the early taverns and coaching inns closely followed that of the breweries, with the final decades of the last century seen as the high point in the number of houses licensed to sell beers for consumption on or off the premises. Since then the total has declined with the loss of around 40% during the last one hundred years, most of these losses occurring in the period from 1950 to 1970.

Although documentation dealing with the early breweries and public houses is extremely sparse, it is the intention of this book to try and record the history of each brewery and public house that has had its bearing on the social and drinking pastimes of Lutonians over the last one hundred and fifty years. A special feature of this book is the vast range of three hundred photographs – many old, rare and unusual.

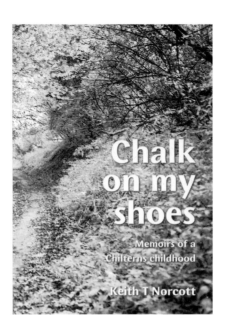

CHALK ON MY SHOES
Memoirs of a Chilterns Childhood

Keith T Norcott

Here is an affectionate remembrance of growing up in the 1930s and 1940s in the villages of rural Bedfordshire and the gentle hills of the North Chilterns, where Bedfordshire and Hertfordshire meet. We are taken back to villages like Lower Stondon and Stopsley and towns like Hitchin and Bedford when life was slower and simpler than it is today. Here too are descriptions of customs and practices that no longer exist, like the "penny picture" shows in the village hall, the local policeman who dishes out summary justice and the Queen of the May celebrations. And central to it all is the guiding hand and indomitable spirit of "Our Mum", who guided the family most of the time, and saw it through the horrors of the war.

Full of stories, anecdotes and impressions of the hills and communities of the area, this is a book to trigger memories in those who know this part of the country, and excite curiosity in those who are coming to it for the first time. The intervening years have seen great changes, but the hills still retain much of the charm they had in bygone days, a charm that is reflected in these pages.

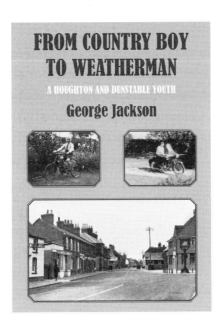

FROM COUNTRY BOY TO WEATHERMAN
A Houghton and Dunstable Youth

George Jackson

A memoir of the author's childhood and teenage years growing up in the village of Houghton Regis. It covers his earliest pre-school memories, his time at primary school in the village and then at Dunstable Grammar School. He remembers family and village life in the immediate post-war years with fondness and humour.

He also takes a mental stroll around the village, as he knew it, stopping off along the way to describe some of the buildings and other features and many of the characters associated with them.

Later the author remembers his first job employed in different departments of the Meteorological Office at Dunstable including working on Meteor, one of the first computers in the country, and a brief period when he was still living in Houghton Regis but working at an operational RAF station at Bovingdon in Hertfordshire. Sporting and motorcycling exploits and a fairly hectic social life in Dunstable and surrounding area are not neglected.

BLITZING VAUXHALL
A Dogsbody's War Diary

Owen Hardisty

This story of Vauxhall Motors and Luton, during the sweltering "invasion" summer and the blitz of 1940, is a view from the ground – and the underground – of daily life in a huge munitions factory, based on the pocket diaries and memories of a 14-year-old who began a 43-year career at Vauxhall as an office boy in April 1940.

It describes at first hand the Luftwaffe attack of the 30th August, and the events of the following months; the seemingly endless daytime hours spent in Vauxhall's trenches and nights huddled in the family's garden shelter. This is a story of hardship and tragedy, illuminated by flashes of humour. The "blitz spirit" is not a nostalgic myth dreamed up by the elderly; it was a living thing in Vauxhall's workshops and trenches, Luton's backyard shelters, food queues and works canteens – it was human kindness and communal solidarity in action.

To quote from the preface by Kelvin Hopkins MP "Owen brilliantly evokes those times and he must be congratulated on a remarkable book."

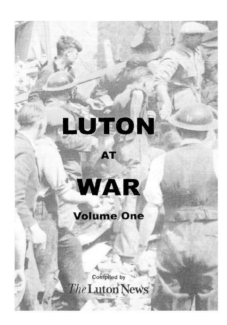

LUTON AT WAR
Volume One & Volume Two

Initially published by *The Luton News* in 1947, the story of how the people of Luton withstood the dark years of war between 1939 and 1945.

Luton and its population have changed so dramatically in the years since the war that now only a few will recall how the town stood up to the trauma of those war years.

Because of strict war-time censorship much of what occurred during those years was not mentioned in *The Luton News*. Once the war was over however, *The Luton News* set about the mammoth task of presenting a complete and vivid picture of war-time life. It tells of the long anxious nights, the joy and the sorrow that made even the most terrifying moments bearable thanks to the tremendous way in which the people joined to help each other.

Written and compiled by the staff of *The Luton News* at the time, it contains the most comprehensive and fascinating pictorial record. As well as being a moving personal account it is also a unique historical document.

This large format paperback is published in two parts.

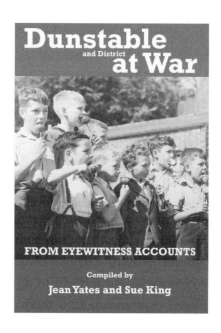

DUNSTABLE AND DISTRICT AT WAR
From Eye Witness Accounts

Compiled by Jean Yates and Sue King

Dunstable and District at War is mainly a collection of personal reminiscences, by people who lived here or who called Dunstable home during the Second World War. Hundreds of recent interviews have recaptured these unique memories that evoke the disrupted, day-to-day life of an archetypal rural town in that unique period of British history. Bedfordshire was at the heart of the Secret War and Dunstable was very much a part of it. The Meteorological Office was based at the bottom of the Downs, and forecasters worked closely with Bomber Command to decide the date for D-Day.

This book tries to give a feel for where Dunstable sat in the wider picture; the relationships it had and the part it played in conjunction with Bletchley Park, Black Propaganda, SOE and our Allies. There is also a section about those of our Allies who sought refuge in Dunstable after the war. And a final chapter recounts a few of the remarkable contributions Dunstablians made to the various battlefronts overseas, including D-Day and the Far East.